THE INTERNATIONALIZATION OF BUSINESS

Also by J. M. Livingstone

BRITAIN AND THE WORLD ECONOMY
THE INTERNATIONAL ENTERPRISE
MANAGEMENT ECONOMICS IN PRACTICE (*with N. Branton*)

Also published by Macmillan

THE BRITISH ECONOMY IN THEORY AND PRACTICE
INTERNATIONAL MARKETING MANAGEMENT

The Internationalization of Business

J. M. Livingstone

Professor, Glasgow Business School
University of Glasgow

MACMILLAN

First published 1989

Published by
THE MACMILLAN PRESS LTD
Houndmills, Basingstoke, Hampshire RG21 2XS
and London
Companies and representatives
throughout the world

Printed in Hong Kong

British Library Cataloguing in Publication Data
Livingstone, J. M. (James McCardle), 1925–
The internationalization of business.
1. International economic integration.
Role of multinational companies
I. Title
33.1
ISBN 0–333–47571–2
ISBN 0–333–47572–0 Pbk

Contents

Introduction

BIG IS BETTER

In any Western industrialized society, many people will work for international firms. These firms may be locally owned companies which have foreign subsidiaries, or local subsidiaries of foreign owned companies. Most people working in the locally owned companies are probably not even aware of the foreign interests: and a surprisingly large proportion of workers in the subsidiaries of foreign owned companies are not even aware of the foreign ownership.

To most people, in practice, the national ownership of the organization for which they work is a matter of some indifference. If, however, the word 'multinational' is introduced, or, even worse, the phrase 'foreign multinational', attitudes may harden. 'Multinational' is now a semantically loaded word; so is 'foreign' and, in most instances, the loading is unfavourable.

The situation is even more acute in the less developed parts of the world, where many of the technologically more advanced industries may be under foreign control. Here the foreign companies are at once saints and devils, bringing in new technology, modern industry and new employment, while, by their very visible presence, carrying the connotation of foreign dominance and neo-colonialism. Local people seek their employment eagerly, since in most instances the conditions of work and wages they offer are better than the alternatives being generated by local effort. Many of the educated elite seek executive or professional posts with them, and yet have a sense of betraying their own national and cultural heritage in the process.

This book is about the international company and the ambivalence its presence and operations create, both in developed and under-developed societies. By and large, the so called 'multinational' is unloved and on the defensive; it is unloved in some instances because, in spite of its 'foreignness', it may be almost indispensable to national development.

One result is that many people employed by international companies in posts of influence are highly defensive about that fact. If they are employed in a locally owned company, they may feel that they are helping to export jobs: if it is a foreign owned company, they feel they are somehow selling a national birthright. Possibly this book has a message of comfort for those working in these large unloved enterprises; the message is that, if in modern conventional thought, small is beautiful, for many purposes, big is better.

CRITICISMS OF MULTINATIONALS

The accusations brought against Western international enterprises are many and varied, but can briefly be summarized under the four headings which follow. It would be dishonest to pretend that the multinationals can be cleared absolutely and without qualification on any: but their reputation scarcely lives down to some of the charges made.

a.   That they interfere politically in the affairs of the host nation

This is by far the most serious charge which is made against the multinationals, and it is a charge which cannot be refuted entirely in every case. There are, however, a number of factors which can be argued in their favour.

When the charge is brought up, the example, and it is almost the only example cited, is the activity of ITT in Chile before the overthrow of the marxist Allende government. Yet it might reasonably be asked, if there are all that many examples to be quoted, why are others not more widely quoted and substantiated? There are in fact others, though not of the same gravity, and incidentally very difficult to document, and mainly relating to refusals to permit a subsidiary to trade with countries at odds with the parent company's home government, but not necessarily with that of the country in which the subsidiary is located. Such intervention by the headquarters in the day to day trading of the subsidiary has, however, if it comes to light, such adverse publicity that the last thing the average multinational wishes to do is get involved in political quarrels of the countries in which their plants are located.

In practice, charges of political intervention by multinationals are the small change of domestic politics. Throughout history there have been domestic crises everywhere, with of course traditional scapegoats to be accused. The multinationals (along with the CIA) are the most convenient scapegoats of the late twentieth century. In the Third World countries, a domestic revolution is as often as not likely to be accompanied by nationalization of foreign assets: indeed, governments may preempt opposition groups by leading the attack. The point here is that any charge of political intervention by the foreign multinationals which are about to be seized is convenient, whether or not there is any substance to the charge.

A pervasive political influence, however, which is often only dimly apprehended by the host community, is in most respects unintended by the multinational. This influence arises simply because the presence of a foreign multinational may be one of the most powerful instruments for change, by demonstrating a political or economic alternative in a relatively stable or even stagnant society. It shares this characteristic with television, which shows even the *favela* dweller in Rio or the slum dweller in Calcutta who can see a TV screen in a shop window what his opposite number in the developed world wants and expects. The awareness of what others have, is a most powerful incentive to challenge existing methods and institutions, and it penetrates not only the Third World but the communist world. Many multinationals, in this sense, are not agents of Western Imperialism so much as examples of the Western way of life. As such they may be much more dangerous than deliberate subversion to the existing social structure in many countries.

This effect, incidentally, is not merely confined to the Third World or the communist world, nor is it merely Western multinationals which have this effect. American practices have affected European practices. Increasingly, in terms of industrial democracy concepts, Europeans will affect American companies, and significantly the success of the Japanese companies (admittedly as yet on a small scale) is likely to affect industrial relations in those parts of Europe and the USA where a tradition of confrontation between management and workers has hitherto seemed to be a state of nature, and immutable. It is not surprising that so many interests which have a stake in a political or cultural status quo, and at the other extreme revolutionaries or reformers who see salvation for their societies in a non-Western ideology, may have cause to accuse the multinationals of interference. Their very presence and success does constitute political interference by showing what appears to be a rosier alternative to existing conditions or marxist revolution.

b. That they destroy local jobs

Again this may be a valid criticism, but it is only a half truth in the sense that multinationals transfer jobs across frontiers and in the process are likely to create as many elsewhere. They are in effect speeding the transfer of certain labour intensive types of work from the developed world, and creating new jobs in the less developed world. They are scarcely doing this with the prime purpose of helping the Third World, but rather to cut down labour costs where these are most expensive. While, therefore, workers and trade unions in developed countries might have an immediate grievance, the critics in the Third World who complain about political intervention and change ought, in most cases, be happier to be at the receiving end, on this occasion. Indeed, since the availability of cheap labour makes the use of capital intensive methods less economical, the multinationals may create more jobs than would otherwise exist, albeit relatively low paid ones in the Third World.

There are of course complications. If the jobs created are to serve the domestic market, i.e. the multinational has closed down export industry based jobs somewhere else, and substituted local production, then local critics of foreign multinationals would argue that it would be still better if foreign imports were replaced by local products manufactured by a locally owned plant, not a foreign one. What happens increasingly, however, is that the new plants will in turn be allowed to export and even supply the original market, at the cost of jobs there. There is very much a swings and roundabouts effect in the process of gain and loss and how the individual feels about it depends whether he/she is on a swing or a roundabout.

Multinationals, in effect, co-operate with the inevitable, in that they accelerate and smooth the process of transferring industry and jobs from one society to another. This is a process which goes on in any event. The chronic problems of steel production shipbuilding or textiles in the developed world in large part arise because less developed nations with appropriate resources want and will have their own plants in those industries. In the cases quoted above they can do so without the multinationals being involved. The job loss in the developed world is inevitable, and the long term salvation for these societies must lie in the proposition that, because they are the developed societies, they will develop new technologies and new job skills as the old industries move away. The drift of traditional smokestack industries from the developed to the less developed world may be delayed, but not stopped, if tariff protection is introduced in the developed world, against low cost imports. But it may be accelerated, where there is no tariff protection, and the low cost imports carry a prestige brand name or trade mark of a multinational company which formerly manufactured the product in the developed country.

There are implications of this acceleration of natural job transfer, which may be hard for trade unions in the Western plants of the international enterprises to digest. First, there is likely to be a continuous erosion of labour intensive jobs in these territories. Second, the conditions under which workers will operate, whether directly in the employment of the international enterprises, or more significantly in the ancillary and supply industries which are not owned by the multinational, may be, by Western standards, quite unacceptable. Yet even these conditions may represent more hope and a better future for the poor of the Third World than they are likely to obtain from any other source. The drift, which is rapidly becoming a stampede, is of the landless poor into the slums of the cities. Huge cities with tens of millions of inhabitants are likely to be the characteristic of the impoverished, not the developed, world: the slums of Calcutta, Mexico City or of Rio being more characteristic than the intellectual power centres, the science parks or science cities in the twenty-first century. The latter will dominate the creation of work opportunities, but the opportunities themselves in the labour intensive jobs are likely to be found in the teeming ant hill cities of the Third World. In many instances the multinational corporation will be a major agent of this process.

c. That, by exporting its knowhow and national technology, multinationals destroy its home country's technical leadership

This is the obverse of the job loss argument: potentially it is more serious, although politically it is less damaging at home. The man or woman in the street can see jobs disappearing but not technology.

There is no doubt, and the point will be expanded later, that the multinational is probably the most efficient channel of technology transfer that has been devised. In that sense the charge is valid from the viewpoint of the developed nations, though the vice becomes a virtue at the other end of the transfer process.

Two points have to be made. As in the job issue, the multinational is, at most, accelerating the inevitable, and, at least, bringing residual benefits for the home country in terms of technology royalties and perhaps orders for capital equipment. But more significant perhaps is the tendency to ascribe other faults in a society to this process. Britain probably peaked as the leading industrial power in the 1880s, and the same process may have happened or be happening to the USA a century later. In the American case, this process, if indeed it is

irreversible, has occurred a generation after the American multinationals emerged in really large numbers and planted, if not the
American flag, at least the American trademark, throughout the
world. It is probable, however, that the American problem is more
insidious, in terms of some loss of self-confidence and a shift in what
are perceived as desirable values. Technology development or
adaptation is, among other things, dependent on cultural values and if
these are changing permanently or temporarily in the USA, then so
also may be the ability to innovate fast enough to stay ahead of the
technology race.

The problem for advanced countries, is not to try to prevent the
export of existing technology, which is after all neither static nor
containable, but to ensure that new technology is developed and
exploited to replace that technology and the related industries which
are ebbing away. No nation can freeze the level and world distribution
of technology at the point which is the most convenient for itself.

d.   That they destroy local culture

The multinational corporation is based on the concept of mass markets
for relatively standardized products, which have been initially
designed for and marketed in the mass markets of the USA, Western
Europe or Japan. There are therefore two ways in which the charge of
destroying local culture might stand up: first, that by more efficient
production methods they destroy traditional local industry and
therefore the communities which they support; and second, because
they demand mass markets to survive, they in effect create mass
demand for their products, i.e. they raise the material standard of
living of the community.

The latter statement exposes part of the implicit base on which the
criticism depends. It is instructive to consider those areas where
culture has not been destroyed, in the eyes of the critic. First, there is
Japan itself, whose culture resisted the impact of foreign industrialization, but which nevertheless was propelled along its own chosen path
by industrialization. It may be that it is industrialization – a
prerequisite for avoiding starvation in most of the Third World – which
changes or destroys culture, but only where the cultures choose to
copy uncritically, rather than adapt. Second, there are the states which
have simply been by-passed by the multinationals. In most cases they
are likely to find themselves either on the verge of starvation or with an
appalling infant mortality rate. The majority of pre-industrialized

societies remain stable and viable on the assumption that most children will die before adulthood. To accept even one form of Western technology, i.e. Western medicine, and in the process reduce infant mortality, produces a population explosion that the existing cultural infrastructure may not be able to sustain. It is by no means certain on the evidence available that all cultures are capable of efficiently operating (and developing further) industrial production and an industrial society, without creating immense cultural strains. If this is so, and that particular society wishes to retain its basic culture, it may have to settle for massive and continuous infusions of Western or Japanese technology via multinationals operating what are in effect enclave industries, isolated from the main stream of society; or simply decide to reject industrial society standards, on the lines of the Iran of Khomeini – a model whose future is uncertain.

The problem for the less developed countries is to examine the technology and decide whether the cost of its introduction and what it may do to the existing creative and social structure is acceptable; whether indeed the local culture can be protected against Western influences. There is in parts of the Third World a national environment which can readily be upset by international business and the prosperity it brings. Many nation states in the Third World are based neither on tribal, racial, linguistic nor cultural homogeneity. They are creations of Western colonial powers which have lost or abandoned control of their own artificial creation, or empires which have been carved out by military conquest and become static when a great leader died or the drive to conquest petered out. Any intense national feeling may be generated in the most heterogeneous society in a struggle for independence or against a foreign threat. But this unity which is strengthened by hardship may not stand fast against prosperity. If the industrial process and international business takes root in one part of the nation state, or if one particular culture in a multinational state prospers while the rest do not, then prosperity and power changes may be created which will rip the fabric of the nation. This process may be seen by the cultures which lose out as destructive, by the cultures which can cope as a natural consequence of their own cultural or racial superiority. The multinational company may become the agent or the victim of the cultural upheavals involved.

THE CASE FOR THE MULTINATIONAL CORPORATION, 'YES ... BUT'

In many respects the current argument about the multinational corporations is a more highly politicized version of an argument which occupied the minds of economists and politicians throughout most of the nineteenth century, namely the free trade dispute. Britain had undergone its industrial revolution in the late eighteenth and early nineteenth century, and had become for several generations the leading industrial power of the world. In the process it had shed traditional theories of economic protectionism, and was the fierce advocate of free trade. Certainly a free trade policy enabled British industry to dominate world markets.

But though the merits of unrestricted competition appealed to the successful British entrepreneurs, its merits were less obvious to countries whose traditional industries were being wiped out by British competition, or which could not themselves industrialize since their infant industries were given no time to grow before being assailed by the longer established British industry.

Such countries imposed tariffs, behind which their own industries could be established. For a long time free traders in general, and British free traders in particular, argued that such protection, as a restraint in trade, was by its very nature ineffective and wrongheaded not only in general terms, but also even for the country which imposed tariff protection. But, as time passed, it became clear that some of the countries imposing such restrictions, most notably Germany and America, were successfully building up industrial bases, which in time passed in size and efficiency that of the original industrial nation, Britain. In retrospect the truth appears to have been that although free trade on a worldwide basis possibly maximized advantages to the world as a whole, and in the process would have sustained British industrial supremacy for a generation or two more, tariff restrictions were manifestly in the interest of some individual national economies, even if the world as a whole was left slightly worse off, and the British economy distinctly so.

This may be the case for the multinational, which can be seen as the modern metamorphosis of free trade, in its unrivalled ability to switch resources from one part of the world to another. The major difference is that while highly efficient transfer of technology can be claimed, there are two potentially interested groups, not one, as in the case of free trade. At the receiving end, so to speak, local industry is threatened unless controls equivalent to old-fashioned tariff barriers are imposed. The danger is not of local industrialization being wiped out, or simply not developing, but of its development being determined by the foreign multinational's interest, in terms of ownership and the type of industrial production which is introduced. At the other end, the process of decline of the traditional export oriented plant industry may be accelerated. The multinational may still make a perfectly valid case that what it is doing is in the overall interests of the world economy, while only incidentally maximizing its own profits. The more directly injured parties at either end are likely to see the problem in different terms, as a threat to their own local interests.

The result is an attempt to impose national controls, the equivalent of the tariff barriers behind which the industries of Germany and the USA were created a century ago.

Not least of the problems in the analogy, and the present situation, is that tariff protection had its failures as well as its successes. Some countries which imposed tariffs against British exports manifestly did not have the success of Germany or America, and may in the event have been even worse off than before. The same may apply to these countries which impose rigid controls on the multinationals, or even forbid the activities of foreign companies within their frontiers. Some countries, and Japan is the shining exemplar, have remarkable success. The fact that some marxist states have moved away from outright denunciation to grudging acceptance of the presence of ideologically obnoxious forms of foreign private enterprise, may be highly significant. The factors which determine success or failure in industrialization, with or without the aid of foreign multinationals, are as much cultural and ideological as technical. There is, nevertheless, a tendency to assume that one's own ideology and culture are quite appropriate to developing the most desired aspects of industrialization and technological development, and to assume that legal or administrative controls will always secure more advantage locally at the expense of the foreign owners of the multinationals. This is not always the result, however.

In summary, a general point to be made is that there is a good deal wrong in economic and human terms in any society, and a good deal about the future which ought to cause concern to the thinking individual. It is, however, a vast oversimplification in most instances to look for a single solution or villain, or even a major one. To choose the multinational for the role simply avoids looking at the real and highly complex world.

Part I

The Growth of International Business

Introduction

The twentieth century, particularly since the end of World War II, has seen a transformation in the manner in which international business transactions are carried on. Traditional exporting and importing has been substantially supplemented by the growth of two alternative policies. These are manufacturing by a company in plants outside its own home territory, and a process which can best be described as the export of 'knowhow' rather than physical products.

Even within the traditional export/import pattern, there have been significant changes in emphasis in that an increasing proportion of what are classified as exports may simply be transactions between the same company operating in more than one nation state: the ability of an international company to do this gives it some possibility of evading controls by individual nation states.

The reason for the various changes will be discussed in terms firstly of American, then European and finally non-Western international companies. A process which began as a by-product of American economic dominance and European weakness after World War II, has developed into something which is a good deal more complex, and which may in the future illustrate a shift of economic power from its traditional base in the West to a wider and possibly more Pacific oriented structure.

1 The Background to International Business

INTRODUCTION

International business, in the sense of trade across frontiers, indeed on a worldwide scale, has existed for thousands of years. But in the decades since World War II, there has been a burgeoning of international business activity on an unprecedented scale, and this has represented a significant change, not merely in terms of scale, but of the nature of the activity. It is largely with the nature of this change that this book is concerned, and above all, with the political background.

In the early decades following World War II, the most obvious phenomenon was the change in emphasis from exporting to local assembly or manufacture. Before World War II there were already a number of companies which would be described as multinationals, in the sense that they manufactured in different parts of the world. They were, however, comparatively small in numbers and scale. The first step in the internationalization of business after the war was simply a very rapid growth in fairly traditional terms, in the sense that more and more companies in one developed country set up their own, or bought over existing, manufacturing facilities in other countries.

In the last decade or so, however, there has been a rather subtle change in the nature and methods of international business. Although the proportion of the new activities, in comparison with the more orthodox multinational manufacturing or exporting, is still small, the future, arguably, lies with the new methods rather than with the older methods.

Why then are these changes coming about, and what exactly are they? It is, in practice, easier to identify the former than interpret the latter. The reason is that in the past multinational business activity has largely proceeded on a twofold basis. First, the transfer of activity was into other countries whose cultural characteristics, ideological views and level of technology were broadly similar to that of the original country: this meant that the Americans were investing heavily in Western Europe. Alternatively, where the move was into different cultures, ideologies or levels of technology, the balance of power was tilted in favour of the multinational or the country in which the multinational originated. The broad pattern of US direct investment in Latin America or European direct investment in Africa and South-East Asia depended implicitly on the realities of power and influence of the north over the south. Even the great ideological split between Western democracy and marxist societies, i.e. the East/West split, did not challenge that concept. The rules simply did not apply, because the conditions did not apply: Western enterprises did not, and could not, invest in marxist societies.

The only significant exception to this general pattern had been Japan. American occupation and tutelage after the war had profound effects on Japanese politics and culture, but did not open up the way for US economic penetration and domination. In a sense, Japan was to be a harbinger of future relationships and methods.

In recent years, this traditional pattern of Western investment has begun to change; first, the emphasis in investment is now switching to non-Western societies where other cultures, different ideologies and vastly different levels of technology exist. In some instances, marxist societies for example, the opportunities for foreign investment have appeared only recently: in many of the societies, both marxist and Third World, however, the balance of the power is no longer unequivocally tilted in favour of the foreign company. Moreover, it can no longer be assumed either that there is common ground about the objectives of industrial activities between the investing enterprise and the host government or culture, or that political dominance lies with the West, or the Western enterprises. New rules are emerging, and new methods of international industrial activity. This book is therefore as much concerned with speculation as to what is going to happen as with an analysis of what is presently happening. It is not too closely concerned with the mechanics of implementing present day business policy, but rather with identifying what are the characteristics of the changing external environment, against which business policy is being formulated.

What then are the factors which have led to the rapid internationalization of business in the post-war years?

a.   Hostility towards extractive industries owned by foreign interests

In many parts of the world there is growing hostility to foreign investment in the traditional extractive industries, where a company based in an advanced industrial society secures supplies of raw materials by ownership of the production facilities. An almost inevitable result is the eventual nationalization or expropriation of the production facilities. These extractive industries had in the main developed in the last century and were intended to supply raw materials from the developing world to plants in the developed world; the majority were American or British in origin, although other European colonial powers developed similar enterprises. In the case of US companies these operated largely in Latin America; in the case of Britain, throughout the world in its erstwhile colonies.

The major type of direct investment up to World War II was either in extractive operations or transport: in many instances the latter, mainly railroads, served to move the raw materials to seaports. There was virtually no industrial activity performed in the host country which could be performed back in the home country where the technology had been developed and markets were located.

The rate of these international operations in the post-war years was dramatic. By the fourth quarter of the twentieth century, virtually all such enterprises had been nationalized or stood in considerable danger of being nationalized – and it is the reaction of the enterprises to this threat which constitutes the more important examples of the second development, to be discussed shortly.

The impetus to nationalization arose from a sentiment in the host country that such foreign owned industries are merely exploitative; that, while they may bring in royalties, they do little or nothing to develop the local economy. To some extent the progress of nationalization is set up by the quantity of sophisticated manpower available locally. It is obviously highly desirable that, if a host government decides on a policy of nationalization, local nationals should be available with the skills to replace expatriate experts. One could expect therefore, that the more sophisticated the industry involved, the longer would nationalization be delayed, until the appropriate technological level had been achieved locally. Politics, however, override technological considerations. In a political crisis it is often expedient to make the foreigner the villain, rightly or wrongly, and nationalize or even simply expropriate foreign assets. On other occasions nationalization takes place because outside pressures compel the host government to act before the time is ripe. Thus for example, the Venezuelan government in the early 1970s nationalized the oil industry, in spite of an agreement which had in effect scheduled nationalization for a decade later. Much of the rest of the world's oil fields were being nationalized in the Middle East. Presumably it would have been regarded as politically impossible to avoid following suit.

Almost inevitably nationalization of the other major raw material followed, namely iron ore production, although manifestly the Venezuelan government found itself short of local experts to run the new state industries.

As it happened, the situation could be contained, in that the government was in a position to agree acceptable terms of compensation with the foreign enterprises and was therefore able to hire back their management expertise on a contract basis. In view, however, of the massive problems and waste of resources which followed in the next few years, as the Venezuelan government tried frantically to accommodate to its new found wealth, and, in the process, frittered away a good deal of it, it is arguable that the country would have been better off to have continued to accept foreign ownership for a few more years, with more modest economic growth, less inflation and the opportunity to train more of its own technical experts. But what would have been economically sensible was probably not politically feasible.

b.   The move from extractive to processing industry

If any such foreign owned extractive industry in the Third World is likely sooner or later to be nationalized, and that probably by the end of the century, the prospect poses a problem for the foreign enterprise. It may try to delay the process as long as possible by conciliation; or it may try to postpone nationalization indefinitely by changing the nature of its industrial activity within the country.

The major complaint of the host government is the tendency of the international enterprise to have the extractive activities in one country and the processing done in its own home base for its own market and markets in other industrial countries. One possible answer for the enterprise may, therefore, be to move its processing facilities back into the region where materials are being extracted, and serve the ultimate markets at arm's length. There are obvious dangers about such a strategy. At one end it may merely ensure that if nationalization does come, the host government will be in possession of an integrated industry rather than merely the raw materials. While the old Anglo-Iranian oil company built the world's largest refinery in Abadan in the late 1940s instead of continuing to ship out crude oil, it did not in the event prevent nationalization in the early 1950s: and the presence of refining capacity made it more difficult to bring pressure on to the Iranians to achieve some sort of settlement or compensation. At the other end, any move to transfer industry from the headquarters to the overseas subsidiaries is bound to cause resentment both at government and trade union level, in the parent country of the enterprise.

The scope for warding off nationalization by those means is therefore relatively limited and depends on a few readily identified factors.

First, that the enterprise has an integrated operation so that it has a processing technique with which to bargain, rather than merely refining and selling semi-finished products. Second, that it has substantial control in the ultimate market, and preferably alternative supplies of raw materials, so that it can effectively exclude the nationalized source of raw material from the traditional market, if necessary. Third, that the raw material input should constitute a significant but not necessarily a major part of the finished product. Many products in the modern world owe their value to the input of knowhow, rather than the cost of the raw material, and it strengthens the bargaining power of the company if both parties know that the enterprise could conceivably carry on supplying its own market with relatively limited supplies of raw materials derived from other sources.

The type of industry which most readily lends itself to this strategy are the various food canning or processing plants, where the ultimate product has a brand name, trade markets, etc. The other range of industries where raw material costs are significant are industries like metal processing or shipbuilding: here, however, market controls by the enterprise or brand names are of little consequence. In the latter group of industries, nationalization of the extractive industry has in many instances been followed by the development of nationally owned plants in Third World countries which significantly challenge established industries in the developed world.

If the foreign company can retain its influence in the traditional markets through its control of distribution channels, trade marks and so on (which in the last analysis depend more on the reputation of the company than the national source of its products) then it may be in a relatively strong position to resist unwanted nationalization. Nevertheless, as has been observed, the price of such bargaining power is a readiness to risk the wrath of parent government and trade unions at home by switching production resources into the Third World and accelerating technology transfer: and at the same time to accept that an extractive industry, reinforced by the technology to process the materials, may be an even more tempting target for nationalization in the future.

c. Substituting local manufacturing for imports

The third major influence in the creation of the international enterprise has been various pressures from the importing countries on their traditional suppliers of manufactured goods, no longer to export into these markets, but to replace these exports by local manufacture, or at least assembly and partial manufacture.

This move, from exporting to local production by the enterprise, arises in part from a variety of factors, only some of which are within the control of the enterprise.

For a variety of reasons there has been a tendency among exporting companies in the developed countries to involve themselves more and more in activities in the foreign markets. Whereas previously such a company might simply have exported through a local agent and abrogated responsibilities once the products were loaded into sea, land or air transport, now it may have to accept responsibility – and a physical presence – in its major foreign markets. Such a presence might be no more than a sales company created to solicit orders on the spot, and accepting the same responsibilities for delivery as any local company. But the commitments might go much further. The company's permanent presence might involve it in installing or servicing the product, assembling it from imported components, even a complete manufacturing operation in the foreign markets; or some intermediate combination of these. The company in effect has a legal presence or personality in more than one country.

The move to multiple personality in different countries, which, as a first approximation, is a reasonable definition of an international enterprise, may have been a response to internal pressures within the company, or external pressures from the foreign market; or again a combination of internal and external pressures.

Internal pressures

The most obvious factor is the possibility of more knowledge and control of conditions in the foreign marketplace when it is no longer treated at arm's length. Even if the company's foreign presence is no more than a sales branch in the foreign market, it has overcome many of the disadvantages of appearing to be 'foreign' and remote to the potential customer.

The latter can meet representatives face to face without elaborate travel arrangements, he or she can negotiate, complain and if necessary pay as if to any other local company. And the enterprise in turn, having its own staff on the spot rather than an agent distributor who is not in their employ and may have rather divergent interests, can hope for more detailed, and hopefully, more objective market intelligence.

Although the permanent presence in the foreign marketplace is bound to be more expensive than reliance on the traditional export channels such as agents and distributors, the move forward may in fact be a recognition that other methods of representation, albeit less expensive, are self-limiting. A distribution channel which does not cost the enterprise money on a day to day ongoing basis of salaries and wages, but simply involves the payment of commission if and when sales are made, is at best an intermittent channel. The export house, agent or distributor have other interests to which they are likely to devote more time. *Prima facie* they are not likely to be able to build up orders to the point where a more elaborate distribution channel under the direct control of the enterprise, becomes desirable; and they have no interest in seeing the market developing to the point where they are eased out.

An increasingly important factor in persuading an enterprise to stake a more permanent claim in the foreign marketplace is the role of research and development. In any technologically dynamic industry innovation and new product development are a *sine qua non*. Even if the domestic market is large and lucrative enough to sustain the costs of research and development, the presence of potential imitators and product pirates in other parts of the world cannot be shrugged off. An enterprise which is not prepared to exploit its technology in other developed markets may find its ideas are being taken up by local companies. Patent rights give only limited protection. The onus is still on the enterprise to sue in a foreign court if it feels its ideas are being pirated, and foreign legislation can be chancy and expensive. Licensing out a product gives more protection at second remove, so to speak, in that a local company paying royalties to use the knowhow has an obvious incentive to protect its rights against imitators. But the only real protection may be the exercise of the local patent by the international enterprise producing on the spot.

Finally there is the issue of seeking more freedom of action, or at the very least, spreading risk. Enterprises where domestic operations are increasingly subject to government restriction, often from a government distinctly unsympathetic to business interests, may find an increasing attraction in moving operations to areas where the government, initially at least, welcomes their arrival. Fewer government restrictions, possibly fewer trade union restrictions too, encourage a situation where the enterprise would not only prefer to produce abroad for the local market, but may even consider supplying its home market from these new plants. The concept of flags of convenience may not only apply to ship registration but to production. The flag of convenience plant is in many instances a legal possibility, and a commercial fact.

These then are some of the internal pressures which may compel or persuade an enterprise away from conventional concepts of production for the domestic market supplemented by exporting to a situation which, at the extreme, may reverse the conventional wisdom and decant industrial productive capacity into foreign territories, not merely foreign markets. What, however, are the external pressures which may reinforce or substitute for the internal?

External pressures

They come from two sources, of which by far the more important is the one already noted, namely a deliberate policy followed by a government which has hitherto accepted imports but wishes to move on to local production. In the modern highly competitive world, exports are politically praiseworthy and economically desirable as a means of encouraging jobs, new and more efficient industry, and as a source of foreign exchange. The problem, however, is that one country's desirable exports are another country's undesirable imports. The latter, if it chooses to reverse the situation, can do worse than bring pressure on the exporting companies to produce locally or at least sponsor local production. How it does so depends on whether it is a developed or undeveloped state, and the power its government has to dictate internal policies.

Developed countries have comparatively limited options in seeking to persuade foreign enterprises to set up plant within their own territories, if for no other reason than membership of such organizations as the General Agreement on Tariffs and Trade (GATT) or the European Economic Community (EEC) will prevent them from sealing off their own markets by tariffs or import controls and thus attempting to compel erstwhile exporters into their markets to manufacture locally or lose the market to someone else who is willing to do so. The only alternative is financial incentives – a battery of cheap loans, grants, tax allowances and the like – which may tempt the enterprise to set up plants. The major snag from the viewpoint of the prospective host government is that not only is the process likely to be an expensive one, but a competitive one. Developed countries which are grouped in economic unions are likely to bid competitively for a plant which will serve not only their own market, but others as well, and in the process bring all the traditional benefit of exporting to the host nation. Even within countries there may be competitive bidding from different regions: a federal state, particularly, may find its state or provincial governments entering into such an auction.

For the less developed country the problems of attracting industry may be greater but the room for manoeuvre is also greater. Not only may it offer the same sort of financial incentives as the developed states, but it is more likely to get away with imposing tariffs to protect its home market without reprisals than would be the case with a developed country. Few, if any, of these less developed countries will be GATT members, even fewer EEC members. The combination of a domestic market closed to imports, plus financial incentives, is a powerful one. But their success depends on two factors. First, that the domestic market is attractive enough, economically and politically, to bring in investment – there is after all no advantage in shutting off imports if the enterprises are not sufficiently attracted by the protected market. Second, there is the question of export prospects. Although many underdeveloped countries are members of trade blocs, their partners in such groupings tend to be much more interested in exporting into the country, than accepting imports from a new foreign owned plant. The trade bloc agreements may specifically exclude such foreign enterprises from any trade concessions. The host country's expectation of export benefits may in fact stem from the willingness of the enterprise to supply some of its traditional markets from its new plant in the host country.

A second, but relatively minor source of external pressure to manufacture within a major foreign market comes from customers, particularly where the product is some type of industrial product sold fairly directly to the customer and requiring servicing. The primary consideration from the customer's viewpoint is naturally this issue of servicing. No customer is likely to relish having to await technical experts or spare parts coming from abroad. To a lesser extent the customer may hope for a cheaper service through local production. This expectation, however, is often not borne out by events. Local production on a smaller scale is likely to be at least as expensive as the mass-produced imported item.

These three major influences, then, of the threat of nationalisation, the transformation of extractive industries into processing ones and the substitution of local production for imports, have produced a situation where manufacturing capacity as well as the technology on which it is based, have become much more footloose: the new dimension which this adds to the market strategy of any company which has any interest in foreign markets is only now being appreciated.

d.   The convergence of consumer tastes on a world basis

A fourth major influence appears at first sight to be working in a contradictory fashion to the three already discussed: certainly it is working at least superficially against the received wisdom of market orientation and market segmentation which is preached so enthusiastically by many marketing men. The influence arises from the appearance of large scale, relatively free trade areas, specifically in Western Europe with the EEC, Northern America where Canada is being absorbed into the American market, and Japan. These three mass markets appear to be meshed into a process of converging tastes, three large markets which are almost one huge market dominating and laying down standards and product tastes for much of the rest of the world. As consumer tastes and industrial requirements within and among the three major markets converge on a high consumption, consumer oriented society, the room for standardization appears first on a regional, then on a global, scale. Particularly in consumer durables, cars, trucks and household furnishings, where there is a reasonable but not excessive element of technology involved, standard products appear which are acceptable in any of the markets and capable of manufacture in whole or in part in many parts of the world, at the discretion of an international enterprise. The automobile industry is perhaps the classic case. As the large 'gas guzzlers' of the American pattern disappear, the compact car of the European or Japanese variety is becoming standard in all countries.

Although there is some evidence of a move in the opposite direction in parts of the Third World, a move which will be discussed in a later section, at least the first three tendencies so far described have been present during most of the post-war years, and there is no reason to expect that they are weakening. Any company which operates outside its own domestic market or even any company which can identify a product substantially similar to its own being manufactured more cheaply or more efficiently elsewhere in the world, has to recognize that the diffusion of technology and market information on a worldwide basis is a process which cannot be stopped or long ignored.

THE POLITICAL RELATIONSHIP BETWEEN THE INTERNATIONAL ENTERPRISE AND THE HOST GOVERNMENT

A major danger for any international enterprise contemplating a move into a foreign country or some similar deal, is to assume that it can automatically strike up the same sort of relationship as it has with the government back home, or even with another foreign government in whose territory it is already operating.

There are broadly three factors to consider. The first is the obvious and conventional political stance of the host government in terms of right or left inclinations in the political spectrum. It is, incidentally, difficult to find governments which would accept the term 'right wing' which, like 'reactionary' and 'capitalist', is now regarded as a term of abuse. By contrast, and more confusingly, many if not most Third World governments claim to be socialist, with varying degrees of conviction and plausibility.

In some instances when an overtly marxist/leninist government is in power, it is reasonable to suppose it means what it says about the abolition of private enterprise, and the foreign enterprise will have to formulate its business policy in that country on the proposition of its own mortality. What then matters are the conditions under which it will temporarily be permitted to continue any operations which involve ownership of production facilities in that territory; how long it will be permitted to operate before the inevitable state takeover; what if any are arbitration or compensation arrangements at that stage. The existence of an overtly marxist type of government might dispose the international enterprise to consider an approach which did not involve ownership at any stage, e.g. licensing, or a system of payment in terms of raw materials or finished products from plant which it had helped to build for the communist authorities.

By contrast, a government which is officially socialist but in practice ignores the ideological implications, may permit foreign private ownership to continue indefinitely. The long term problem for the enterprise is that, as has been noted, some day the host government might begin to take its ideology seriously.

The second factor is more difficult to define, but may be more important than the conventional left/right dichotomy. This is the presence or absence of *étatisme*, the extent to which a society assumes that the state is expected to provide leadership in the commercial and industrial fields. As is pointed out in a later chapter dealing with various public enterprise organizations, the phenomenon of *étatisme* is at least as likely to occur in a corporate state which has fascist tendencies as in an officially socialist state. There is a semantic problem in discussing the situation, because 'fascism' is now used as a generalized term of abuse rather than in its strictly accurate sense of a system of authoritarian government, to which the term 'right' or 'left' cannot easily be applied, originating in Italy, but copied in a modified form elsewhere.

Quite apart from the cultural roots from which *étatisme* may be derived in many parts of the world, there is an intellectual attraction to many ambitious and idealistic men and women, who would accept the appellation technocrat. A society which values the technically qualified and throws the weight of the state behind their plans, is only incidentally right or left wing. The political terms are almost irrelevant, as is the issue of the extent of private ownership of the means of production which is a conventional method of defining the political stance of a government. What matters in this context is control, rather than ownership, and the technocrats tend more naturally to work with the administrative machine, than with the official shareholders. Corporate states in this sense are to be found in Europe. France is perhaps the most obvious; Italy too, might be regarded as a corporate state, tempered by anarchy. The pattern is to be found in wide variations from Japan to Brazil. The prerequisite may be a sense of cultural difference, even superiority, in comparison with a foreign enterprise, even if the latter enjoys a technological superiority. This sense of difference may be at best a sense of patriotism, at worst unjustified arrogance. It cannot easily be quantified, but it does exist in many societies and is highly relevant to how the foreign enterprise will be treated. The spectacular growth of the Peugeot car company from a minor producer to a national giant, by the absorption of Citroen, then to an international giant, by the absorption of Chrysler's European interests, was sustained consistently by the French government, not merely on economic terms but as a means of replacing foreign multinationals operating in France by a French multinational dominating the French market and extending its (and French) influence elsewhere.

A favourite device of a state with corporate leanings is the creation of parastatals or state holding companies with which the foreign enterprise may have to deal. Such parastatals, when consistently backed by government, are very powerful; without such backing or in the event of failure of governments to follow consistent policies, the parastatals are in a much weaker situation *vis-à-vis* the foreign enterprise. The role of these parastatals has grown significantly over the past decade or two, but their problems and implications are as yet not fully appreciated by international businessmen. Some of these issues raised will be discussed in Chapter 3.

By contrast with the corporate state philosophy there may be the *laissez-faire* approach where governments, regardless of their official ideological stance, in effect opt out of any serious degree of intervention. Arguably, in spite of the size of its bureaucracy, this is the US model, and what might be termed 'the Thatcher model'. Much of the relevant legislation affecting business is intended to increase competition rather than increase state control. Regulation of abuses or alleged abuses, is not the same as a regulation of industrial corporate philosophy. Regulation is of a negative nature designed to cure abuses rather than advance a particular national policy. Businessmen are more likely then to regard the administrative machinery as a potential adversary, rather than as an ally and mentor.

The foreign businessman in this situation has a free hand, probably free of many of the restrictions on his activity he would experience at home. Thus pollution controls or even safety standards in Third World countries are certainly not rated anywhere as important as in the developed world. The danger to the foreign enterprise arises from adverse publicity and a comparison between standards set in the home territory, and the host, rather than from government intervention. This means in practice that criticisms tend to be concerned with wage rates and any other observable feature, rather than on technical specifications or safety standards, pollution emission, etc., which are not readily made into a headline catching story, unless in a particular instance, like Bhopal, the results are catastrophic.

The third factor to be considered is political stability. Prosperous democracies tend to be politically stable; so too do communist dictatorships or other authoritarian governments if they can provide a reasonable standard of living. In this situation, the important difference is not between right wing and left wing governments, good or bad regimes, democracies or dictatorships, but between strong governments and weak ones. This factor of stability helps to explain the chimera of joint ventures between multinationals and communist governments. Whether it is politically desirable in the national interest, or even the interest of the whole free world, that some of the collaboration with the more sinister regimes should be permitted, is, of course, a very valid question. There is little doubt, however, that at least in the short term interest of the foreign company, it is expedient that any government with which it treats should be stable, even if it is unpleasant.

Thus three factors listed represent a vast oversimplification of the situation. The point which needs to be made, however, is that in many instances the more obvious factors, particularly the ideological stance of the host government, are not, at least in the short term, necessarily decisive. The long term implications of an ideological stance, however, have to be considered with some care; and it is useful at this stage to consider some of these implications, by drawing a parallel between the motives and actions of the individual enterprise and that of host governments.

CORPORATE POLICY IN INTERNATIONAL BUSINESS

All commercial management implies decision taking in uncertainty, and nowhere is this more striking than in the area of international business.

At the time of writing, international business and the international enterprise are on the defensive. The American multinationals are under attack even at home from trade unions who resent job loss, and from consumerist groups who regard their activities with a jaundiced eye. Some of these multinationals which entered the European market with enthusiasm a few years back, now contemplate withdrawal; and the Third World echoes with charges of bribery, political interference in the domestic affairs of their host countries and worse by the multinationals. It is possible to argue that international business faces a period of consolidation rather than of retreat after a generation of precipitate and *unplanned* advance. It is conceivable, however, that the world political climate has turned permanently hostile and that the international enterprise will be hard put simply to survive until the end of the century. But whether the present pause is a prelude to further development or the beginning of the long retreat back to the domestically based enterprise, it is important to identify the factors which have led to the present situation. This involves examining issues from the viewpoint of the two major protagonists, namely the international enterprises and the host country, within whose territories its subsidiary operates. There is a third viewpoint, namely that of the parent country in which the enterprise originates. Its importance cannot be ignored but generally does not rank in significance with the other two.

It is a major argument in this book that the adjective *unplanned*, identified in the previous paragraph, is a key factor. Even a cursory examination of what has happened in the field of international business since World War II suggests a degree of confusion and a lack of consistency on the part of both enterprise and governments. Some conflict of interest between the international enterprise and the host or parent government is almost inevitable. For the host government in particular, which is prepared to permit a foreign enterprise to operate within its territories, the possibilities of conflicts are obvious. All that people of good will on both sides of the bargaining table can do is recognize where such conflicts are likely to exist and ensure that their effects are minimal compared with the expected advantages. But if some conflicts are inevitable, others are unnecessary and arise essentially from the lack of a consistent policy on one or both sides.

How can unnecessary conflicts arise? A major factor is probably the circumstances under which so many domestic enterprises transformed themselves into international enterprises in the quarter century which followed the end of World War II. They appear to have done so in an unplanned and unco-ordinated manner, reacting instinctively to events and opportunities, with the result that a number of fundamental problems were left unresolved at the time when the original move into international status was made.

The author has argued elsewhere that much of what might be termed the multinational explosion of this period was an inappropriate response to transient problems. Typically, many American multinationals appear to have moved into Europe in the following manner. They found a ready market in a war devastated Europe, which was particularly convenient because of the excess capacity built up to supply the needs of war. Quickly, however, they found that although Europeans desperately needed their products and technology, they lacked the hard currency, namely the dollar, to pay. The next step was to go into local production in Europe in the hope that European governments would permit repatriation of profits, even where they would not release hard currency to pay for imports; moreover, there was the intriguing possibility of earning hard currency by exporting in turn from plants in the soft currency areas. Thus, as an initial irony, a move to use surplus capacity in the home plant led to the creation of more capacity in the European subsidiaries. The second irony was the fact that within a remarkably short time of the new plants being created, the hard currency problem had disappeared: indeed over time one or two European currencies become harder than the dollar. It can be argued that the creation òf the American manufacturing stake in Europe played a part in changing the relative hardness of the US dollar and some European currencies. But even so, the relative changes were almost certainly not foreseen by the managers who decided to go international in response to the situation, as they read it at the time. As it happened, the advent of the European Economic Community then ushered in a period of growth which the American companies were well able to exploit – in circumstances which were quite unlike those originally envisaged. The fact that 'going international' proved in most cases to be a highly successful move should not obscure the fact that by the time success was assured, the original reasons were historical irrelevances. By the same token, the current problems which have caused some enterprises to retrench or even pull out of Europe were not apparently foreseen at the time, nor have they necessarily been dealt with in a consistent manner.

'GOING INTERNATIONAL' AS A SHORT TERM RESPONSE

The previous section *inter alia* outlined a generalized scenario of why some American companies moved into Europe when they did. It is helpful, at this stage, to outline some of the reasons which can readily be advanced to explain why large enterprises of different national origin 'go international' in various parts of the world. Some of these reasons, it may be argued, are as transient as the European hard currency shortage, which lay at the heart of American developments; others may have more permanent validity but have wider implications than were necessarily seen at the time.

Such short term 'non-policy' decisions can be summed up as reactions to changing circumstance, generally unfavourable, but occasionally opportunistic. The sort of situation typically might be a crisis in existing methods of handling a market: e.g., the unexpected loss of an agent or distributor at a highly inconvenient moment; a valued client being angered by avoidable delays in transport or delivery; the decision of a rival company to set up a subsidiary in a competitive market and the threat of being cut out of the market if the host government offers it protective barriers against imports; or an approach, out of the blue, by a foreign company seeking a joint venture partnership in the local market. Because the crisis or opportunity may arise in an acute form, suddenly instead of as a gradual process, an immediate and positive response may have to be taken – and this is often an immediate success. But the long term implications in that market or in others may emerge only years later; and, perniciously, they may appear as a series of apparently unconnected crises each of which is tackled in an *ad hoc* manner, rather than as a general problem requiring a generalized and consistent solution.

The term 'non-policy' was used of such short term reactions, simply to emphasize a point to be developed in the next section. This is that they may be made without reference to an overall policy by the company. They are not necessarily wrong decisions: some may even be right for the wrong reasons. But if they cannot be fitted into an overall policy, they pose a severe threat of loss of control by the parent company management.

LONG TERM CONSIDERATIONS

The point of the previous section was to suggest that responses which lead, almost by accident, to an international status may make sense in the short term, but pose difficulties in the longer term; difficulties, moreover, which are not always correctly diagnosed, let alone treated. To consider why this is so it is necessary to compare what might be termed the ethos, and the methods of implementing such an ethos, available to both the enterprise and host government. This involves a study of what are defined here as 'business philosophy' or 'policy and corporate strategy' on the part of the enterprise, and 'ideology' and 'culture', together with national planning, on the part of the host government. It is the contention of this argument that the terms applied to the individual company have their counterparts in government. If two sets of terms cannot be reconciled, then the long term prospects of the enterprise within the host government's territory are dim.

In passing, it is worth emphasizing that this book is neither a study of politics nor a political polemic in the sense that the author attempts to avoid value judgements on a number of issues in business and politics where few readers are likely to be wholly neutral. Thus the reader might have a strong opinion for or against an enterprise which, as a matter of principle, decided never to deal with communist regimes; or with a national government whose policies are deemed unacceptable for some reason in the parent country of the enterprise. On the other side, a potential host country might hold, as a self-evident proposition, that private enterprise was inherently evil or historically doomed, and so on. Such premises are never likely to be proved or disproved to the satisfaction of all parties. These beliefs are intuitive rather than rationally argued, and a book on business policy as well as national policy is not likely to shake deeply held beliefs of a moral or political nature. All that can be attempted here is to indicate some of the factors to be considered – in terms that are as apolitical as possible; and then to try to identify in a situation what is immutable to one side or the other and what is negotiable, and proceed from that point.

CORPORATE POLICY AND CORPORATE STRATEGY

What follows in the next few paragraphs applies in particular to Western enterprises, and some qualification will have to be made in the case of their non-Western equivalents. In company terms, the author will define 'corporate policy' and 'corporate strategy'; and in host government terms, 'ideology', 'culture' and 'national planning'. All of these terms tend to be interpreted in widely different senses by different writers. The definitions given below are terms used in this book: they do not command general acceptance.

Corporate policy (or philosophy) is the sum of a group of precepts which explicitly or implicitly determine the conduct of the enterprise. These precepts may have a variety of objectives, ranging from the most mundane commercial detail to the highly moral. For convenience these might be grouped under three headings.

Technical precepts: that any new activity be confined to 'the business we are in', to use a phrase coined by a well known writer on management. If, for example, the company produced television sets, it might decide it was in the entertainment business and accept as valid an excursion into other forms of entertainment from bingo halls to sports clubs; or it might decide its expertise was in the electronic industry and decide on a move into medical diagnosis or telemetry. It is not the intention here to decide which is the better policy – merely to observe that it could be dangerous to go off in both directions at once.

Another topical example is to be found in the role of oil companies whose oil fields in foreign territories have been nationalized or expropriated. Should they regard their business as being in marketing expertise in oils; should they diversify more into petrochemical industries, shouldering their way into areas which have previously been the province of the chemical corporates like Dupont, Monsanto, Dow, ICI, Hochst, Bayer and the like; or should they define their business as being energy and move into non-oil sources, coal, nuclear power and the like? Several such enterprises have hedged their bets by securing a stake in more than one. They are generally big enough and rich enough to do this, at least in the short run. But as the various interests and technologies diversify they will have to choose. In this sense, the choice establishes or confirms this aspect of corporate policy.

Financial precepts are a good deal easier to delineate. One very mundane precept might be that a new venture had to show prospects of yielding a certain minimum net return, or paying for itself within a certain specified period. In the international context such criteria might have to be relative to the cost of local borrowing or the local rate of inflation. The acceptable length of time for a full pay back also might depend on the political and economic conditions prevailing in the host country, and so on.

Other financial precepts might be less rational in short term monetary terms, but be none the less firmly held – a decision, for example, never to set up a subsidiary abroad unless 100 per cent financial control and ownership remained with the parent company; or at the other extreme, a decision always to insist on the participation of a local financial interest. A variant on this is the policy that nothing should ever be done which involved any significant change in the financial structure of the enterprise, such as might alter the ownership pattern.

Political and moral judgements might relate to staff, products or markets. In terms of *staff* this could be a decision not to operate in territories where staff practices of the home territory could not be applied. Examples are to be found in areas of discrimination, e.g. by race, colour, religion or sex. At a less controversial level, there might be an insistence that certain posts anywhere in the world would be held by the nationals of the enterprise's parent domicile. *Products* might be unacceptable if they were judged in some way to be undesirable or wasteful of resources, e.g. war materials, certain pharmaceutical products, cigarettes, etc. *Markets* might be banned on ideological or political grounds, e.g. no business to be done with a group, a nation or an ideology which was unacceptable to the top management or owners, over and above any legislation on embargoes imposed by the parent government. In the latter connection it may well be that business policy takes account of the opinions of the parent government, even where these opinions do not have the sanction of law: response to host government opinion tends to be less spontaneous.

Such precepts in corporate policy, explicit or implicit, would be known to the top decision makers. Policy as such is not immutable or eternal. It may evolve slowly or by deliberate decision. But it should not be violated for the sake of a short term tactical response to a crisis, particularly if this follows from a decision at junior management level which somehow slips past at senior level.

Corporate strategy: if the above definition of policy is accepted, then 'corporate strategy' or 'planning' might be defined as the means by which the corporate policy is implemented. It would involve the establishing of criteria by which new products or market decisions could be assessed, the preparation of short and longer term objectives preparing the various production, finance and marketing plans, certainly on a year by year basis, possibly on a rolling four or five year plan; and of course a system of monitoring results and where necessary adjusting plans accordingly.

It is possible for an enterprise to have no coherent corporate policy because there are no obvious causes of uncertainty which would require a precept to be formulated. It would be possible to have a corporate policy but no conscious corporate strategy, i.e. the enterprise simply reacts to ideas put up by management on an intuitive basis, or responds in an *ad hoc* manner to events. It is impossible, however, to have a corporate strategy without in the process evolving guidelines or corporate policy.

Even if the definitions given above appear somewhat unusual or indeed perverse, the concept of rational planning and the need for consistency appear so much commonsense as to make their being spelt out superfluous.

This section started with the comment that what followed applied almost exclusively to Western enterprises. In the present context it is impossible to do much more than scratch the surface in dealing with the strategy and motivation of non-Western enterprises. Two types of these are perhaps particularly worthy of note, namely the Japanese international enterprises which are beginning to rival the American in importance, as well as one or two of the 'Little Dragons', namely the newly industrializing economies and in particular Taiwan and South Korea. Some of the motivations of such non-Western enterprises will be touched upon in Chapter 2, but for the moment it can be noted that these, and particularly the Japanese enterprises, appear to march to a different tune. To revert, however, to the Western enterprises, what is being argued here is that implicitly or explicitly such enterprises have their own Western based corporate cultures and ideologies, which are more commonly described as corporate policy, strategy, etc. and that these may have to be reconciled with the larger cultural or ideological assumptions of host countries. This may not always be easy, particularly if the host country is not a Western one.

IDEOLOGY, CULTURE AND NATIONAL PLANS

Just as an individual company then, may have a corporate policy, explicit or implicit, and a corporate strategy by which to implement it, so the host government may have its equivalent in terms of an ideology embedded in a culture and possibly also a national plan. 'Ideology' and 'culture' are terms susceptible to a variety of interpretations, but in brief the definitions to be used for these terms are the following.

An *ideology* is a systematic body of economic, political and ethical doctrines which are adopted by a society or imposed on it by a ruling establishment. A *culture*, by contrast, is that body of economic, political and ethical beliefs which have historically evolved in the society. There is therefore in the first concept a deliberate decision if necessary to shape the culture; but also a tendency for the culture to absorb the ideology.

The implication of these definitions is that while ideology is the more important in the short run, it tends to be influenced by and to influence the underlying culture so that the same economic and political doctrines produce strikingly different results from culture to culture.

It is a matter of argument how far every nation possesses a consistent ideology or indeed a single prevailing culture. Western societies in general do not have a very clearcut ideology which can be separated out from the local culture, although there is a case for saying that those countries which have a written constitution or an extant bill of rights have at least the rudiments of an ideology. The situation is directly comparable with companies whose policy is at best implicit. In most parts of the Third World, however, an ideology is virtually *de rigueur* even if ignored in practice, and any local culture is prized. Certainly in the communist world there exists an ideology which officially abhors private enterprise and should therefore regard the presence of an international enterprise as totally unacceptable within its own frontiers.

If a nation state with a recognizable and consistent ideology is considering the use of the foreign international enterprise as an instrument of national development, it would be well to consider whether such an organization operating within its society is compatible with the ideology that nation professes. If it is not, the government may have to think again, or consider to what extent, if it cannot reconcile the activity with its ideology, it may have to change its ideology.

National plans. The second part of the pattern, the implementation equivalent to corporate strategy, is the national plan. As with an ideology, a national plan or a series of more specific objectives in creating particular industries is a not too infrequent feature of Western developed societies, and almost a *sine qua non* in Third World and communist economies. Generally, such plans set priorities in terms of the industries or technologies to be developed over a given period, and provide an indication of what the market will be like for certain products or what type of investment is being sought.

Again, as with corporate strategy at the company level, any national plan which is more than window dressing will have a fairly specific timetable, including intermediate objectives against which progress can be monitored. Unfortunately, even more than in the case of corporate strategy, targets are missed, slippage occurs and targets are downgraded. The more complex and detailed the plan is, the more serious the 'knock on' effect of a missed timetable.

An appreciation of the national plan, if this exists in detail, is important to the enterprise in three ways. In positive terms the plan may indicate the types of products, particularly capital goods, which are to receive priority. Second, if the plan lays down that certain industries are to be developed, it may warn the enterprise that the time has come to move over from exporting to local production – or to seeking new markets as the old one closes up behind protective barriers. The third, largely negative, aspect is the extent to which a subsidiary of an international enterprise can, if it chooses, evade the intent of any national plan, simply because of the room for manoeuvre which the enterprise possesses because of the legal personality.

THE PROBLEM OF THE DORMANT IDEOLOGY

From what has been said, it should be clear that there are ideologies in existence which are profoundly hostile, in theory, to private enterprise but which in practice tolerate or even welcome its presence within the territories over which the ideology is applied. It may be that any concession is a deliberate short term exception. This is a situation which the enterprise can cope with, provided it is given a clear indication of the period during which the ideology is being suspended. It may even be that the ideology is simply withering away whatever the official policy may be. The most difficult situation is that of the dormant ideology which is rather unexpectedly revived as a result of a political upheaval – a 'purification' movement which may apply ideological values which have been tacitly ignored. Such revivals are typical of Third World countries which have a built in political instability. At the very least, when such conditions appear possible, it is as well to have some contingency planning in reserve.

CONCLUSION

Much of what has been written so far may appear to the practising businessman to be remote and academic. There are after all many senior executives who would be hard pressed to identify the particular business policy or corporate strategy followed by their own organization. Moreover, though they may be well acquainted with their foreign contacts whether agents, joint venture partners or government officials, they may have little or no grasp of how their own enterprise fits into local ideologies or politics.

There are, however, serious implications about a failure to identify what the enterprise really wants to achieve by entering into that particular market, and what the long term intentions are of the host government in respect to its own operations.

2 Production Centres and Markets

INTRODUCTION

There are about one hundred and fifty nation states in the world, any one of which in theory could be both the source, i.e. the home country, and a potential foreign market, i.e. the host country. It is convenient to treat all of them as falling into one of four groups. These are, Western developed societies, Japan, the underdeveloped societies and the communist societies.

(1) The Western developed nations include most states in Western Europe and North America. All are predominantly European based cultures and are among the richest areas of the world, politically stable and growing in prosperity.

A subset of this group may be some Western developing nations, which again have dominantly European based cultures, are relatively underpopulated and are heavily dependent for their prosperity on the export of raw materials. Examples are Australasia, some countries in Latin America and, more controversially, South Africa. Their aim is industrial development, i.e. to join the ranks of the developed nations, and in pursuit of this, they are inclined in the short run to impose or increase trade barriers to protect and encourage their infant industries: hence the multinational enterprise engaged in exporting to these countries has seriously to consider setting up manufacturing plants within these states.

(2) Japan is not only the industrial giant of Asia, it is potentially the leading economic power of the twenty-first century. Over a wide range of technology it is on a level with or superior to most countries in the first group. It is at the same time profoundly non-Western in culture and traditions, and is at present the only non-Western society which has been able to absorb Western technology and match Western performance without in the process adopting Western cultural values. It is incidentally a role model for a number of developing countries which have achieved varying degrees of success in imitating it. It is, for example, possible to argue that a subset of the Japanese model exists in some Pacific Rim economies, namely Korea, Taiwan, Hong Kong, Singapore and possibly even Malaysia and Thailand. All are significantly different from Japan, but have still a number of factors in

common with that country, including a respect for age and authority which is Confucian in origin in some instances, intelligent and highly motivated workforces and a readiness to imitate Japanese methods.

(3) The underdeveloped world, the third group, is the most populous and at the same time most heterogeneous, comprising most of Latin America, Africa and Asia outside the communist bloc. In many instances overpopulated in terms of their resources, poor and politically unstable, the countries concerned pose substantial problems for the international enterprise, which may be unable or unwilling to invest in these areas because of the poor political or economic prospects awaiting foreign investment.

This group is steadily becoming more heterogeneous, in the sense that some of the larger countries are becoming economically more successful and may in time reasonably be added to the category of developed countries, Western or non-Western in cultural background. At the same time, however, a large number, possibly the majority, may be regressing rather than developing. Their population growth exceeds their industrial growth, and the individual citizen or family becomes worse off over time.

(4) The fourth group is the communist world, posing substantial ideological problems, yet having some attractions for the international enterprises, because of their potential wealth and their political stability in comparison with many countries of the third group.

WESTERN DEVELOPED SOCIETIES

Two groups of such markets, namely Western Europe and North America, together with Japan still dominate the world economy and represent the richest, as well as the most competitive, areas for the international enterprise. And in spite of the strains of prolonged world depression the tendency to falling trade barriers has been maintained. There have, however, been significant developments.

The first of these might be described as a tendency towards greater equality. Previously, if the Western developed nations dominated the markets of the world, the United States dominated the Western developed nations. This is no longer as pronounced a characteristic as it was in the early 1970s. Western Europe has emerged relatively stronger. Germany, for example, has attained a standard of living fully comparable with the United States. The fluctuations in the value of the dollar which is still effectively the world international currency has incidentally made the financial strategy of the typical American international enterprise much more complex, and has propelled such enterprises into a situation in which their interests may clash with that of their own government in that murky area of international finance.

Another developing characteristic of these groups of dominant economies is the remarkable growth of common standards, tastes and product acceptability. To a large degree this has implied the acceptance of American standards and tastes, the tendency towards mass consumption societies. The influence is, however, not only one way; the extravagant energy consumption practices of the Americans are likely to be replaced by the more economical European standards. As these societies move towards American living standards, they are not entirely losing the habits of thrift and caution engendered by a history of hardship, and this pattern is being reinforced by the exhaustion of some of the hitherto abundant indigenous natural resources on which American prosperity was in part based. America is becoming, like Western Europe, a substantial importer of raw materials, with the restraints and potential worries about paying one's way in the world that this implies.

An enterprise in a Western developed society whose production methods are based on a technology adequate enough to have prosects outside its own domestic market has various international options available to it, but is simultaneously subject to various external constraints.

The situation can be summarized in Diagram 2a. Initially the enterprise has three major options in the international field, namely to export, to assemble or manufacture in the foreign market or markets (the situation designated in the diagram as the 'international production' condition), or thirdly to follow the no-ownership/licensing option. As the diagram indicates by use of broken lines between the three choices which are crossed over, the divisions though logical in theory are by no means clearcut in practice.

The vertical or north–south co-ordinate indicates the degree of market information and control which potentially becomes available to the enterprise as it moves into more elaborate organizational structures. For example, at the north-west corner of the diagram one could envisage an export strategy based on the use of an export house, which bought products ex-factory, paid the manufacturer as a domestic purchaser and undertook to transport and market the goods abroad: the manufacturer could even remain ignorant of the ultimate foreign market in which his/her products were being sold, let alone the price and distribution methods being used there.

42

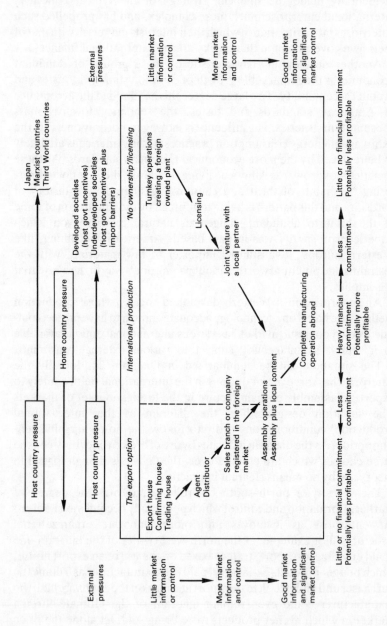

Diagram 2a International Production and Marketing in the Western Developed World

By contrast the horizontal west–east axis could be used to measure factors, namely the degree of financial commitment and risk and also the degree of potential profitability. These are measured outwards from the centre. They tend to confirm what is in most instances a commonsense assumption that organizational strategies which involve little knowledge of or control in the market, i.e. the export house situation in the north-west sector, or the licensing situation in the north-east, are also likely to be the strategies involving least financial commitments and risk, but also affording least potential profit.

The pros and cons of the various export channels shown in the first option, and of no-ownership/licensing strategy shown in the third option are sufficiently detailed elsewhere to require little elaboration at this stage. Suffice it to say that the diagram can be read as a 'trade-off' between risk and reward in the international field.

These three options as thus outlined might be described as being available to the enterprise in a political and economic vacuum. Unfortunately the situation is complicated by the presence of external pressures, which must now be considered.

a. External pressures

The major external pressures are represented as arrows in Diagram 2a, in the main indicating pressure to move from exporting to local production or licensing. This pressure comes from the marketplace, i.e. from the government of the importing country and to a lesser extent from the customer there. The several reasons why these sorts of pressure build up can be summarized in the proposition that for most governments, exports are good, in that they create or sustain jobs, enable levels of production to be kept up to the point that the technological base of the country is reinforced, and foreign currency is earned by sales abroad; conversely, imports are bad in that they represent lost jobs, increase the difficulty of introducing new technology based on mass markets or at the very least lower the scale of output, cost valuable foreign exchange and so on.

From the point of view of the importing country, a local production operation by the foreign enterprise, or a no-ownership/licensing strategy which transfers 'knowhow' without foreign ownership, have much the same desirable effects in terms of jobs, technology and foreign exchange implications, although the latter no-ownership/licensing strategy might be politically more acceptable. This strategy requires that an acceptable technological level already exists or can readily be built up to absorb the new industry, as well as the political will by the potential host government to insist on the option. The diagram has a three pronged arrow instead of a single arrowhead to indicate the countries where the pressure to adopt this option will be most readily applied to a foreign enterprise, namely Japan, marxist economies and some Third World countries. In all three cases, however, the statement requires almost immediate qualification. Japan built up its industrial strength after World War II, by making it extremely difficult for other industrial nations to export directly to its markets, and by excluding direct foreign investment if at all possible. From the foreign enterprise's viewpoint licensing was likely to have been the only way to earn money in this market. The qualification to be made is that Japanese policy has been amended under heavy external pressure.

In marxist societies the same principle tends to apply, backed up by ideological convictions, which denounce private ownership of productive resources, including foreign ownership, and hold simultaneously that while the technological level of the marxist society may be for historical reasons lower than in Western societies, a marxist society would prove to be inherently superior to the Western. It only requires that a technological 'graft' took place, and in a short time a socialist society would out perform a capitalist one. 'We shall bury you', as one Soviet leader remarked, rather prematurely, as it turned out. These societies therefore are in the main interested in buying technology rather than products, with the emphasis being on high technology, turnkey operations, however, as much as purely licensing. The marxists wish to buy not the product, but the plant which makes the product. Again, in recent years, several of the countries have modified their policies and allowed some foreign investment.

Insofar as Third World countries follow the no-ownership/licensing route, their model is probably Japan rather than the marxist societies, although their political sympathies may lie nearer the latter. The obvious point about the Japanese example is its success, i.e. the Japanese absorbed the technology and then out-performed their mentors, whereas marxist societies are hardly doing that with unqualified success. The Japanese success may be an unattainable ideal for most Third World countries, in that the level of existing technology may simply not exist already, or even more important in the long run, there may be a substantial cultural block which inhibits a successful transplant. Nevertheless, mirage or no, the Japanese strategy is seen as an ideal to be imitated.

The local production option may range from assembly to manufacture with 100 per cent local content, from a joint venture (or an indigenization strategy, i.e. one where local equity shares are sold to local investors) to a wholly owned subsidiary. The arrow in Diagram 2a which represents the pressure on the enterprise to move from exporting to local production is shown to divide into two prongs. The reason for this is to emphasize the different type of pressure operating on the enterprise, depending on whether the foreign market is a developed industrial country or a less developed one. In the case of the developed society the pressure may include financial incentives: these may be regional grants from central government or federal states in the case of, for example, the United States. In the last resort this pressure might go as far as the imposition of import restrictions such as the US government has from time to time threatened in the case of Japanese motor vehicle imports. Such restrictions in the case of developed countries are likely to be very much a last resort. In the case of the automobile industry, the US government achieved some inward investment/assembly not only from the Japanese companies but also Renault in partnership with American Motors, and Volkswagen. In the case of developing states, exempt from the non-tariff legislation implicit in membership of groups like GATT or the European Community, incentives may be reinforced or replaced by sanctions against imports, import controls, tariffs and the like.

The major pressures are those driving the enterprise away from an exporting strategy to local production in the marketplace or licensing. There may, however, be a countervailing pressure, namely from the home government of the enterprise, but reinforced by local hostility to a foreign enterprise, to compel it to revert from the international enterprise condition to exporting. Additionally, the commercial difficulties of British Leyland or the US Chrysler Corporation compelled them to close down or sell off foreign operations in the 1970s and serve what remained of the foreign market by exporting.

Such a retreat may be welcomed by the home governments of the international enterprise as a means of reverting to the advantages claimed for exports, principally the increased job opportunities which may be created in the home plants. Legislation on tax allowance which discriminated against the earnings of foreign subsidiaries may reinforce the tendency. The Hartke Burke legislation proposals of the early 1970s, supported significantly enough by the US trade unions, was a typical example of the sort of pressure which may be brought to bear. In spite of this legislation, however, no government in the West has pressed this issue so far as to compel its enterprise to wind up production abroad; in that sense, at least, pressure from a home government may be less than pressure from the host.

Finally, to complete the cycle it is necessary to show the reverse flow of products from areas of licensing or foreign plant sites back into the home territory of the enterprise. This flow is likely to arise in part as a means of payment or recovery of financial assets committed to a foreign operation. In the case of a no-ownership/licensing arrangement with a marxist economy chronically short of hard convertible currency, payment may be in kind. Typically, a turnkey operation might in time be paid for with the products of the plant. The difficulties of many chemical plants in the West in the 1980s were undoubtedly due to a flood of semi-processed materials built in East Europe with Western technology and now selling competitively back into the West European market. Similarly West European designed, East European built, motor vehicles are becoming relatively common in the European Community.

In the case of wholly owned subsidiaries, whether in the developed countries or the Third World, it may be the policy of the enterprise to transfer products depending on obsolescent technology or cheap labour assembly operations, and then supply its traditional markets from these new factories, using of course the familiar brand names on which its reputation was built. The implications of this 'runaway' industry on the Western industrial base may be profound. It is not merely the spread of technology which threatens many Western industries: it is the fact that the products continue to appear in the West under familiar brand names, although the manufacturing plant may be on the other side of the world.

b.   Internal pressures

If the external pressures are broadly in a west–east direction on Diagram 2a, it is likely that the internal pressures carry the enterprise in towards the central international enterprise condition, i.e. a south-east direction in the case of the export option, and a south-west in the case of the no-ownership/licensing strategy. Two reasons for this are discussed in Chapter 3, but briefly can be summed up as a condition where more knowledge of the market, and self-confidence on the part of the enterprise, might persuade it to a greater degree of financial commitment to secure a long term place in the market. Clearly the internal pressures conflict with the external in many instances, and ensure that the decisions to be taken by the enterprise are based as much on political as corporate strategy factors.

JAPAN

The Japanese international enterprises are a fascinating mixture of long term planning under national directives, and short term expediencies in response to pressure from the countries to which they have exported too successfully.

In the first instance they operate internationally in a relatively limited range of industries, most obviously electronics, motor vehicles and latterly construction companies. In part, at least, this relatively narrow concentration appears to indicate a successive unfolding of parts of a national strategy, to which major industrial groupings conform under the overall guidance of the central planning authority in the area, the Ministry of International Trade and Industry (MITI). Generally the groups are of two sorts, although the difference is historical rather than functional. There are the Zaibatsu, pre-war groupings which were dissolved under the post-war American occupation, but in many cases were reconstituted afterwards; and industrial groups created only in the post-war era, like Keiretsu. Often such groups, both Zaibatsu and Keiretsu are constituted round a bank. Mitsubishi, Mitsui, Sumitono and Fuji are typical examples of long established Zaibatsu. The post-war Keiretsu are frequently centred round a large industrial company, e.g. Hitachi, Matsushita, Nissan, Toyota, Toshiba and others. In both situations an important feature is a close link between a bank, an industrial group and a general trading company, the so called Sogo Shosha. The centre of power will vary between groups, but with interlocking directorates, and a sense of common interests in the upper hierarchy of management in all these elements, and with top civil servants, often based on the individuals concerned being graduates of the same prestigious universities. The result is a community of purpose which serves the national as much as the group interest.

The perverse feature of the Japanese groupings is that they become international, so to speak, by default. The Japanese have been far more reluctant than the Americans or Europeans to venture abroad on a permanent basis. They react to threats of sanctions from governments whose domestic interests are threatened by the too palpable successes of Japanese exports. But wherever possible they confine themselves to exporting using the Sogo Shoshas.

The success of Japanese policies in international business can scarcely be overestimated. In many respects the most significant developments of the 1980s have been in the rise in importance of Japan and in the role of their industrial groups, whose very success has destroyed the 'low profile' policy of an unpublicized advance into foreign operations and international status, while the domestic market remained substantially immune from foreign participation or even imports. The hostile criticism of Japanese methods, and pressure both from the US and the European Community have led to a moderation of Japanese restrictions on foreign investment or imports to Japan. It is becoming more possible for the foreign enterprise to secure a foothold in this market, though the bureaucratic and cultural obstacles remain formidable.

It is apparent, however, that an increased willingness on the part of the Japanese government to accept foreign imports is not by itself enough to permit foreign companies to penetrate the market significantly by more exporting there.

In one aspect, at least, Japanese policy may be changing, and that is in respect of the internationalization of the Japanese enterprises. The rapid rise in costs is likely to compel the Japanese to seek lower cost production facilities elsewhere, anywhere from Brazil to the United Kingdom or even the USA. A decade ago, Japanese foreign investment tended to be in extractive industries or low cost cheap labour operations in South-East Asia. Now, in response to growing hostility to Japanese export successes at the expense of domestic producers in the developed world, Japanese owned plants are becoming more common in Western developed societies. The Japanese international enterprise with manufacturing capacity outside Japan is likely to be far more important in the remainder of the twentieth century than in the past.

Diagram 2b representing the options open to the Japanese international enterprise might be regarded as a variant, or distortion of, the diagram applying to Western enterprises (2a). All the familiar features are there but their importance is substantially changed. One obvious example is the dominating role of the Sogo Shosha or trading house. Strictly this could be regarded as the equivalent of the export house used by small Western enterprises, or by large enterprises in very small or unimportant markets.

The Sogo Shosha, then, plays a dominant role in Japanese exports compared with which the other distribution channels fade into relative insignificance. The tie-up among the three elements, however, goes

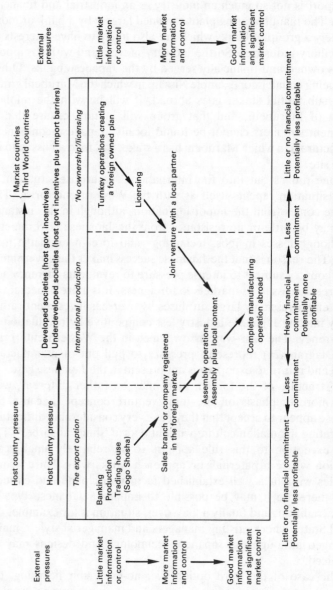

Diagram 2b *International Production and Marketing – JAPAN*

further, as the Japanese enterprise is subject to the pressure to move across from exporting to local manufacture. For what the Japanese may export is not so much an industry as an industrial and financial system. The manufacturing plant is owned largely by a bank or more accurately a group of banks which are also likely to have interests in any ancillary industries. So the industry moves, and with it support services owned and financially served by the Japanese banks. Other things being equal, if for example Nissan, in which the Marubeni group have a substantial stake, goes abroad, it will be with the implicit consent of Marubeni, and that group will in turn ensure that if component suppliers cannot be found locally, Japanese component manufacturers in which Marubeni has a stake, will follow Nissan to its foreign site.

As one moves out into the international enterprise situation, a similar situation repeats itself as with the Western enterprise. The pressure comes from the importing nation, although in this instance there may be little or no resistance from the Japanese government, even though losses in jobs, technology and foreign exchange may follow. The reason is that the Japanese success makes the government of that country subject to intense pressure to revalue its currency and allow freer access to its markets to foreigners. It is more expedient to reduce embarrassingly large surpluses by overseas investment rather than by making Japanese industry less competitive by revaluation of the currency. The east–west arrow which in the Western enterprise case (Diagram 2a) represents pressure to pull out of manufacture abroad and return to exporting is not present in the Japanese case.

The structure of the foreign plant may be rather different, with rather more emphasis on the joint venture concept, because the Japanese appear to accept that they have very considerable difficulties in operating in an alien culture without a local 'shock absorber'. The major exception to this rule appears to be relatively small scale operation where a paternalistic approach works well; Third World countries without a well established factory discipline and culture, where therefore it may be possible to impose a Japanese type of factory tradition; and finally a 'buy-over' situation is for example, the United States where existing managers and managerial style remains unchanged although the Japanese technology and designs may be introduced.

In the case of the third option, i.e. no-ownership/licensing, the Japanese emphasis appears to have been more on the turnkey operation backed up by managerial support, than on licensing as such.

There are two possible reasons for this. Japan is notoriously short of raw material and its efforts in this direction tend to have the aim of creating alternative sources of raw materials. Whether the turnkey operation is in the extraction of natural gas from Siberian fields or the creation of a chemical complex in Saudi Arabia, the literal pay-off for Japan is the raw materials which can in time be supplied as payment. Japan's licensing of its own technology appears to have been effectively limited by the rapidity with which Japanese enterprises exploit their own developments on a worldwide basis although reciprocal licensing of the type discussed elsewhere is becoming more significant.

The major distinction in approach between the Western and Japanese enterprises may be the role of the government: in the Japanese case the powerful Ministry of International Trade and Industry which provides effective and unchallenged guidance to the enterprise. The Japanese enterprises act almost as an extension of government policy to a degree which is almost inconceivable in most Western society, with the possible exception of France.

Because of the close relationships between industry and the state in Japan, it is possible to perceive more of the joint planned corporate and national policy in this instance than appears to apply to international enterprises originating in the United States or Europe.

There appears to have been two stages. The first post-war drive was to secure raw materials, i.e. what might be defined as a belated but accelerated effort to set up extractive industries. This phase lasted until about the early 1970s, and probably helped to explain the evident unpopularity of many Japanese enterprises operating in the Third World generally and in South-East Asia particularly where wartime memories persisted. In time, the Japanese appear to have decided to avoid the dangers of ownership of extractive industries and contented themselves with assisting other economies to develop the raw material supplies required by Japan.

In the long term, of more significance has been the spread of manufacturing capacity from about 1970 onwards. In the beginning, as has been suggested, this seems to have been a pragmatic response to problems of payment in developing countries, problems which were eased if the foreign exchange costs of imports could be reduced by assembly operations. However, as hostility to Japanese success has spread to the developed world, assembly operations and local manufacturing has been applied there. There have been experiments in several of the ownership strategies discussed. In the United States,

Japanese strategy has often been to buy over existing companies, in Europe to build from a green field operation, often on a minor scale; and most recently there have been experiments in a new variety of joint venture, namely the British Leyland/Honda link-up to produce specific car models for the European market, or Datsun's link with Alfa Romeo.

Finally, it is noteworthy that the Japanese model is being imitated very consciously both by South Korea, Taiwan and more tentatively by the Philippines and Malaysia which are setting up trading companies on Japanese lines. The first two will be the subject of a later section, on the Pacific Rim NICs. It is doubtful whether these economies will go all the way down the Japanese route, let alone achieve the same degree of success. The latter must be due as much to cultural adaptation as to the structure of the enterprise. But at least in the Korean example the operation of turnkey projects represents a marriage of industry and national policy which goes even further than the Japanese have achieved. This is in the mass supply of labour as well as technology: work on an international turnkey operation appears to rank for the Korean labourer as the equivalent of national service. This may be practical for a country whose living standards are appreciably lower than that prevailing in Japan, but may not be so practical as prosperity spreads.

Finally, to revert to Diagram 2b, it is worth emphasizing that though there is external pressure on the Japanese enterprise to move away from exporting to local production or licensing, there is little or no pressure being applied by the Japanese government or trade unions to move back from overseas operations to simple exporting. The reluctance is to move outwards in any event: Japanese companies would much prefer to stay at home in their own environment, and have to be encouraged by the Japanese government as well as pressured by the importing nations before they will move out of Japan. Japanese enterprises are very responsive to the wishes of the Japanese government: they would very rapidly respond to any instructions to return home.

THE NEWLY INDUSTRIALIZING COUNTRIES

As was suggested at the beginning of the chapter, some of the countries popularly known as the newly industrializing countries (NICs), and particularly those with a common Confucian background who are consciously imitating the Japanese pattern, may be considered as a subset of the Japanese pattern. They are sometimes referred to as the 'new Japans'. The most spectacularly successful are those countries strung along the East Asia edge of the Pacific Rim, and they will be discussed in more detail in the next section, but there are arguably others, such as Brazil and possibly Mexico and Egypt. They have all achieved a technological base which enables them to produce a wide range of products which do not involve the most dynamic technology, i.e. they can sustain mature industries, where no great new technical breakthrough is likely, e.g. steel making, shipbuilding, even car production, a wide range of electrical equipment and appliances, etc. They can even produce components for more sophisticated technology where their labour costs are relatively low and a market is assured, i.e. through a foreign international enterprise producing more sophisticated equipment elsewhere. A majority are pro-Western, or at least anti-Soviet, although there are exceptions, and additionally they tend to have authoritarian governments.

Their attitude towards inward foreign investment varies, but in general is harsher the more obvious the intention of the enterprise to exploit the domestic market rather than export. Thus large and rich countries tend to require dilution of foreign ownership through joint venture, or indigenization legislation, except where there is a strong expectation of foreign exchange earnings from export. Where the domestic market is small or insignificant the bargaining power of the host government is reduced, and foreign investment may be actively encouraged as a means of entry into the lucrative markets of the Western developed economies.

An interesting expedient pioneered by Mexico but potentially applicable elsewhere is the 'in bond' system. Here the government permits duty free imports of raw materials or components from a developed society, in this case from the United States. After processing is completed, they are re-exported back to the originating country, where they are taxed only on the 'value added' component, not the total value. This is a particularly appropriate system where there is ready access to the major industrial economy; as has been seen, Mexico with its proximity to growth centres in the USA is a prime example. But relatively cheap sea transport makes much of the Eastern edge of Asia readily accessible to Japan and the west coast of the USA. Not only are American companies heavily involved in these operations, but Japanese electronics and vehicle producers are also showing an interest. The main resistance to such a policy by an international enterprise is likely to come from the trade unions in the developed country, where jobs are perceived to be lost.

A characteristic of the successful newly industrializing country is likely to be a rapid rise in the standard of living and therefore a corresponding rise in costs. Just as Japan developed from a low cost, low quality economy to a high cost, technologically innovative one, so, it may be argued, will some of these newly industrializing countries. The crunch, if it comes, will be when higher wage costs have to be matched by technological innovation to compensate. Some countries with rapidly growing populations may postpone almost indefinitely the rise in the cost of labour, since they have every reason to prefer more, to better paid, employment. Brazil, Mexico or even Hong Kong fall within this category. Others, like Singapore, with a small population and a government willing and able to restrain growth, may in fact seek wage cost rises at some stage to accelerate the process of increasing technological content in their products. This certainly was the strategy before the recession of the 1980s.

THE PACIFIC RIM NICs

Although the industrial and commercial institutions of countries like South Korea or Taiwan are often consciously modelled on Japan, their differences from their role model may in the long run be more important than their similarities, and they are likely in time to develop their own business culture and practices. But at the moment it appears that, for example, the Korean Chaebols, industrial groupings centred on family interests but fostered as instruments of growth by the government, owe much to the Japanese Keiretsu model, with their trading house aspect. In the same way the Taiwanese government has encouraged the formation of trading groups based on the Japanese Sogo Shosha. But it cannot be said that either of these two experiments has as yet shown the coherent philosophy and success of the Japanese model.

Singapore has in many respects been more adventurous. Not only has it adopted the Japanese pattern extensively, but in the late 1970s and early 1980s the government deliberately forced up wages to accelerate the change from a low cost, labour intensive society to a high technology, capital intensive economy. The experiment faltered in the mid 1980s in the world recession when Singapore was worse hit than the other NICs, in part because of this adventurous policy.

Hong Kong and the special economic zones of China

The situation of Hong Kong is of course dominated by the implications of its reversion to mainland Chinese control in 1997. Its industrial and commercial development is unique for the area. From the nineteenth century onwards industrial, but mainly commercial, development was led by the 'Hongs', those commercial groups financed and dominated by expatriates, Jardine Matheson, the Swire group in its earlier form, *et al.* By the late twentieth century, many of the smaller Hongs were being taken over or overtaken by local entrepreneurs, in many instances financed by the accumulated savings of the extended families or clans. Although there is plenty of evidence of massive investment overseas, particularly in North America, the Hongs and their indigenous successors have not as yet developed any coherent strategy of internationalization of business, save perhaps in shipping lines, and in the take-over of some traditional industries in the West, such as textiles or even some electronics. What is possible in the longer term, provided that there is no great change in strategy in Beijing is that such enterprises will use the growing production facilities in the special economic zones set up by the Chinese government to encourage inward investment particularly as an export earner. Hong Kong may in time evolve its own variety of a trans-ideological enterprise, matching up cheap labour intensive production skills in the South China provinces and the special economic zones, with the entrepreneurial genius of the overseas Chinese based on Hong Kong.

THE UNDERDEVELOPED WORLD

The underdeveloped world comprises much of Latin America, Africa and South-East Asia and spans the range from the primitive to the rapidly developing economy which is likely to catch up with European standards of living within the foreseeable future. The situation has been confused by the rather bland assumption of reasonable homogeneity and a community of interests at least against the Western developed world, expressed in membership of the United Nations Conference on Aid and Development (UNCTAD), of non-aligned conferences and so forth. The reality has always been different: there is at least as much variety within the underdeveloped world as elsewhere, and incidentally as much political and economic conflict.

In terms of their interest to the international enterprise, these hundred-odd nations can be further divided into subgroups. One very obvious of such subgroups distinguishes between those which permit foreign investment and those which do not, and within the former subgroup there is the question of whether any plant may be 100 per cent foreign owned or whether a policy of indigenization is likely to be imposed. These issues will be discussed in more detail in Chapter 3.

Of more immediate relevance, however, is a consideration of whether the individual nation state is large or small in population size, and rich or poor in terms of natural resources. Such measures are clearly relative, nor are they really independent of each other, but by applying the two pairs of attributes, a fourfold classification emerges.

As a fairly arbitrary cut-off point, one might define a country as large if it had a population of at least 30 millions. The population explosion of the Third World makes any such definition a very vague one, but the point about such a population size is that if there is any element of disposable income it is at least possible to argue that a domestic market exists which could sustain the output of some modern industries. A country of such a population size could, for example, sustain some form of vehicle production which amounted to more than simply the assembly of imported kits.

The second attribute, namely the degree of wealth, is equally hard to define. However, insofar as wealth in underdeveloped countries depends on the production and sale of raw materials, one might regard an underdeveloped country as being relatively rich if their sales give a *per capita* GNP roughly comparable to that of an industrialized state of Western developed world.

(1) The first group then comprises states with a large population which are potentially relatively wealthy. They have resources to match their large and growing populations, and even if they do fail to turn this wealth into a high *per capita* income, it is often failure imposed by their governments rather than scarce resources that condemn a high proportion of their population to a marginal existence. The obvious examples are some of the more populous oil exporters, e.g. Nigeria, Mexico, and possibly Indonesia which, while having officially a very low *per capita* income for 150 million inhabitants, still represents a relatively wealthy small urban population. Such states may be in a position to put up tariff barriers or other restrictions in the knowledge that their domestic market still would be attractive enough to persuade the former exporters to set up production facilities. A major problem for the international enterprise which does so is that in time a process of nationalization, or more probably, of indigenization may take place

when the host government insists on the dilution of foreign ownership by the sale of equity shares to local individuals or institutions. The initial policy of the enterprise may be to introduce obsolescent products, using equipment which is being phased out elsewhere: if, however, the economy is large enough to absorb several producers, then the competitive situation will be such that more up to date models will be introduced.

Again it is difficult to generalize about conditions in these countries. An obvious attraction of this type of market is cheap labour combined with an attractive 'base load' domestic market on which subsequent exports can be built. At the same time it has to be recognized that the social structure of some of these countries is under immense strain, particularly if uncovenanted wealth has suddenly arrived in the form of oil revenues. Typically the price of oil soars to the point where unearned wealth damages much of the traditional national infrastructure, but at some time later the oil price collapses and the country is left with a partially ruined system which has not yet been replaced by a Western type. Inflation and corruption are only the outward signs. Just as significant may be the partial collapse of the national infrastructure, which grew up to cope with a poorer and less frenetic society. Interminable hold-ups in every form of communication from road traffic congestion to inefficiencies in telephone or telex, hold-ups and congestion in ports etc. make a mockery of the more sophisticated planning, based on the fallacy of assuming that the experience of planning in one society can be readily applied anywhere else.

Governments in such countries tend to be optimistic, indeed arrogant about their future prospects. The assumption is that an abundance of the raw materials so desperately required by the developed world will enable them to industrialize, to acquire and improve on the latest technology, to reach the front rank of the industrialized nation before the raw material or the demand for it runs out. The problem is that for these nations it is on occasion almost too easy to pay their way and enjoy a high basically unearned standard of living without the need to become competitive. Such nations tend to find that inflation rapidly erodes any competitive edge and possibly long term reserve assets. The result of allowing expenditure to rise to meet income is, as has been suggested, disaster if the demand for the basic raw material collapses or the materials run out. Nigeria in the late 1980s became a horrendous example of that phenomenon. Such economies whose oil reserves, for example, are estimated at say 30 years of current demand are running a race with time. They have to create alternative means of creating wealth, presumably through industrialization, before their earning capacity from raw material sales is exhausted. It is by no means certain that all will succeed in industrializing in time.

(2) The second group of underdeveloped nations are those with the classic symptons, namely a large mass of the population at subsistence level, inadequate natural resources to pay for industrialization, and hence political instability. The primary attraction for the international enterprise, namely an adequate base load domestic market, may simply not exist. Foreign investment may therefore consist of assembly operations, licensing or some combination: or more occasionally an industry based on cheap labour and geared to exporting from the outset.

Insofar as such societies have less obvious attractions for the international enterprise, it may be possible to obtain some financial concessions from the prospective host government, particularly in the form of export incentives. At the same time however the fact of political instability and an unpromising economic prospect may make investment a risky business, calling for a strategy which emphasizes the idea of a rapid return on investment at the expense of longer term prospects.

(3) The third group at first sight appears to be the most fortunate, namely countries with small populations but vast natural resources. The classic examples of such societies are most of the Middle East Oil States. The *per capita* income of such states is among the world's highest: they may not even be particularly unstable since the wealth can finance the 'buying off' of all but the most ideologically committed rebels, and insofar as they are vital to Western interests, they are in practice well protected against external aggression.

The long term prospects of these societies is dubious: certainly they have limited attractions for international enterprises interested in setting up manufacturing facilities. The major difficulties are simply the degree of wealth, the expectations created among the citizens and the degree of inflation. In many of these countries, the vast majority of the working force consists of immigrant labour, since manual work is regarded as degrading by the *nouveau riche* inhabitants, and the cost of such labour is constantly rising. The consequence is that labour costs, and for that matter, any other local cost is going to be very high. In a sense, although the host government which is anxious to industrialize may be willing to protect the home market by import restrictions, any industrial development which follows is likely to be very costly and quite uncompetitive in the international market place. So far as industrialization is concerned, too much wealth may be an even greater obstacle to development than a little.

This type of industrial development is to be found typically in a country like Saudi Arabia where vast sums are being spent by the authorities on projects of industrialization. It is to be feared however that the outlook for these projects may be bleak unless they continue to be linked to abundant and virtually freely exploitable natural resources, resources which are not inexhaustible. The problem may be accentuated by cultural problems which militate against the creation of a Western type industrial culture. But even in the case of European based cultures such as exist in Venezuela, the implications of massive natural resources are not all encouraging. The depopulation of the countryside, the need to import foodstuffs into a large and relatively fertile country suggests the possibility that expensive industrial projects based on raw materials may never be competitive and may in fact absorb most of the income generated by the sale of raw materials. Once these run out, the prospects for the new industries may be bleak. Some observers would indeed make the same observations about UK oil resources.

The role of the international enterprise in these societies is therefore, and probably should remain, relatively limited to advice and contract management, rather than a permanent commitment in a territory whose immediate market, though rich, is small, and which is not likely to be increased by exporting. Some at least of these societies which are seen as the most lucrative in the world may also be the most transient.

(4) To be a small community with few natural resources, i.e. one of the fourth group, might appear to be a recipe for a grim fate. In fact a suprising number of such communities, particularly in South-East Asia have used their apparent disadvantages with remarkable effect. The first point is that smallness may have some advantage in enabling a government to pursue policies to attract inward investment, or encourage exports, which would invite reprisal if indulged in by major societies.

What such communities may have as a raw material is initially at least simply cheap labour, and this has made them the natural areas for assembly operations which can be done more cheaply by hand than by automation. As rising wage levels and the influence of trade unionization make their presence felt in more and more of the industrialized countries there is a temptation for the international enterprise to transfer production facilities to these territories while retaining control of technological development by keeping research and development at home. Whereas products from many of these countries would have an unfavourable reputation as being cheap and unreliable, the trade mark or brand name of a world famous company will count for more than the origin. Electronic equipment manufactured in South-East Asia under well known names is an increasingly familiar phenomenon. In some respects the lack of the base load domestic market can be turned into an asset by the international enterprise which can ensure the product is designed for its traditional market, and which through the control of the distribution channels in the foreign market, is in a strong position *vis-à-vis* the host government.

There is likely to be even more use, by international enterprises, of such societies in industries particularly where the value content of assembly is high in relation to transport costs. These are the runaway industries which threaten jobs in the developed societies and which so concern governments and particularly trade unions in traditional areas, as well as highly innovative industries where the rate of development makes the enterprise reluctant to introduce capital intensive methods which may rapidly become obsolescent.

As a source of international business, the underdeveloped world cannot be said to compare in variety or sophistication with the developed world.

A growing type of industrial export from underdeveloped countries is what might be termed the unidentifiable product, often a component which is being produced for an enterprise in the West, which ensures its acceptance by branding or incorporating the component in a more sophisticated product. This gives access, albeit on a limited scale at minimum profit to Western developed markets. The most obvious basis of commerce in many instances is raw materials, which may or may not be controlled by foreign enterprises. Foreign enterprises tend to be dispossessed of these extractive industries as and when the technological processes can be taken over by local individuals or fixed foreign technicians. Indeed the process may be encouraged by the enterprises themselves, who may prefer captive suppliers, to their own local plants. In the present context, however, it is the nationalized industries, generally previously foreign owned, which are seen to enter the international field firstly as exporters of raw materials, but later as exporters of semi-finished products, i.e. from iron ore to sheet steel, from copper ore to copper ingots and so on, as the former host governments attempt to attract the processing industries away from the developed world to which raw materials were previously shipped.

The export channels for such raw materials are relatively simple, as is shown in Diagram 2c. Either products are being sold through the commodity exchange markets, or through some process of price fixing to large scale industrial buyers in the West. In most cases the distribution channel is short and simple: all the commodity organization does is put on a minimum price. OPEC in its more successful days was the best example of this.

A problem about semi-processed materials is that, almost regardless of the cheapness of local raw materials and perhaps fuel, low technical efficiency may make the products relatively uncompetitive in the world market. Barter deals or sales into a relatively protected regional grouping may be the most practicable way into a limited international market.

The major type of manufactured goods being exported from these countries are relatively low quality, relatively unsophisticated consumer durables, which may sell in other parts of the underdeveloped world, often through bilateral deals between the governments, or at the lower end of the market in the West. Although these manufacturers depend on the ability of the government to attract processing industry from the developed world which previously processed the raw materials and so tend to rely on imported technology, they find it very difficult to move 'up market'. The process of moving up market is, however, not impossible. Older readers might care to reflect on the image of Japanese products a generation ago, i.e. cheap and inferior, and how the image dramatically changed as the Japanese reputation for quality, and the price which could be commanded, rose accordingly. At least four countries which one or two decades ago would have been grouped in the underdeveloped world – Hong Kong, South Korea, Taiwan and in particular Singapore – are attempting to follow the same route and are likely to succeed.

In some countries the enterprises were originally foreign owned and were expropriated during a political crisis – much Indonesian locally owned industry is a good example, which largely dates back to the Dutch colonial era. One result of a takeover during a political crisis, namely the loss of foreign technical experts is critical enough: in most cases however the expropriated companies are then run by indigenous managers whose political connections count for more than technical competence. The level of efficiency which the nationalized company then achieves may simply not be high enough to be internationally competitive.

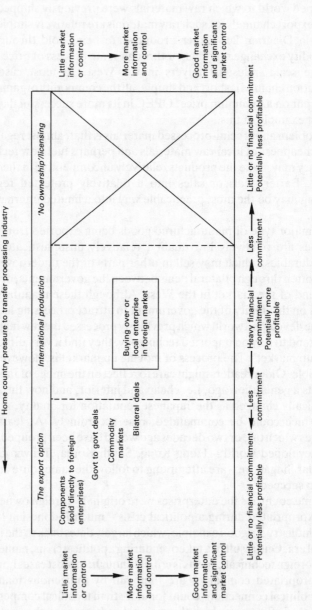

Diagram 2c *International Production and Marketing – the Underdeveloped World*

What has been described this far is the export option situation for Diagram 2c. There is no licensing option although, as has been noted, some of the more advanced industrially, like South Korea, offer 'turnkey operations' on capital projects.

The middle option of production in other markets scarcely exists save in two respects. One or two international enterprises are beginning to emerge in underdeveloped countries like India which have production or at least assembly operations elsewhere.

However, insofar as the governments of countries like India tend to see the operation of international enterprises within their territories as presenting problems, their attitude towards their own multinationals is at best ambivalent. Potentially more important however may be the fact that some of the rich underdeveloped nations are embarrassingly endowed with foreign exchange assets which are losing value through inflation. An obvious use of such funds might appear to be to buy into foreign industry – either buying over the industries which process and distribute the products based on the raw materials, or other industries whose technological development makes them particularly interesting. Examples of this type of development have been Libyan purchases of shares in the Fiat car company, or reported plans to buy over refining capacity and petrol distributors in some European countries: or Iran, in the days of the Shah, attempting to buy his way into European heavy industry.

The theoretical promise of such developments are boundless. A few weeks' revenue of, for example, Saudi Arabia would equal the market value of all but the largest US multinationals. Even the net value of a company like General Motors could readily be matched by Saudi oil exports in a relatively short time.

There are, however, two obvious limitations to this tactic of the underdeveloped world buying into international business. In the first instance, no government of a developed nation would accept the buying over of its key industries by foreign interests. Minority holdings only would be permitted, and certainly not controlling interests. Second, the acquisition of relatively smaller or less sensitive companies does not really make the owner a genuine international business organization. Ownership by accident of unearned wealth is not a basis on which to acquire real control. Control implies knowledge of the technology, and a Third World owner, whether private individual or state holding enterprise, lacks that technology. Investment in this situation flows into finance and property rather than the technologically dynamic sector of an economy. This is a point which will be developed in the next chapter.

MARXIST SOCIETIES AS A SOURCE OF INTERNATIONAL BUSINESS

The communist world now provides a complete variety of technological standards from the primitive to the highly sophisticated. As a political system marxism is now far from monolithic even with the political bloc in Eastern Europe dominated by the USSR. The style of industry, of trading and of relationships with international enterprises elsewhere are changing at a bewildering rate.

Nevertheless, there are certain characteristics still common to all. First, an economic system whose internal pricing methods are significantly different from those in the Western world: a tendency to subordinate the interests of the enterprise to the needs of the state: the use of the state trading enterprise as the main channel for foreign trade and, as a consequence, a complex system of exporting, quite unlike anything experienced in Western societies. Above all, of course, there is the ideological issue of ownership, and the ultimate incompatibility of a privately owned international enterprise operating within a society which regards private ownership of the means of production as anathema.

It is an open question as to whether Western governments should permit or encourage the degree of collaboration with societies whose ultimate objective is to destroy the Western system: it is an equally open question on whether the ideology of the marxist states can resist the encroachment of capitalism at its most dynamic. But what is clear is that from the point of view of the Western international enterprise, the key factor in their relationship with communist societies is not the ideological aims of these societies, but rather their political stability.

Although there are as yet no exact equivalents in marxist countries to Western or Japanese multinational companies, the operation of marxist societies in international business, whether in competition with or in collaboration with the non-marxist groups, is highly significant and growing in importance year by year (see Diagram 2d).

The major channel for foreign trade in communist societies has been and is likely to remain, the foreign trade enterprise (FTE) acting under the aegis of the Ministry of Foreign Trade. Depending on the size and industrial complexity of the particular economy there may be between

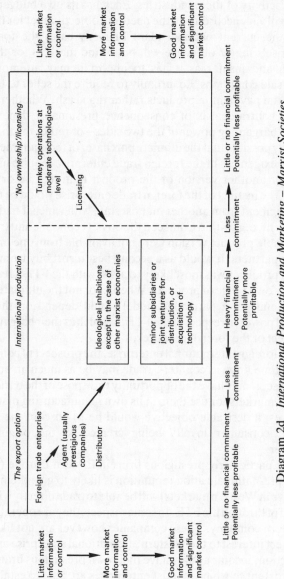

Diagram 2d International Production and Marketing – Marxist Societies

20 and 40 such organizations each dealing with a specific industry or range of industries and responsible for the great bulk of export and import activity of these industries. Each has its own budget and tasks, which will vary according to the need and objectives set for the industry under the current national plan. In many cases the foreign trade enterprise's major objective will be to find markets for the industry abroad, and insofar as it has to import it may attempt to attach contra-sale conditions, i.e. broadly to require the seller to take at least part of the payment in products rather than cash. Whether or not this type of contra-deal is of consequence presumably depends on the relative bargaining power of the two sides – or rather the three, for it is perfectly possible that the ultimate purchaser of the equipment may find that the exigencies of the foreign trade enterprise require him or her to settle for another version of the product than that he or she would desire. The instinct of the foreign trade enterprise would be to purchase the equipment from another marxist state with which it had a trade-up agreement, e.g. within Comecon the Soviet economic and trading bloc. If a suitable product version were not available from one of its marxist trading partners, it would as a second best resort buy from whichever foreign producer was most likely to assist with the FTE's requirements to sell its own range of products. Whether or not the ultimate user could prevail and get a particular model would depend on their relative political power in respect of the FTE, as much as their bargaining power in respect of the foreign producer.

For a foreign international enterprise, the prospect of contra-, or as it is sometime known, counter-, trade may be as much an advantage as otherwise. It may have the opportunity to dispose of the barter products in other markets, or use them in its own manufacturing plants. In both instances, a desirable objective would be to obscure the source and prevent consumer loyalty being created to the original marxist producer.

Some particularly prestigious firms in Eastern Europe (often firms whose pre-nationalization reputation is likely to give them a competitive edge in Western markets) will be able to trade directly with the West instead of through the FTE. In some respects they are operating much as a Western company. These companies however are not likely to be of any direct interest to the Western international enterprise as a source of production, insofar as they have their own prestigious brands.

The extent to which marxist enterprises are able to establish a clear brand name and image in Western society varies enormously. In general they have very limited acceptance and reach the public in the case of consumer goods through the more obscure retailing channels. There are exceptions where, in for example the case of watches or cars, they may be advertised in a manner and with panache rivalling that of any Western producer. This, however, seems very much to be the exception rather than the rule, and probably depends on the extent to which good advice from Western sources overrides the ideological distaste of playing the capitalist game. Capital equipment fares particularly badly in a competitive situation. Quality is often indifferent, and after sales servicing even worse. Sales of such equipment tends to be confined to the Third World and depends on ideological compatibility as well as the readiness of the communist producers to accept barter payment.

Although the last few pages describe the situation up to the late 1980s it would be dangerous to be too dogmatic that this situation will last. Economic reforms attempted by Gorbachev are altering the structure and their supporting institutions with bewildering speed, and it is possible that in a few years' time many enterprises will be able to bypass the Foreign Trade Enterprise system, and conduct their foreign trade in much the same manner as do Western enterprises.

Finally in this context it is worth noting that the FTE system has been adopted by a number of countries which, while not formally marxist, are of a left wing, or at least anti-Western, persuasion.

Again, it is a little difficult to generalize about the role of international production in the context of the marxist world. There are instances of joint ventures to develop technology within a communist society, but clearly the possibility of selling up production facilities in foreign countries is fraught with ideological problems. Some marxist societies however appear to be willing to experiment in joint ventures with Western or Japanese enterprises in Third World countries. In the case of those involving international tendering on turnkey operations they may more properly be seen as a variant of the 'no-ownership/licensing' option.

The 'no-ownership/licensing' option is one which has attractions for the communist world under two sets of circumstances: first, that they have no means of earning foreign exchange more directly; and second, that the level of technology is not too high. This tends to translate into turnkey operations in Third World countries in areas such as steel making. The resultant product is likely to be robust, rather than sophisticated.

The foreign trade enterprise whose responsibility is handling licensing may be concerned to sell knowhow. There are two practical difficulties: first, that the level of technological innovation in marxist societies has tended to be low in non-strategic industries: and second, in the latter, security considerations constrain the amount of useful knowhow they have available to license out.

Finally, and significantly perhaps in the Western marxist concept a proto-multinational enterprise pattern is beginning to emerge, albeit from very small beginnings. This is to be seen in the proposals for assembly operations in such potentially lucrative markets as North America for Soviet produced vehicles; if, as anticipated, this led to sourcing of components from local companies, the era of the genuinely trans-ideological enterprise would be brought significantly nearer.

The preceding paragraph used the qualification '*Western* marxist', since the same pattern does not necessarily apply in Asian marxist economies. The Chinese have shown a readiness to experiment, and are apparently willing to compromise ideological purity to obtain Western technology. The authorities may even be prepared to permit 100 per cent foreign ownership of subsidiaries which export, or a minority shareholding in subsidiaries supplying the domestic market for a period of up to 15 years with promises of fair compensation in the event of nationalization at the end of this period.

It is difficult to generalize about China in the midst of the New Economic Reforms of the early and mid 1980s. From being arch imperialists during the Cultural Revolution in the 1960s, Western enterprises have become in some respects the panacea, bringing in new technology, and opportunities for Chinese enterprises to enter world markets directly, instead of through the Soviet style foreign trade organizations which were adopted in the early 1950s. The major problems facing the foreign enterprises are twofold: first, the inflated expectations of many of the Chinese enterprises now seeking foreign partners, in that these enterprises may have a somewhat simplistic idea of what a partnership with a Western organisation, unaccompanied by a readiness to impose Western financial and managerial disciplines on their enterprises, may achieve; second, the Chinese government (and the individual enterprises) have generally failed to come up with a specific *quid pro quo* for the foreign partner.

There are two probabilities, one of which has developed against the intention of the Chinese government. This is that a foreign enterprise may enter into a joint venture/licensing arrangement with a Chinese enterprise and then may concentrate in meeting an almost insatiable demand within the Chinese domestic market. Thus, instead of supplementing China's foreign trade earnings by assisting in exporting, it may drain off that country's foreign exchange reserves. Such a situation has become possible because so much discretion on the expenditure of these reserves has now been decentralized to the municipal level. These municipalities which have the authority to license joint ventures may, for example, be fobbed off with obsolescent models of Japanese TVs or other electronic or electrical gadgets. The Japanese partners find a use for obsolescent models and dies, the Chinese partners and the municipalities which control them still make large profits. But this was hardly the original intention of the Chinese authorities.

The second possibility exists in terms of products which can be exported to secure hard currency to pay the foreigner, instead of asking them to accept virtually inconvertible renminbi, the local currency. The problem for the foreign enterprise is to ensure that any products or components thus supplied are of an acceptable international quality. In a situation of a captive domestic market, where virtually any products can be sold, it is difficult to persuade the Chinese partner that, in the outside world, the consumer has alternative suppliers, and will not accept the same quality standards that the Chinese consumer is used to.

REGIONAL GROUPINGS

Introduction

There is a *prima facie* case for saying that any attempt to set up a regional grouping anywhere in the world is important to the international enterprise, in terms both of the opportunity and threats posed by such groups.

The opportunity is to be found in the prospect of increased market size represented by the amalgamation of several smaller markets already mentioned; a situation which may justify a move to a more integrated production facility in the market. The threats, however, are more numerous and complex. The first of these is that the co-ordinating authority may feel better placed to impose greater restrictions on the operation of the enterprise, most typically perhaps in indigenization or joint venture requirements; second, there is likely to be a deliberate attempt to favour locally owned enterprises within the region, the so-called *empresa multinacional* of the Andean group which is not a multinational enterprise in the conventional sense, but simply one owned and operated from within the group, having trade relations with other countries in the group. Finally, there is the possibility that, notwithstanding the provisions of the regional agreement, restrictions will be maintained in the potential export markets, even against exports originating in the regional grouping.

There are in effect three major group types, namely the European Economic Community (EEC), or more strictly, the European Community (EC) and the European Free Trade Association (EFTA) on the one hand, representing the Western developed economies. Second, there are the Third World groups, of which the Andean Pact, the economic groups, and the Association of South-East Asian Nations (the ASEAN Pact) are typical. Finally there is Comecon (otherwise known as the CMEA, or Council for Mutual Economic Assistance) group, the political and trading bloc dominated by the USSR.

There are unlikely to be any more in the developed countries; there may well be others in the Third World. Of the two developed national groupings, only the European Community is of particular significance and will require to be discussed in some detail. EFTA, by contrast, is a vestigial grouping of relatively disparate nations, whose major *raison d'être* is that its members, largely for political reasons, have been unable to join the European Community and are attempting to increase the level of their trade and co-operation.

There have been several attempts at regional groupings in the Third World, most of which have collapsed or are at best moribund. There seem to have been at least three adverse factors at work.

Although such groupings have been inspired by the EC, their resemblance is at best superficial, since, although they tend to have timetables for integration on EC lines, the timetables have not been backed up by the massive and detailed bargaining which preceded the Treaty of Rome, the foundation of the Economic Community. Such complex regional grouping arrangements require a long period of preparation.

Second, there is the phenomenon already alluded to, that most countries contemplating such unions tend to see them as representing opportunities for increased exports, rather than as a source of competitive imports.

The third factors arises from the second, namely that imports from other developing countries in a region suffer from two drawbacks. They have neither the advantage of familiarity or a patriotic impulse on the part of the purchaser, nor do they have the prestige of being imports from the technologically developed countries: products from the latter source, as has been noted, may even carry a premium over apparently similar local items. Third World groups do not appear to have developed regional loyalties to anything like the degree achieved in the EC.

There are two characteristics of the Third World groups which are of particular significance to the international enterprise. The first is the appearance of sectoral development, largely pioneered by the Andean group, and now being studied by others. This concept will be discussed in greater detail later in the chapter, but basically consists of allocating new industries on a regional basis, rather than permitting them to appear at will anywhere in the group. Second, there are the common policies laid down to determine the most attractive conditions which will be allowed to foreign enterprises within the region. These may be limitations on the amount of government aid or tax concessions which may be given by any member nation of the grouping, requirements for the sale of equity, holding locally, limitations on the repatriation of profits, and so on. The intention is not to standardize concessions, but to establish maxima. The Allende government, while Chile was an active member of the Andean Pact, was clearly intent on eliminating foreign direct investment, and in this sense the rather severe limitations on investment suggested by the governing body were more generous than the Chilean government would accept.

It is not likely that the Comecon group will have much significance, or represent much opportunity for the Western or Japanese international enterprise to tap the whole of this potentially vast market. Foreign trade is rigidly controlled not only from the centre, but also in terms of individual national plans. While international enterprises can and do make what are in effect treaties with individual members, there is no suggestion that such an agreement in one Comecon country would give the foreign enterprise access to any other member country's market.

Bearing in mind the general principles of regional groupings it is useful to look at some individual groups in more detail.

The European Community

Of all the regional groups the European Community is by far the most significant not merely in its general political and economic impact but also in terms of its implications for the international enterprise. If such an enterprise is outside the day to day control of national government then it is logical to argue that an international organization can be a better vehicle of control. Certainly in at least three spheres the Community is having a profound effect on the structure and market strategy of such enterprises. These three spheres are the harmonization of company law, the prospect of a consistent regional policy and competition policy. It is worth examining these three areas in some detail.

a. The harmonization of company law

The European Communities Commission has as one of its primary objects the harmonization of company law. This is an obvious method of securing increased integration within the Community, and affects non-EC as well as EC based enterprises insofar as they have established production facilities within the Community. An interesting aspect of such harmonization is that the changes in strategy and structure which are or will be required by Community legislation are liable to have effects elsewhere, not only by deliberate duplication of the legislatory provision, but by a simple demonstration effect as national governments, trade unions and other groups become aware of the possibilities.

The harmonization of company law has in the past proceeded along two parallel routes. The more ambitious of these was the possible creation of a European Company, the *Société Européene* or the *Societas Europa*. This would have been a form of legal incorporation available as an option to local registration as a national company under existing national company law. However, although the proposals for such a European Company statute date back to 1970, progress has been very slow, and the more obvious progress has been made along the second route.

In this instance the European Communities Commission has issued a series of directives. The effect of such directives, once they are adopted by the Community, is to require the member states to bring their existing company law into line within some two to three years. A number of directives have already been ratified and cover such issues as common standards for disclosure of information, the capital structure of companies, domestic mergers and the protection of employees and creditors in such a situation, and the presentation of annual accounts. Additionally some others as yet unratified present potential problems to non-EC based multinational enterprises, for they require a level of administration and disclosure of information that any international enterprise could expect to command. One such relates to employee involvement in management, or codetermination, which has global implications. Its widespread adoption in the Community involving, as it does, employee representation and participation in management decisions, could affect the freedom of manoeuvre of international enterprises through the world.

As significant, albeit in a more subtle way, is a directive which requires consolidated accounts from international enterprises on a standard basis throughout the European Community. Where the standard of accounting practice and the attitude to presenting honest accounts varies startlingly throughout the Community the more honest international non-Italian enterprises may find themselves at present in difficulties in countries such as Italy, where published accounts are frequently perceived as opening bids for tax purposes. Conversely it would be unwise for an Italian subsidiary operating in northern Europe to adopt the same accounting conventions as its parent company regarded as acceptable in Italy. Such directives if enacted would lay bare the financial practices of an international enterprise – no doubt to the gratification of the national tax authorities as well as the EC Commission.

b. Regional policy and the international enterprise

Virtually every member or aspirant member has its regional problem and is interested in using foreign enterprises as one means of solving the problem. To grasp the size of the issue it is useful to consider the European regional problem as a whole, rather than examining regional issues country by country. In short, western Europe can be seen as possessing an industrial heartland stretching from the Midlands of England to the Ruhr and the Paris basin. There are one or two satellite concentrations like the north Italian plain but this is the general pattern. The rest of western Europe, and particularly the periphery from Scotland and Ireland, through Spain, Portugal, Sicily and the Mezzogiorno, Greece and Turkey are areas in danger of being drained of industry by the centripetal attractions of the vast centre complex. They are likewise in danger constantly of becoming a source of labour rather than industrial regions in their own right.

National governments have regional policies designed to reverse this drift. The British government has its development areas with various financial concessions to keep employment opportunities open in Scotland, the north of England, Northern Ireland, Wales and the west. The Italians have similar policies for the Mezzogiorno and Sicily.

Sometimes, however, the problem is not a regional one, but a national one. Arguably the whole of the Republic of Ireland, Portugal or Greece are regional problems requiring aid. Since any of these countries, whether the problem is regional or national, are anxious to attract industry, and particularly foreign industry, they tend to bid competitively against each other – each seeking a national solution to what is arguably a western European problem. Even countries outside these already listed, namely the members or the aspirant members of the European Community, have the same problem of the gravitational pull of the European heartland, whether relatively small countries like Austria or Sweden whose economic interests lie in association with the heartland, but whose political neutrality poses problems, or even Comecon members like Poland, Czechoslovakia or Hungary, whose economies are in effect wrenched out of their natural international markets by the military power of the Soviet Union.

Insofar as there is no common regional policy, then, the foreign enterprise which is relatively footloose can find itself in a very strong position to play off one government against another not only within the European Community but even among the non-Community members, Western neutrals, Comecon members or Yugoslavia, for whom the west European market poses such prospects and threats.

How far is there an effective regional policy within the European Community which might prevent this competitive bidding to attract foreign, particularly non-EC investment? It has to be said that the record so far has been poor.

EC regional policy has two aspects. First, it has its own finances which can be used to support developments. These however are tiny compared with sums being spent by national governments. The European Commission's attitude towards national governments' policies represents the second aspect. One or two principles have emerged. First, that the aid must be 'transparent' in the sense that its value can be readily calculated by an outside adviser: as we shall see this is an ideal rather than a reality, in that national governments are remarkably coy about giving details of deals; second, that certain practices such as export subsidies or discriminatory tax practices are ruled out. Here, in a curious way, the small aspirant members have an advantage, in that if they are in the practice of giving out such concessions before they become members, they may be able to secure a waiver of EC requirements for a transitional period.

The weaknesses of regional policy   Although competing bids based on regional incentives occur on a regular basis, the most widespread, public and most documented example is now about ten years old. But the conditions which enabled the companies concerned, two American car giants, to play European governments against each other, still prevail.

The success of the Ford Motor Company or General Motors in securing massive financial assistance from governments during the 1970s thus provides a cautionary tale of the shortcomings of regional policies in western Europe.

A generation ago Ford was probably the first of the motor vehicle manufacturers to move overtly from a national to regional based market strategy – to move towards a degree of specialization in its European plants which required standardization on European models. The main Ford marques in Britain and Germany were brought into line and a European strategy began to emerge. At the beginning of the 1960s the British plant was integrated into the European strategy by the buying out of local shareholders: by the early 1970s the main plants in Britian, Germany and Belgium were being supplemented by the creation of production facilities on a very large scale in Spain, and to a lesser extent in Portugal.

The fact that Ford were now operating on a European basis made the acquisition of a Ford plant even more attractive to national governments, since they brought the possibility of foreign exchange earnings as well as employment: the possibility of Ford's holding a competitive bid situation were obvious.

One of the earliest of such bids was for a new engine plant supplying many of the European factories. In the event the plant location chosen was in South Wales, which by what might be regarded as a happy coincidence was a region in which the then Prime Minister and several other government ministers had their constituencies. The triumphal announcement by the government did not, however, make clear what the cost to the British taxpayer was going to be, on the official grounds of commercial confidentiality. Unofficial estimates put the bill to the taxpayer at somewhere between £80 million and some three times that amount. The smaller figure was inherently unlikely for it appeared that the British government had simply outbid any rivals. An official announcement some two years later suggested that the costs up to that time (early 1979) had been in the neighbourhood of £320 million.

The next round of competitive bidding was to come in 1978/9 when Ford announced its intention of building a new plant in the 1980s with a vehicle production capacity of over a quarter of a million vehicles per year. It appeared to Ford that within three or four years, it would be unable to meet the anticipated European wide demand for its cars. It had three choices. The most straightforward was simply to step up investment in Spain, into which it had moved a few years previously. A second choice would have been to increase capacity in the older established plants in the United Kingdom, Germany or Belgium. The final choice was to go to a greenfield site, in a European country which had as yet no substantial motor vehicle industry and might therefore be prepared to bid substantially for such an industry.

The conditions laid down by Ford were a remarkble comment on the bargaining power of a multinational company in a competitive bid situation *vis-à-vis* governments. They wished any host government to meet up to 35 per cent of the investment costs, to offer reduction of tariff duties on imported capital equipment for the plant, a reduction in rates, cheap loans and subsidies for the training of manpower. In the case of Spain where it had agreed to substantial restrictions on the sale of cars in the domestic market (i.e. an emphasis on exporting), it wanted restrictions on sales within Spain to be lifted, along with revisions on Spanish import requirements. In a sense this was a logical and inevitable development, in that if and when Spain joined the European Community, it would not have been permitted an indefinite extension of these protective measures in the home market. In comparison with much of car sales in western Europe, the Spanish domestic market was considerable.

It is probable that Ford would have preferred to expand in Spain particularly if that country were to become a member of the European Community, as eventually happened in the 1980s. At the time, however, the Spaniards reacted slowly and reluctantly. Relationships between the post-Franco government and the multinational had soured. The Spaniards appear to have felt they were being rushed into making concessions to the Americans they could not give to their own hard pressed industry; moreover, the relatively docile labour force which had appeared to be so attractive a few years before were becoming as militant as any other European workforce.

The British record of labour unrest and relatively low productivity, the German and Belgian pattern of very high labour costs, may have helped to point the Ford company towards a greenfield operation.

The Austrians made the first greenfield bid, or more accurately gave out the first signal. An Austrian parastatal indicated that it was seeking a joint venture arrangement with a car manufacturer both to create jobs and to cut down the very high import bill from elsewhere, particularly Germany. In fact, it was fairly clear that Ford would not really be interested in a joint venture deal, which would have been quite inconsistent with its European strategy of 100 per cent ownership in order to give freedom of action in its market strategy. Nevertheless the signal was there. Austrian taxpayers' money was available if a suitable deal could be arranged, the Viennese local authorities were ready to give production facilities and the government was ready to provide training facilities. A site near Vienna free of charge and grants of over £300 million, with guarantees of training facilities was offered. At this stage the French government intervened, apparently on the direct instructions of President Giscard d'Estaing. The new economic policy followed by the Barre government requiring the massive closedown of steel plants in the Lorraine basin and the political unrest was considerable. One obvious solution was the new vehicle plant: after all, Ford were scarcely represented in France at all. The bait being offered by the French appeared to be some £250 m in grants, etc., with the implication that the chauvinistic French motorist would be far more likely to buy a locally produced Ford vehicle than an imported one. Certainly the readiness of the French government to spend money in attracting the American companies alarmed and angered the two major French consortia, the nationally owned Régie Renault and the privately owned Peugeot Citröen.

Ford were in the meantime emphasizing that Spain was by no means excluded as a possibility: the Ford plants in Spain and Portugal were being integrated into Ford Lusitania, which could be rapidly integrated into the whole European strategy if and when Spain and Portugal became EC members. Perhaps not surprisingly the Portuguese government now began to enter the bidding, although this was seen as very much the outsider, since one result of the Portuguese revolution of 1974 was the drafting of legislation which made it virtually impossible for an employer to dismiss any worker. The Portuguese government were clearly ready to amend the legislation as well as providing subsidies, tariff protection and all the usual incentives.

As it happened, Ford decided to delay a decision on building new plants for the time being and instead chose to expand their existing facilities. Nevertheless, they were now in the happy situation of being wooed with varying degrees of hope and desperation by four countries, three of whom were EC members or aspirants. Their competitive bidding illustrated graphically the need for some consistency on regional policy in the Community if the international enterprises were not to retain the whip-hand. In the event, in the face of an approaching recession, Ford postponed its proposed new plant and decided to spend a reduced amount in expanded production facilities at its existing plants.

The pattern was repeated for General Motors in the late 1970s and early 1980s. By a series of bargaining encounters they created component plants in Spain, Austria and Northern Ireland, some $2 billion investment in total. In each instance they were being substantially subsidized by the host government on the somewhat vague promise of new job creation.

c.   Competition policy in the European Community

Competition policy in the European Community derives essentially from Articles 85 and 86 of the Treaty of Rome, the former in general dealing with issues of restrictive practices, the latter with monopolistic conditions. The policy is not directed specifically against incoming international enterprises, i.e. those originating in, say the USA or Japan. Some of the most severe measures have been directed against EC originating enterprises.

In this sense EC regulations are at once less limiting than those operated by any other regional grouping, and at the same time more specific. The Council does not attempt to lay down the sort of conditions in ownership, e.g. sectoral allocation of industry, sourcing or repatriation of profits which are increasingly to be found in other regional groupings, but at the same time it deals with, for example, pricing policy in various parts of the Community with a sophistication which would be quite impossible in a regional grouping of less developed countries.

Article 85 is intended to prohibit actions by enterprises which prevent, restrict or distort competition, and covers agreements affecting relations between enterprises inside and outside the Community, and applies to public sector as well as private sector enterprises.

Article 86 affects the international enterprise in opposing any abuse of a dominant trading position by a company: almost by definition such an enterprise would be a large international enterprise. Examples of the application of Article 86 are to be found in the US Chemical Solvents Inc. case, where that company and its Italian subsidiary decided to cut off supplies of the basic chemicals required in manufacturing an anti-tuberculosis drug to an Italian manufacturer of the drug, because the subsidiary was going into direct manufacture in competition with its former customer. On an appeal from the unfortunate customer, Chemical Solvents and its subsidiary were ordered to resume supplies.

A more confused result followed from a Commission decision that an American company, Continental Can, was likely to abuse a dominant position in the market for cans in that part of Europe by its buying up interests in German and Dutch companies. Although the European Court did not uphold the decision it did in effect support the proposition that purchases of this sort required close attention under Article 86. Any international enterprise, EC based or not, has therefore grounds for caution in extending a powerful market situation into a dominant one, simply by buying out smaller local companies.

Decision on products so diverse as bananas and Scotch whisky have further extended the application of EC rules by making discriminatory pricing illegal. Potentially, at least, such decisions could impose significant restraints on a European marketing strategy based on partitioning markets for purposes of differentiating prices.

Proposals currently under discussion but not yet having the force of law include a requirement for prior notification to the European Commission of large scale mergers.

In summary, it can be argued that EC policy such as it is, is not specifically anti-multinational, but is designed to give greater protection both to employees and customers from problems arising from the size of an enterprise rather than its multinational nature. Arguably the problem posed by such legislation, as alluded to earlier, is the possibility of imitation without preliminary discussion, by other regional groupings. Blanket requirements on, for example, employees' rights, market share, etc. introduced on a general 'anti-foreign' principle in Third World regional groupings could prove more destructive than the original EC decisions.

A major criticism of EC competition policy is that it may become outdated, insofar as competition may increasingly have to be measured on a worldwide basis, not merely on intra-Community basis. Thus the American government appears to be taking a more relaxed stance towards mergers, etc. within the USA, if alternative competition elsewhere in the world continues to ensure adequate competition. The European policy continues to be literally more regional than global in its outlook.

REGIONAL GROUPINGS IN THE THIRD WORLD

The adverse factors which so far have rendered the regional groupings of the Third World largely ineffective, namely inadequate preparations, the one-sided attitude favouring exporting to, but not importing from, one's regional partners and the relative lack of prestige of the manufactured products which are exported have been commented upon. It may however be useful to examine some of the current regional groupings to ascertain how much they have learned from past failures, and how attractive they may be to the foreign international enterprise.

a.　The Andean Pact

By far the most interesting of such groupings is the Andean Pact, set up in 1968 and comprising initially Bolivia, Chile, Columbia, Ecuador and Peru. Venezuela joined in 1973 shortly after the Pact began to operate, but Chile withdrew in 1976 following the accession of the new military government, which refused to accept some of the limitations on the treatment of foreign investment insisted upon by the Pact. Most of the relevant conditions applying to foreign investment are to be found in the famous Article 24 of the Commission of the Cartagena Agreement, the constitutional instrument of the Pact. Article 24 sets out the principles applying to foreign investment trade marks, licensing, payment of royalties etc.

The effect of the agreement was not in effect to lay down standard rules applying to foreign investment, but rather to lay down the minimum (relatively severe) constraints and maximum concessions. Members could impose more severe restraints (as did Chile under the marxist Allende government), but not more favourable. It was in fact the desire of the right wing post-Allende government to offer freer access to foreign investment which led to the Chilean withdrawal. The general principles included the gradual indigenization of majority holdings, through a request to sell off equity to local interests over time, limits on the repatriation of profits, etc. The attraction for the foreign enterprise was the vastly enhanced market, and the concept of sectoral development, i.e. that industries would be allocated to one or other of the member states, with access to the whole market, instead of all members seeking to set out the same new industry on the basis of exporting to all the others.

There have been serious problems which turned partly on the political variety of the regimes (and sometimes their stability), their ability to attract foreign investment in any event, and the level of technology already existing. Initially Chile and Peru were both extreme left wing and most hostile to foreign investment, Columbia the more moderate and Bolivia simply politically unstable. In the next few years, both left wing members moved sharply to the right, with Chile moving out of the Pact completely. So far as ability to attract investment was concerned, Chile and Columbia were relatively well developed and, given a favourable political climate, could attract foreign investment. Bolivia and Ecuador by contrast, being more underdeveloped, needed more help to get any investment and wanted the sectoral principle.

Finally, there was the complication of Venezuela, whose role as a relatively rich oil producer made its accession to the Pact a political, rather than an economic decision. A moderate social democratic government presided over a relatively high cost producing economy, which would be an attractive market to poorer members of the Pact, but not the most obvious source of cheap exports.

In spite of the limitations, sectoral development and the potential size of the market may enable the organization to be selective on admitting foreign enterprises and impose rigorous conditions on technology and export requirements in such foreign enterprises.

Largely because of the internal political fluctuation of member states and the impact of world recession, which has lessened the confidence of member states in their ability to impose restrictions on foreign enterprises while still attracting them, the future of the Pact clouded: nevertheless, the concept of a united front with a limit to the concessions to foreigners, rather than the competitive bidding which has been a feature of the European Community and the concept of sectoral development of industry, possibly points the way to future developments in the Third World.

b. ECOWAS (Economic Organization of West African States)

Compared with the Andean Pact, Africa has made little progress in creating economic zones or presenting a united front in dealing with foreign investment issues. Economic unions in north and east Africa have foundered on political quarrels among member states. The most important at the present moment is ECOWAS, founded in 1978.

It has to be said that ECOWAS has immense problems to resolve. Its 16 members include former English, French and Portuguese colonies with few common traditions: it ranges from free enterprise to marxist, from very large states like Nigeria to very small, with a corresponding range of technological standards. It is dominated by Nigeria, which is a giant in the group, and which is regarded with suspicion and fear by several others. There are plans for a free trade area, but at present no co-ordinated policy towards multinationals. Its prospects for survival, let alone success, are doubtful.

c.   ASEAN (Association of South-East Asian Nations)

The ASEAN pact dates from 1967, but in comparison with the Andean Pact, with which in fact it has often been compared, its progress has been slow and its attitudes towards foreign investment remain rather confused. In fairness it has to be said ASEAN was seen as much as a political grouping for defence as a potential economic union and the heterogeneous nature of its members (Indonesia, Malaysia, Singapore, the Philippines and Thailand) made co-operation difficult. Indonesia dominates in size almost as much as Nigeria dominates ECOWAS.

The impetus for closer integration and sectoral development along Andean Pact lines, comes particularly from Singapore and to a lesser extent the Philippines, who are industrially the most advanced and have potentially most to gain from access to the huge Indonesian market. Indeed it can be argued that one major threat to the economic development of ASEAN into a trading bloc has been the excessive success of the Singapore authorities in obtaining sectoral concessions for their own industries and by implication, the Japanese and other non-ASEAN companies which have set up plant there. What is particularly significant about the ASEAN area for the foreign company is not merely the size of the market and its political stability, but the relatively good economic prospects of its members if they can avoid political disaster. Singapore was, during the 1970s and much of the early 1980s, one of the most successful of the newly industrializing countries; the Philippines, Malaysia, and Thailand may well achieve that status in the next few years, while Indonesia, the giant of the area in population and resources can reasonably expect to be a front rank power in the twenty-first century.

A major development within ASEAN may be the development of trading patterns derived in part from the Japanese pattern of the Sogo Shosha or trading house, linked to industrial groups. Plans envisage an ASEAN Finance Corporation combining Western concepts of banking and loan finance with functions of the Sogo Shosha: it could fulfil a twofold function: first, to supply finance, possibly in a partnership situation with foreign enterprises operating in the region; and second, advance the so called 'Bumiputra' objectives of Malaysia and Indonesia to spread equity ownership among the non-Chinese inhabitants, and so give a better power balance in these multinational states.

Part II
Ownership and Strategy

Introduction

A locally registered company in a country like Britain may be wholly or partly foreign owned; at the same time it may be only one part of a much bigger multinational operation. Foreign ownership and an international scale of operations may enable such a company to operate to a different set of rules and objectives than a purely domestically owned and operating company.

The ability of a multinational enterprise to operate according to its own rules, rather than to the wishes of a national government, may vary with the political will of the government and the sophistication of the latter's administrative machine. Developed countries believe they may be able to control the activities of multinational companies by legislation, efficiently administered; less developed countries may have stronger views on what they want foreign companies to do for them, but they believe they can control them only if they achieve ownership or at least part ownership of the local plant. This causes potential conflicts which will be explored in this part of the book.

3 Alternative Ownership and Market Strategies

INTRODUCTION

There are two broad marketing strategies which can be followed by the international enterprise. These are determined by the ownership pattern and, in turn, affect its product policy.

First, it may follow a genuine global strategy, in terms of sourcing and production as well as markets. In this situation it has every incentive to standardize its products and possibly add a degree of specialization on an international basis. It is not likely to confine the production of a product to any single national source – such a degree of specialization would render it particularly vulnerable to trade union and other pressures – but it will certainly be able to move away from a situation where every national plant has to produce a complete range of products.

A global strategy of this type implies an ability and willingness to switch production facilities and market sources on a global basis, and this in turn requires the elimination of local financial interests, i.e. joint venture partners or shareholders in a locally registered company. Such interest cannot be unfairly penalized and need not be excessively awarded, if the company chooses to switch production facilities or access to particular markets, from one country to another.

The alternative is local production (indeed local products for local markets). This, it might be argued, is a form of market orientation which is acceptable locally. It means however that the enterprise is international, only incidentally, in terms of ownership. There are dangers of lack of control and a distinct probability of loss of ownership. To be an international enterprise in any real sense implies tensions arising from the need to avoid excessive conflicts between local interests at sudsidiary level and the interests of the enterprise as a whole: nevertheless, these tensions are probably a necessity for survival.

OWNERSHIP STRATEGIES IN INTERNATIONAL BUSINESS

An international enterprise may follow one or more of four main ownership strategies, in every case either by necessity or choice. The significance of any particular strategy lies in the degree of freedom in business policy and market strategy which it makes possible.

The four strategies can be summed up as:

(a) a 'no ownership' strategy in respect of foreign operations;
(b) a joint venture strategy with a local partner or partners drawn from the private or public sector;
(c) an indigenization strategy, i.e. one where a substantial part of a foreign operation by the enterprise is owned by a number of local citizens, who are, however, equity holders rather than active partners;
(d) a 'wholly owned' strategy where all, or virtually all, of the foreign operation is owned by the enterprise.

It is perfectly possible for the enterprise's overall policy to include elements of all four, depending on the conditions existing in various parts of the world where it wishes to operate. In general 'no ownership' or 'wholly owned' strategy is likely to leave the enterprise with most freedom of action, to build up or run down operations in various parts of the world, to allocate or transfer markets from one plant to another, possibly in a different country. A joint venture or indigenization strategy, by contrast, makes it more difficult to take a global view of the interests of the enterprise, for there are local interests which might be inequitably treated or excessively rewarded by any attempt to exercise the freedom of action described in the previous sentence.

With this generalization in mind it is convenient to examine the four strategies in more detail, following the routes shown in Diagram 3a.

a. A 'no ownership' strategy

A no ownership offers at least four possibilities namely the 'turnkey' operation, the subcontracting of the production of components, a group of variants which are not readily defined, and finally the licensing option.

1. The turnkey operation

It can be argued that a 'turnkey' operation is simply an export of capital equipment, very much like building a dam or even a supertanker. But if the turnkey operation is planned and carried out not so much by a construction company specializing in large scale

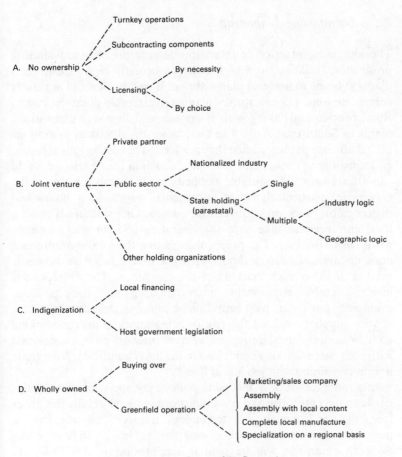

Diagram 3a   *Ownership Strategies*

capital works as by a company which manufactures and sells products rather than the plants which manufacture the products, then the situation is rather different. Fiat in the 1960s effectively delivered vehicle producing plants for the USSR and Poland, rather than selling vehicles. The result has been a second generation of vehicles deriving from Fiat technology, but over whose distribution and sale Fiat had no control once the original agreement had expired. A turnkey operation which may be backed up by technological and managerial support services can be seen as a transfer of technology in an industry scale, as opposed to the more limited licensing operation which relates to a single product or small range of expertise.

2. Subcontracting components

The increasing practice of international enterprises of transferring production facilities from high cost (particularly high labour cost) plants at home to low cost plants abroad is well known and adversely commented on. US enterprises may have assembly plants in Puerto Rico, Mexico and, along with European and Japanese enterprises, plants in South-East Asia. The fact, however, that such operations attract adverse publicity when they are seen to be costing jobs at home, and substituting imports for local production in the developed world can attract very unfavourable publicity in the home country of the enterprise, particularly when subsistence wages, long hours and unacceptable work practices can be quoted. One solution is to let a local entrepreneur take over the operation and contract assembly work out to him/her. The prerequisite is that the local entrepreneur does not have access in their own right to the lucrative domestic market or other such markets of the enterprise. The enterprise is buying assembled components rather than completed products. It can eventually put on its own brand name and has the advantage of a captive supplier, without the risk of being attacked for the working conditions of the local entrepreneur from pressure groups concerned with political or working conditions in the host countries or from trade unions concerned with job loss at home.

In a more subtle way the same policy may apply in relationships between the enterprise and communist countries. Normally this arises from the consequence of a technology transfer deal whereby, as payment for assisting in creating a new plant say in eastern Europe, the Western enterprise will be paid in the products. Such deals are examined in more detail elsewhere but the fallout may logically point to a 'no ownership' policy, if such a communist assembly source is available. At least one leading critic of the multinationals has argued trenchantly that such deals not only cost Western trade unionists employment but also contribute to the continued suppression of genuinely free trade unions in the communist world – exactly the same criticism levelled against multinationals operating in countries like South Africa.

Much the same situation applies, *mutatis mutandis*, in many enterprises' attitude towards investment in the Western developed countries. Faced with the prospect of extensive and expensive limitations on their freedom of action by employment protection legislation or even the pitfalls of legislation on equal opportunity covering sex, colour or race, an enterprise may feel there is little incentive to become or remain a local employer, and may choose instead to rely on buying in components rather than manufacturing them. Although this can be described as a 'no ownership' policy, a more accurate title might be a 'no employee' policy in those countries where the scales appear to be weighted against the employer.

A variant may arise where there is a tendency to bring in measures of codetermination, i.e. the practice of giving workers and salaried managers a share in the running of the enterprise, along with the owners. Codetermination may exist in two forms. The first might be described as a rational well thought out philosophy of power-sharing with an ideal of industrial democracy, as has been pioneered in several countries in western Europe, notably West Germany. The second might be a woollier statement of interest in a revolutionary minded Third World country, where the government is aware that to nationalize a foreign enterprise with high technological content or access to foreign markets might prove disastrous, but yet is under pressure to convince its supporters that a vital change has taken place. It therefore may install workers' representatives on the board etc.

International enterprises can live with the first situation and in the case of the second, simply hope that economic realities will penetrate even in the most revolutionary situation. But the longer term implications of a legal requirement for codetermination in one plant, or other plants elsewhere, might cause an enterprise to seek alternatives to production in that market. A diluted form of no ownership through disinvestment appears to be occurring in parts of western Europe where some internationals, particularly Americans, are closing down national plants within individual countries in the belief that the local markets can be served well enough from elsewhere in the Community or even directly by exporting from the home plant in the USA.

3. Ad hoc *ownership and mixed patterns*

There are also variations of subcontracting, which can scarcely be regarded in the same light, for the scale of the components is so great as to constitute a new pattern, and even the term 'subcontracting' is scarcely appropriate. Thus there might be a company in a developed country with foreign associates, rather than contractors or subcontractors. The main principle which runs through a variety of such arrangements is that the company has considerable technological assets at its disposal but does not choose to become a multinational on a permanent basis: sometimes it may be a product division of a multinational which does not wish to become a multinational in that product area.

Some examples may suffice. A giant American aircraft manufacturer like Boeing is not a true multinational in the sense of maintaining substantial manufacturing capacity outside the United States. But it could and does on occasion operate a 'no ownership' policy of contracting out the manufacture of components on an international basis. The aircraft will be designed by Boeing: the design work might be done entirely in the USA, or alternatively some of the design work could be carried out elsewhere if it were cheaper to hire designers elsewhere. The entire manufacturing process could if necessary then be contracted out to other manufacturers in the USA or abroad. Not only might such a policy be cheaper than laying down new production lines in the Boeing plants in the USA, but it would increase the prospect of sales of the aircraft to countries where the sales created at least some employment in locally owned factories.

The second example can also be drawn from an American operation. The Industrial Gas Turbine Division of the American General Electric is a recognized world leader in this field, but the sale of a gas turbine is essentially a turnkey operation, in that the turbine is the core of a power plant. Rather than attempt to sell turnkey operations throughout the world, either from the USA or from subsidiary plants, General Electric has established associated relationships with some half a dozen major companies in western Europe and Japan. It does not own these plants in whole or in part, but nevertheless exercises some control over them in the area of industrial gas turbines. It will sell to any of its associates. The value may be between 10 and 20 per cent of the whole turnkey operation cost, but General Electric will retain the right to approve subcontractors employed by its associate companies and monitor the quality control specifications. The associate companies are likely to be competing against each other, or even on occasion against General Electric for a turnkey project tender, but whoever wins the contract anywhere in the world is likely to be one of General Electric's associates – and customers. Such an arrangement is difficult to classify, although one could describe such an associate company as a foreign distributor 'writ large'.

Yet another variant on the no ownership, no jobs strategy is that followed in many parts of the world by the Japanese electronics group, the Sharp Corporation. Although Sharp had several wholly owned or jointly owned foreign subsidiaries, its strategy in most parts of the world is a variant on licensing. In brief, in the Sharp strategy the company will sign a fixed period technology transfer contract with a local firm. This is likely to include quality checks by the Japanese company, but no equity holding by them, or direct control in the local company. In most parts of the Third World where this policy is applied the products, most noticeably TV sets, will sell under the Sharp name, although in the case of an agreement in a developed country with its own well known brand names, this is not necessarily the case.

The system works without necessarily creating potential rivals (which may be a weakness on conventional licensing deals) because Sharp makes a policy of continuously updating licensing so that the local partner is happy enough to renew a contract knowing that the technology level is constantly being raised without its having to incur heavy research and development expenses. In the circumstances the name Sharp on the products is a guarantee of quality, and as such is a valuable asset in the form of what is loosely termed 'intellectual property'. Some of the incipient threats to this no ownership strategy will be discussed in a later section on such property rights in Chapter 4.

4. Licensing

A company with marketable technology, knowhow or simply a well known brand name may choose to export this intangible, rather than the product, i.e. it may license out its abilities against payment by royalties. The decision to licence may be taken out by necessity or by choice.

The first variant of such a strategy is where there is a political or ideological objection to direct investment, emanating from the potential host government. A few years ago it was relatively easy to identify countries where such a situation existed, namely in overtly marxist economies, some intensely nationalistic states and Japan. Today, however, the situation is much more complex and is changing so rapidly that it is difficult to be dogmatic.

(1)   The policy toward foreign enterprises in marxist countries is very far from being monolithic even within the East European Bloc dominated by the Soviet Union. In general the more Western oriented countries including Poland, Rumania, Czechoslovakia and the German Democratic Republic, appear willing to contemplate some form of joint venture arrangement, while the more Soviet oriented and

the Soviet Union itself remain more cautious, not to say suspicious.
(Even here in the Gorbachev era, as has been noted earlier, there are
signs of relaxation.) Yugoslavia is the most liberal of all European
communist countries in this respect. Outside Europe the situation is at
least as complex. Until the death of Mao Zedong and the subsequent
disgrace of the 'Gang of Four', China was the most rigidly orthodox of
all the marxist states in respect of the prohibition of foreign investment.
The extraordinary about face of the late 1970s created a situation where
foreign investment appeared not only to be acceptable, but positively
welcomed. The special economic zones of south China were in effect
capitalist enclaves, more comparable to conditions in Hong Kong a
generation before than in a late twentieth-century marxist state.
Vietnam has shown willingness to allow foreign investment, albeit on a
limited span of time, with provision for nationalization on agreed
compensation terms after 20 years.

   In spite of the exceptions which have been made, the concept of a
private foreign enterprise being allowed to operate indefinitely in an
officially 'socialist' society progressing towards a communist ideal
according to marxist theory is impossible. In the long run, either the
private enterprise is eliminated from the system, or the ideology itself
has to change. The international enterprise has therefore to consider its
long term strategy in marxist countries, as being by necessity 'no
ownership'. This does not mean that no relationship between the
enterprise and the marxist economy is possible, merely that it is not
likely to be based on conventional definitions of ownership; and if the
situation does not permit the enterprise to have a permanent ownership
stake in the operation; it may find it has created its own competitor.

(2)   Very nationalistic states in the Third World may present an even
more confusing picture. In general, however, countries most hostile to
foreign investment are likely to have recently nationalized foreign
holdings in the extractive industries, and moreover, have nationalized
them in the context of a political crisis rather than on particularly
rational economic grounds. The typical country is possibly politically
unstable and the situation is likely to be volatile. Insofar as there is
economic rationality behind the policy, it will probably stem from a
belief in the merits of technology transfer via licensing – a conviction
that what Japan achieved in the post-war period can be achieved by any
other state. Such a conviction, as has been noted earlier, is likely to be
associated with a grossly overoptimistic view of the ease with which
technological skills can be acquired.

In this circumstance the enterprise may be forced into a licensing agreement, *faute de mieux*, so to speak. Even where this is against the overall policy of the enterprise, there are two considerations worth noting: the first is that a failure to achieve the expected results through licensing may in time convince the host government of the advantages of a more overt foreign stake in the operation; the second is that this type of operation is likely to be confined to relatively inefficient and costly production for the domestic market of the licensee. It is not likely to lead to the creation of a rival exporter as happened in the Japanese example.

(3)   The third situation where 'no ownership through licensing' may be the policy is in Japan, although here the situation is less rigid than a decade ago. Japanese legislation and, more important, an implicit government policy, ensured that international enterprises were effectively excluded from producing in Japan and had to license out their products. The very success of the Japanese has, however, made their policy more prominent and forced them to bow to foreign pressure. An increasing range of industries are being opened to direct foreign investment. It remains true however that while the legal barriers are going down, political pressure and cultural barriers are increasing.

b.   A joint venture strategy

To examine the varieties of ownership strategy systematically it is necessary to impose a structure which can at times draw a slightly artificial distinction between one ownership condition and another. This is particularly the case with the joint venture, which on the one side blends into a licensing situation and on the other into indigenization. To clarify the situation it is useful to define the term 'joint venture'. In the present context it occurs where a foreign enterprise has one or more local partners in a subsidiary company. The foreign company normally supplies technology and knowhow; the local partner or partners local knowledge of the market and possibly useful political contacts.

The idea of insisting on, or at least encouraging, a foreign enterprise to find a local partner is a popular one. Certainly from the viewpoint of the foreign enterprise it has the advantage of giving easier access to a foreign market and possibly more local goodwill. The disadvantage, as has been noted, is that the existence of local interests may prevent the enterprise following a global strategy where the overall interests of the enterprise may conflict with these local interests.

In practice the requirement by a host government that a foreign enterprise enter into a joint venture is rarely absolute – save in the case of a marxist government – certainly not in the case of high technology industry or industry which may be export oriented. There may, however, be considerable political pressure to enter a joint venture arrangement, and particularly in the Third World, the partner may be an individual or company with acceptable political connections.

The fact of political acceptability of the local partner in a Third World country may create an interesting situation, in that the local partner may take a relatively nominal part in developing the operation, being primarily concerned to give political acceptability. The local partner may even be simply a *'prestanombre'*, i.e. a name lender who is necessary purely for political purposes.

This situation of the nominal partner is not likely to exist in a developed country in quite the same way in that there is not likely to be the same necessity to conciliate or buy the support of the local government. In one sense however there is something of an obverse situation, where a public sector organization puts finance into the operation without in any sense participating in running the operation. This joint venture structure is probably seen as politically more acceptable locally than the situation of giving money as an outright grant to a foreign company to persuade it to set up a plant in, say, an area of high unemployment. This takes the discussion into the role of the parastatal organization and this is discussed in more detail in the appendix to this chapter.

There is a tendency for many joint venture operations to prove temporary: one side or the other will buy its partner out if and when there is an obvious and chronic clash of interest over, for example, the allocation of markets or the introduction of new technology. The most stable long term joint venture operations are probably those involving the financial institutions in the host countries as the local partner. They may choose not to buy out the foreign partner over time because he/she will continue to be a major source of technological innovation: on the other hand they are not likely to be under financial pressure to sell up themselves, and they are likely to have a substantial hold on the domestic market in any event through their financial stake elsewhere.

The reasons for the implicit transience of a joint venture arrangement are complex, but in summary they are that as local expertise and the level of technology grows, particularly in an industry where the rate of technological development is slowing down, then the complementarity of expertise by the foreign partner and market knowledge and connection by the local partner breaks down. In the case of some Third World countries there is almost a pattern whereby joint venture policies are imposed rigorously with only a minority holding of the foreign partner, the policy is relaxed when the difficulties of technology transfer become apparent, and are then re-imposed once the major obstacles have been overcome.

Local partners

There are three types of local partner available to the international enterprise.

i. A private sector company   The first of these is simply a private sector company within the country which is seeking technological and possibly financial aid from a foreign partner. As has been suggested elsewhere, the advantages of such an arrangement are immediate, in giving quick access on a knowledgeable basis to the local market. Any disadvantages tend to be long term, in that a local interest may limit the freedom of action of the foreign partner; moreover, it is not impossible that the ambitions of the local company may be relatively limited and exclude, for example, an expansion to the point where family control was threatened.

ii. Nationalized industries or parastatals   The second situation is a joint venture with a nationalized industry, a parastatal or other state holding organization. Such parastatals while apparently holding very strong cards may in practice be in a relatively weak position *vis-à-vis* the foreign partner since they may be subject to considerable political pressures to maintain jobs regardless of viability, and the foreign partner may be able to extract considerable concessions, such as could never be offered by a private sector partner which could only accept an arrangement which was likely to bring it a profit in commercial terms.

It is worth noting that the term 'joint venture' may be something of a misnomer in that it is highly unlikely that the parastatal will take an active part in management as would be the case with the private sector partner. In the non-Anglo-American structure of a two-tier company, the parastatal's interests would be confined to the supervisory board rather than the board of management. In the Anglo-American type of company the parastatal might at most nominate non-executive directors.

A variant of this situation is growing in importance, namely the collaboration between ailing state owned companies, and more successful foreign enterprises whose success makes them vulnerable to restrictions on exporting to these more lucrative foreign markets where they have been threatening the existence of the locally, nationally owned company. In general the idea of collaboration becomes attractive if there is a foreign market which can be tackled. The most spectacular of these joint ventures has been the prospective collaboration between British Leyland, at the time effectively state owned, and the relatively small (in Japanese terms) car producer, Honda. A less successful example was the attempt at collaboration between Alfa Romeo (owned ultimately by the Italian parastatal the Istituto per la Riconstruzione Industriale) and Nissan.

There are two situations where this joint venture approach may lessen the relatively weak bargaining power of the nationally owned partner. First, when the holding company is at arms length and the negotiations are carried out directly by its wholly owned company, rather than the parastatal (and by implication by the politicians). Second, when the joint venture tends to relate to specific product types, i.e. a particular range of cars, rather than a permanent joint venture.

iii. Other holding organizations and other financial institutions   The third situation is likely to be encountered in economies where there is neither any extensive banking system nor alternative sources of raising finance, such as the stock exchange, available, but where the existing financial institutions may seek direct investment opportunities. These, for the sake of convenience, are here classified as 'holding companies', though they may include such diverse institutions as pension funds or insurance companies with substantial sums to invest.

One factor which may inhibit the growth of a sophisticated banking system in a Third World country is persistent and variable inflation which makes it very difficult to lend or borrow at fixed rates of interest. Banks or other financial institutions such as insurance companies or pension funds have little incentive to lend and every incentive to invest directly. They will therefore resist bids to borrow or even to invest through the purchase of equity shares, in favour of a direct stake as a joint venture partner. There is a spiral effect in some instances. The more local enterprises they own or have a stake in, the more bargaining power they will have in respect of an international enterprise contemplating investment in the area to serve the needs of the local enterprises. This is a pattern to be observed not only in the Third World but in countries such as France or Belgium where the *société générale* is an obvious source of funds but one which may not choose to lend on the same basis as an American or British commercial bank, preferring instead a direct stake in a local company, which it may set up jointly with the foreign companies. As in the case of the parastatals, it may wish to limit its representation to the supervisory board of the jointly owned local subsidiary; but it is also likely over time to command the services of highly qualified executives available for board of management functions.

These holding companies are likely to come under pressure from the state to invest in the areas which are perceived to be in the national interest, but they can if necessary resist such pressure. It might back a project on social grounds, but it would not have to. This greater independence of the holding companies in part at least arises from their more non-political origin. Their funds come directly from the public not by grace of the government as public funds arising from tax revenues.

The *société* form, then, is an instrument of state policy in a more limited sense with a degree of independence often lacking in the parastatal agency. This relative independence from political pressure, e.g. to save jobs, gives them more bargaining power in dealing with international enterprises. They can effectively insist on some form of share participation as the price of making funds available, or alternatively settle for a covered loan if they have doubts about the viability of the project. Such options are not so readily available in countries where the banking system is less directly concerned to obtain shareholding rights or where an active stock exchange provides the enterprise with an alternative method of funding a local operation.

The discussion of public or quasi-public sector organization has been largely confined to western Europe where a wide variety of forms is to be found. The same developments are to be found in Third World countries which in principle favour the nationalization of foreign assets (particularly extractive industries). In a rather half-hearted way they tend to work towards parastatal forms as a means of administering the vast resources which in some cases they have become heir to. The parastatal form is also used increasingly as a vehicle for industrial and regional developments and these agencies may in time, and once they have appreciated the practical difficulties which arise when local technology is inadequate, be prepared to deal with international enterprises on a partnership basis, even though local capitalists continue to be anathema.

The *société générale* form, which is attractive for the small saver, is much less common. There may be relatively few small savers, and those with wealth to save may be suspicious of lending to an impersonal organization with manifest links to government. Lastly, inflation or monetary depreciation common in the Third World make sustained savings in such economies economic madness in the absence of adequate indexation.

Finally, to end on a note of cynicism, virtually all states have some form of honours system and badges of distinction: titles and honours are eagerly sought by the vast majority of executives. The ultimate sanction, therefore, a government may have over its autonomous or semi-autonomous organizations may be an awareness among the chief executives that, if they accommodate ministers in political difficulties, they will be rewarded, even if the results are commercially unfortunate. But if they place commercial criteria above industrial embarrassment they will remain honest but unhonoured.

Diagram 3a indicated various subdivisions which could be identified within the joint venture structure, involving not only nationalized industry, but the so called 'parastatals'. The complexities are such, however, that the thread of the main argument in the chapter could easily be lost, so for convenience the discussion on the public or quasi-public enterprises has been relegated to an appendix at the end of this chapter.

Miscellaneous and ad hoc *licensing and joint venture arrangements*

The point has already been made that it is in practice sometimes difficult to draw a precise distinction between licensing and joint ventures – or indeed an indigenization policy, which is discussed next. In the meantime however it is useful to look in passing at a number of specific arrangements or negotiations in progress which fall into the borderline between one ownership pattern and another and which cannot easily be classified. They are significant not merely because they are difficult to define, but because they may be the harbingers of new patterns for the future.

The most striking perhaps is the form of co-operation which currently exists between Volkswagen and Nissan to produce the former's models in Japan, not merely to multiply Volkswagen sales in the Japanese market by five- or sixfold, but also to permit the export of Japanese manufactured Volkswagen elsewhere, to enable the two companies to exchange technology and also to strengthen the distribution channels of both companies throughout the world. The implications of such an arrangement could be far reaching. From Volkswagen's point of view it provides an unassailable *entrée* into the Japanese market which no other foreign manufacturer is likely to achieve: from the Japanese point of view it simultaneously bluntens the criticism of the foreigner about the impenetrability of the Japanese market and lessens the prospect of a united European front in dealing with Japan. It would in a sense be the obverse of the Japanese deals with British Leyland and Alfa Romeo to produce Japanese models in western Europe, but would be potentially far more important.

There are a range of other and less spectacular *ad hoc* situations, which might or might not be defined as joint ventures, but which illustrate the tendency of even large multinational enterprises to enter into specific arrangements with other multinationals on an *ad hoc* basis, to produce what might be regarded as a universal product. Illustrations abound in the motor vehicle industry: the US giant's arrangements with the Japanese, General Motors' stake in Isuzu, a relatively small car company, not only rounds out its range of light commercial vehicles in its home market in America, but enables it to feed in variants of its European designs, the Opel/Vauxhall ranges, into other Japanese dominated markets under a more acceptable marque. Ford has similar links with Mazda with similar objectives, and even for the production of automatic gearboxes with Nissan, Chrysler and Mitsubishi, and so on.

The European car producers are now increasingly following the same policy. Volkswagen links up with Fiat and Chrysler. Renault's links go much further than its joint ventures with Peugeot (part of the PSA Group), to co-operation with Volvo, and others. Alfa Romeo of the IRI Group co-operates with Fiat and the French Saviem (a subsidiary of Renault) in the manufacture of diesels, and so on. Renault, Citröen and Swedish Volvo co-operate in an engine manufacture in France.

In some respects, the increase of these *ad hoc* joint ventures involving multinationals co-operating with other multinationals rather than a local domestic partner, have aspects of international treaties as much as joint ventures – and their importance is growing as the costs and scale of production reach continental rather than national scale.

c. An indigenization strategy

In strict terms indigenization is often a restraint rather than a strategy in that there are few advantages to the policy of giving a large number of local equity holdings, and substantial disadvantages. There might be a case for giving a minor holding to an individual who had served the enterprise well at an earlier stage: an agent, for example, whose services when the company simply exported to the territory were the basis for a subsequent move into large scale local production. More cynically, a small equity holding could be seen as a method of buying the goodwill of a local politician or key figure. In both cases the proportion would be so small as to pose few difficulties if the enterprise subsequently chose to follow a policy which would operate to the detriment of the local interest. The latter could be compensated at no great cost. If, however, a significant proportion of the local equity were to be held by substantial numbers of local individuals the limitations would be much greater. A change in policy would require a very expensive operation to buy out all local interests – if indeed this could be done.

The difference between indigenization and the joint venture situation depends on two factors: the numbers of owners involved, and their degree of participation in running the local enterprise. It is possible to envisage a joint venture with two, three or four local partners, but as the numbers increased, active participation becomes more impractical, and beyond that stage equity holding involves little or no active participation.

In a sense, indigenization is a form of nationalization without, however, the local equity holding accruing to the public sector, when it would become virtually indistinguishable from the joint venture with some variety of parastatal discussed in the last section.

There are two sources of an indigenization strategy. First, the international enterprise may have decided to finance its foreign venture by floating a company in the new territory exactly in the way that a new domestic company might seek a stock exchange quotation. This type of indigenization, where a controlling interest is retained by the enterprise in exactly the same way as the owners of a private company which had decided to 'go public', would tend to retain a controlling interest is now comparatively rare. Second, the host government may insist on such an approach. Indigenization is a policy in Third World societies where this type of investment financing via the stock exchange is unusual. Generally, the host government simply passes legislation requiring the company to sell off shares to local buyers, or legislates to discriminate against wholly owned foreign enterprises. Examples are to be found in all three of the underdeveloped continents, from the requirements of the Andean Pact legislation in Latin America, Nigeria or Kenya in Africa, India or

Malaysia elsewhere. Often the government not only requires the company to sell off shares but lays down prices and conditions. Again there may be the usual qualifications, namely foreign owned enterprises bringing in significant new technology or generating foreign exchange through exports may be exempted or more leniently treated.

There are a number of responses available to the foreign enterprise, some of which shade rapidly into law-breaking. The most desirable, however, is to try to ensure that if shares are being sold, they are going to pass into the hands of individuals who will be able to protect the interests of the enterprise. Critics then complain that it is in practice almost impossible for a local citizen without the appropriate political connections to buy shares. Relatives of politicians and civil servants are often to be found in the share register. To accept or indeed to encourage this is arguably questionable enough. What is even more insidious is the wider use of the *prestanombre* condition already alluded to, namely that the enterprise will find front men who, for a price, will allow their names to appear as shareholders, while ownership and control remain firmly with the foreign enterprise.

A complication from the point of view of the enterprise can arise if its shares fall into the possession of sections of the community who may be viewed with suspicion or disfavour by the host government, for this disfavour may rub off on to the enterprise. One example might be where a left wing government was in power and its opponents among the rich section of the community bought shares, precisely because they felt a foreign connection was financially more secure. A large share premium could be regarded as an indication of hostility.

More common, because more subtle, could be the position in a multicultural society where only one section of the community bought shares. In Malaysia, for example, the tendency has been for the Malaysians of Chinese descent (and to a lesser extent the Indian minority) to buy shares while the indigenous Malays, because of cultural and even religious qualms, did not. The dangers of one community holding virtually all equity shares available, and the other, i.e. the majority, holding none is obvious. In this situation the Malaysian government, following its 'Bumiputra' policy of fostering shareholding etc. among the 'Bumi' Malays, in effect buys shares on their behalf to prevent the Chinese or Indian community replacing the foreign shareholder. This was part of the New Economic Policy announced in 1970. This involved a 20 year plan to ensure that by 1990 at least 30 per cent of the equity available in Malaysia would be in the possession of the Bumi Malays: by this time too the non-Bumi inhabitants could have held up to 40 per cent and the remaining 30 per cent might be held by foreigners. Even when this plan was still being rigidly enforced it was claimed, for example, that even where Bumi Malays have acquired equity shares the most desirable were being allocated to the politically well connected. The pitfalls for the foreign enterprise in this sort of situation are great.

The combination of an indigenization programme with cultural inhibitions on the ownership of equity shares was bound to pose serious problems in a multicultural society such as Malaysia. While the 20 year plan envisaged a more equitable distribution of equity shares among the various ethnic groups, the political philosophy of the government favoured free enterprise, and this was to prove potentially incompatible with the Bumiputra drive. Before the plan was halfway through, it was becoming clear that cultural or religious factors were not being overcome by legislation on its own, for the Bumiputras were not buying into the industrial and commercial enterprises on an individual basis to anything like the extent necessary to achieve a balance of ownership. Perforce, to achieve its aim, the government found itself relying more on institutional buying, creating what amounted to parastatals to represent Bumiputra interests. These parastatals tended in practice to attract much the same criticisms as many other parastatals especially in the Third World, namely of inefficiency and vulnerability to political pressure. Only in a very limited sense could it be claimed that industrial and commercial power through ownership was being achieved by the Bumiputras. They might in theory, and collectively, have to end up owning their 30 per cent, but the more dynamic and efficient institutions were likely to remain with the Chinese and other minorities.

By the late 1980s the plan was being effectively shelved, since it was failing to achieve its targets, and was discouraging badly needed foreign investment. But as long as the plan remained in suspense, so to speak, rather than rescinded, the disincentives to foreign investment remained real.

From the viewpoint of the enterprise, indigenization effectively limits freedom of action in global terms, and if persisted in represents an effective threat to its continued existence in global terms, as opposed to a series of operations scattered throughout the world, all partially owned by the headquarters company, but none of the subsidiaries really being under control of the centre.

In this sense indigenization could be a threat to the enterprise that internationalization is not. It would probably suit the enterprise better if it were issuing shares in the parent company rather than local shares, to become in a sense an internationally owned as well as an internationally operating enterprise. Such an arrangement in fact is unacceptable in most countries since the existence of such shares which could readily be exported would make a farce of any currency controls it wished to employ.

When, then, should an enterprise accept and encourage indigenization, given the choice? If it is prepared to accept that it cannot, on the basis of the indigenization programme, integrate the relevant production facilities into a global market plan. It follows from this that the domestic market must be large enough on its own account to make the operation worthwhile on a 'one off' basis, and/or that the plant is located in a high cost area where it would be unlikely that successful exporting could be achieved in any case.

The most widespread use of an indigenization strategy is to be found in countries like India and Nigeria. It is useful to look at the principles on which these countries are operating their policies, because if they are successful they may well be imitated elsewhere.

In the case of India, the key legislation is to be found in the Foreign Exchange Regulation Act of 1973 which has the objective of reducing foreign ownership to a maximum of 40 per cent, with the usual provision of exemptions where there are significant net advantages to the Indian economy, through export earnings or technology transfer.

The effect of the act, which has been amended slightly in subsequent years, is to set up three categories of foreign enterprise. The first category covers the key sector activities, capital goods, petrochemicals etc., which involve a high input of new technology or substantial exports. A high percentage of share ownership may still be allowed to foreigners. The second group are those which re not so widely committed in the key industries but have nevertheless significant interests in them as well as significant exports. Here the foreign holding may still be up to 51 per cent. There are various 'gateway' exceptions for companies with substantial exports, but little involvement in key industries etc. There are of course problems of defining key sectors of industry, advanced technology and what exactly the value and ratio of exports is – problems which are probably not helped by the formidable Indian government bureaucracy.

The final group of companies which do not contribute heavily in key industries, technology or foreign exchange earnings operate at the 40 per cent equity rule and are probably vulnerable to further dilution of equity over time.

One or two major foreign companies have simply refused to dilute control through indigenization, and have pulled out. The best known of these are IBM and Coca Cola. Others have gone along with the legislation, and in some cases have made a deliberate effort to export to the point where they will qualify to retain a majority shareholding.

In the case of Nigeria the indigenization decrees which were first issued in 1974 and have subsequently been revised now create three categories of foreign companies. The first category is for those enterprises which are seen to be providing neither new technology nor significant export earnings, e.g. domestic retailing or distribution networks. Here the intention is that such companies have to be completely Nigerianized, i.e. they must be sold off to local citizens. There is some evidence of evasion (bribery is not unknown in Nigeria) by the use of name lenders, i.e. Nigerians who would be willing to act nominally as owners while the real power lay with the foreigner: more difficult to deal with has been the change of nationality by owners to become official Nigerian citizens, a device which appears to be practised particularly by Greek or Lebanese owners.

The second and third categories require a maximum of 40 or 60 per cent foreign ownership; the categories are rather confused but in effect turn on the perceived contribution to Nigerian development in terms of new technology or foreign exchange earning.

The future of joint ventures and indigenization policies

The Indian and Nigerian examples have been quoted because they represent the most clearcut and consistent policies in large and potentially wealthy economies in the Third World. But they are by no means unique. Many Third World countries have such ambitions, and rather similar illustrations could be drawn in such disparate economies as Brazil, Mexico or Indonesia. These, and even more, the smaller countries may however be constrained by an awareness of the ability of the multinationals to move productive capacity into their territories, if conditions are sufficiently attractive, and bring more rapid development than might occur if development were left to local efforts. There is arguably a race between technological and administrative sophistication on the one hand and national self-confidence on the other: in general the larger the Third World country, the more self-confident it is likely to be, with or without justification. It may be, that as these countries become capable of competing in the world market on their own account, and in the process develop their own multinationals, they may feel that ownership of any plant operating within their territory, is not a prerequisite for control. But if they persist in joint venture or indigenization requirements, the thrust of multinational investment may have to be directed to the smaller economies which have less to offer in terms of a domestic market, but more to gain from export oriented foreign subsidiaries.

d. A 'wholly owned' strategy

This strategy is possible where the subsidiary is virtually exempted from local partners or equity holders with locally issued shares. Here it can be argued the enterprise can operate globally, disposing of its assets and its markets in the way which is to the overall interest of the enterprise. The appropriate strategy may be to maximize profits, or move assets and liabilities around the world as the economic and political situation warrants. This freedom of manoeuvre has its obverse; it is the wholly foreign owned enterprise which is the ready object of local hostility.

The concept of whole ownership however can exist at two levels. The enterprise wholly owns the subsidiary; but who owns the enterprise? In strict legal terms, ownership is likely to be in the hands of the equity holders, generally a host of private owners, but conceivably a public holding pattern may operate. The major dilemma for the enterprise is, as has been noted, that while its operations are international, its ownership is not. In most instances the country of registration of the original enterprise will tell all about the nationality of the equity holders. Arguably a wholly owned strategy is most acceptable when ownership of equity shares is distributed proportionately among nationals of all the territories within which it operates. Such a move however is an ideal rather than a reality both because of cultural difficulties in getting acceptance of the concept of equity holdings and because of governments concerned, both home and host, who would see in the widespread exchange of shares a means whereby national financial controls could be averted.

A 'wholly owned' strategy can be achieved in two ways, namely a 'buying over' or a 'greenfield' operation. 'Buying over' implies that a local operation already exists, which may be owned by another foreign enterprise or by a local interest. Often the company which is being bought over is already well known to the foreign enterprise. It might, for example, be that the local partner is an established joint venture or a company which has licensed 'knowhow' or products from the foreign enterprise. This 'buying over' strategy is a controversial one in many parts of the world: it is liable to be regarded locally as an action to suppress local competition and concentrate on industry in foreign hands. Even where it is legal to buy over a company in this way the foreign enterprise might well hesitate before risking unpopularity. It is sometimes politic to accept local competition rather than appear as the monopolistic villain. Many developed countries will have administrative procedures to vet such takeovers: many Third World countries simply prohibit such foreign takeovers.

A 'greenfield' operation, i.e. building a new plant from the foundations, is politically more acceptable, although it may be difficult to attract local skills in the industry as managers and shopfloor workers. In practice it may be possible to 'grow' local talent if the process does not start with a 'turnkey' operation where a new plant literally rises from a greenfield site. The progression instead may be the setting up of a sales office to which maintenance or technical staff, as well as sales staff are appointed. There may then be a steady progression based on a timetable agreed with the host government, of assembly of imported components, a rising degree of local content in the assembly operation and finally a plant independent of any imports whatsoever. It is significant that such agreements between foreign enterprises and host governments may, in time, balance permission to import components or repatriate profits against foreign exchange earnings for the host government from the export capability of the new plant. The fact that an export capability may exist, and be compatible with the global strategy of the enterprise, can be a powerful card in the hands of the enterprise when it is dealing with a host government.

OWNERSHIP POLICIES AND MARKETING STRATEGIES

This chapter began with a brief reference to the marketing strategies of the enterprise. There are at the extreme two marketing strategies which might be followed by an international enterprise. As with so much else in business decision taking, the possibility of following either extreme course without compromise is remote, and most enterprises will have marketing strategies somewhere in between the extremes, with the relative position between the extremes determined by the particular market and product. Nevertheless, it is useful to consider the two strategies in their purest form.

The first is literally to have a global market strategy. Here the whole world is seen as a series of markets and a series of production centres which have to be linked in the most expedient way. There is in this situation no distinction between the domestic market and the foreign market. That one market happens to be that of the nationality of the parent company of the enterprise is an irrelevance. There is certainly no reason to assume that this is the most important market, or that the production facilities at home are the most important. It is indeed possible that over time the historical home market may be served by production facilities elsewhere, distributed through a sales company. Production and investment are planned on a global basis.

It would be difficult to identify any international enterprise as having achieved that degree of detachment from national interest, but it is at least arguably the end product of several current developments, e.g. the existence of international enterprises originating in small countries whose domestic market or production facilities are negligible in a review of its worldwide activities and assets: the potential of a European company firm, whose national origin is less important than its European span of activity, even the relative decline in world terms of some countries like the USA and the UK which have pioneered the international enterprise.

The second market strategy is the disparate approach, i.e. to establish individual production facilities for individual markets, with no attempt at exporting from the plant in one country to the market place in another, and no attempt to achieve any degree of specialization on an international basis. This strategy is a logical first stage of a move into import substitution in a traditional export market under pressure from the government of that country. If the market is relatively small and production relatively costly and inefficient, it may be the only stage, and possible only in conditions of tariff or other import protection.

How do these extreme market strategies relate to ownership strategies? In effect a global strategy is possible with ownership condition A, as defined earlier in the chapter and summarized in Diagram 3a, i.e. the 'no ownership' or 'no employee' approach, but most likely under condition D, i.e. the 'wholly owned' situation. The disparate market strategy is possible under all four ownership conditions, but is virtually obligatory under conditions B and C, i.e. joint ventures or indigenization, for the simple reason that it would not be possible to switch the right to supply a market from one plant to another if there were local ownership interests in the plant which might be harmed by such a move.

There is therefore an inherent conflict between local interests and an overall global strategy which might require the enterprise to move out of ownership conditions B and C to D, or at a pinch A, if it could safeguard trade marks and distribution channels into the market place. If joint venture or an indigenization situation are virtually legal requirements of host governments, exemption may have to be purchased by promises of substantial and continuing injections of technology or guaranteed foreign exchange earnings. Even where there are no legal problems, the costs may be considerable and the enterprise may have cause to regret an earlier ill considered move to seek local financial participation.

The 'no ownership' condition, A, is the least common, but is potentially the most intriguing as a means whereby political or ideological obstacles can be circumvented, and unorthodox sourcing strategies may be possible. The last two decades of the twentieth century may see the evolution of ownership strategies, which would have appeared extraordinary in the mid century situation, when the international enterprise first made its massive impact in the world scene. If the international enterprise cannot evolve such ownership strategies as are compatible with the political ambitions of the host governments, particularly in the Third World, their further development, outside the industrial West and Japan, may be stinted.

CONCLUSION

It is possible, indeed probable, that an enterprise would use more than one marketing strategy depending on the circumstances prevailing in various parts of the world. It has to be recognized that, where ownership and control are diffused to a local level, restraints on freedom of manoeuvre appear. The probable future pattern is for wholly owned subsidiaries to be practical only in the Western developed countries, joint ventures in the communist countries and joint ventures and indigenization in many parts of the Third World. Potentially the 'no ownership' strategy has applications everywhere because of such factors as hostility towards ownership and employer status in many parts of the world. What may matter most in the long run is access to markets via prestigious trade marks or research and development rather than physical assets in foreign countries.

APPENDIX

Public or quasi-public enterprises

As was noted in the section on joint ventures, an international enterprise which is moving into a new market or initiating a programme of development in an existing market may have to consider increasingly the possibility of a joint venture or another participation deal with a local partner; often this local partner turns out to be a state owned or controlled organization which is not necessarily a clearcut nationalized industry. The implications of partnership with such organizations are vast. They were alluded to very briefly earlier, a much more detailed discussion of the implication could be the subject of several volumes, but some of the issues can be noted here, if not discussed in detail. This section therefore discusses organizations, whether whole industries or single companies, which are owned, controlled or substantially influenced by the state – the public or quasi-public enterprises. Their numbers have been growing fast in recent years and there is no reason to suppose this growth will cease: although there is some reason to expect their growth rate to slow down, they may grow even more rapidly in the Third World. The international enterprise has increasingly to accept their existence, either as partners or competitors, and learn something about their strengths and weaknesses.

Three factors largely account for the growth of these state organizations:

(a) In many parts of the Western developed world socialist or corporate state planning increased rapidly in the 1970s and early 1980s. There is in some respects a ratchet effect permitting the process to go forward but preventing it going into reverse. A left wing or corporate inclined government may take steps to increase the scale of public sector enterprises, e.g. by nationalizing private industry, while a successor government, for reasons to be discussed, finds it difficult to reverse the process and return public enterprises to private hands. In a mixed economy Western nation the balance between the private and public sector has until fairly recently been moving in favour of the latter, and the efforts of right wing governments in the mid 1980s to reverse the trend appear in many cases to be a good deal less successful than the original efforts to set the trend.

(b) In the Third World the predominant ideology is socialism, and this, whether marxist or social democrat, implies public ownership of the means of production, or at the very least control of the 'commanding heights' of the economy. Arguably even in marxist terms it would make most sense for pre-industrial societies in the Third World to go through a phase of *laissez-faire* capitalism, even if the ultimate desired end was seen to be communism. Nevertheless leaders of these newly emergent nations perceive capitalism as the enemy, and take the moral and technical superiority of socialism for granted. When, as often happens, they find this self-evident proportion does not always work out, they may turn to the capitalist world: not, however, to their own native capitalists, but to the foreign enterprise, often using the latter as an instrument of wealth creation, but in partnership with their own public sector enterprises which remain officially the heirs to the future.

(c) The last factor is the increase of marxist states, now comprising one third of the world's population. In theory all, in practice most, of the production facilities are state owned and the markets rigorously guarded; but even here, increasingly, sometimes reluctantly, sometimes enthusiastically, the marxist authorities are turning to international enterprises as one means of solving their problems.

This section will deal largely with the first of these groups, namely state enterprises in the Western world, and those in western Europe in particular. The Western economies in general are the richest markets of the world: although at most they comprise one quarter of the world's population they absorb three quarters of investment by international enterprises. If state enterprises are on the increase in these markets, the international enterprise will have to accommodate them.

The forms of public and quasi-public enterprises

As with many other aspects of the subject of international business policy, it is necessary to structure the discussion, albeit at the risk of making distinctions which are rather artificial. Nevertheless, it is convenient to look at these public or quasi-public enterprises under three headings; their political nature, their strengths and weakness arising from this substantially determine their relationship with international enterprises. These three categories might be defined as:

(a) nationalized industries;
(b) parastatal agencies, state owned but many having the same legal structure and some of the characteristics of private enterprises;
(c) state guaranteed holding companies, relying largely on funds from private savings but under the influence of central government.

Most of the examples cited here will be drawn from western Europe, which yields a variety of all three categories. The Third World presents an even wider range depending on the political and cultural background; while examples can be given it is difficult to categorize for this group.

a. Nationalized industries

At their most traditional, these tend to be public utilities which in most Western countries are owned and run by the state or local authorities. With them may be lumped other industries which have been deemed at some time or other to be of such consequence to the public interest that they have been taken into public ownership. That is the theory at least: what has often happened is that, following a financial crisis under private ownership which threatened jobs in politically sensitive areas, or because the previous owners have in some way offended the government, the enterprises have passed into public ownership. In most Western nations the major state railway and airline system falls into this category, as do many communications networks.

The scope for joint venture or similar arrangements between these nationalized industries and international enterprises are relatively limited for two reasons: first, by their nature the nationalized industries are powerful monopolies which command substantial financial resources or at least have access to public funds; second, by choice or political expediency they do not always operate on the commercial criteria required by a private enterprise, domestic or international. The arguments about the function of nationalized industries are well enough known to require little exposition. Briefly, however, the defenders (and some of the customers) of nationalized industry tend to emphasize their social role in the community. Thus they are often excused from operating in the most commercially efficient methods, i.e. those maximizing profits. Precisely because of their monopoly position and their licence to operate without overdue concern about profitability they may be inefficient and overmanned – certainly they are not obvious candidates for close co-operation with international enterprises with a prejudice in favour of making a profit.

Surprising as it may appear, the terms of reference of some nationalized industry boards are so vague as to be a licence to do practically anything. It is often in what might be described as maverick activities that co-operation with international business becomes more practical, simply because the only justification of these maverick activities must be a commercial one, and the executives concerned often lack the technical or marketing background in the areas into which they are straying. Disciples of the theory of marketing myopia might argue that the British National Coal Board's (NCB) early venture into oil exploration in the North Sea represented far sighted appreciation of the concept that the NCB was in the energy rather than the coal business. The real story may be less logical: namely, that commercially aggressive executives saw opportunities for investing in an industry which, with some plausibility, could be claimed to be relevant to their main interests but where they were not likely to be burdened by 'social responsibility' claims. No one was likely to argue that the NCB had a social duty to retain redundant oil workers in worked out wells, in the way they had in the past been saddled with redundant miners in unprofitable coal mines. They could logically justify their intervention in the oil business only on commercial grounds: not surprisingly, lacking oil technology, they rapidly acquired partners in the field of international business, and US oil companies found themselves the unlikely partners of a British nationalized coal industry. In much the same way the NCB ventures into the production of artificial fibres appeared on the surface a rather improbable development which could hardly be described either as socially desirable or a natural development from their existing technological base. Again they had to find a foreign partner, not least, one suspects, because any British private company going into the deal would fear ultimate absorption. Probably only a handful of NCB executives or employees would even have realized that their nationalized board was in a joint venture relationship with a Dutch company to produce nylon material, but for the fact that their main plant was destroyed with considerable loss of life in a highly publicized accident.

In summary then, nationalized industries as such in most Western countries do not readily go into partnership with international business enterprises, at least so far as their main activity is involved. Extraneous or unrelated ventures are a different matter.

b.   *Parastatal agencies*

The growth of the parastatal concept has been one of the most significant developments in extending the reach of public sector industry in many Western states. Indeed with the growing disenchantment among the general public in many of these states with the practical results of straightforward nationalization, the parastatal agency approach is likely to be the main method of increasing public sector industry in the future.

In a very considerable risk of oversimplification, it might be said that the objectives of a nationalized industry are primarily social and political, and the objectives of a parastatal, economic and commercial, although elements of the objectives of each tend to invade the others. In particular the parastatal, as will be argued, is likely to have its aims compromised to serve political interest over time.

The parastatal agency, then, is a state sponsored organization which takes over existing private enterprises or creates new enterprises often resembling in legal form the type of company which is normal in the private sector of that particular country. The majority or all of the shares of any such company may be held by the agency on behalf of the state. The agency's funds are initially provided by the state rather than by private shareholders or commercial institutions; it may borrow money on the national or international markets by selling bonds. The major advantage of this type of organization is that since its industrial or commercial holdings conform to the norms of a company and are not directly responsible to a government ministry it is not so subject to the same political pressures and criticisms from the government that happens more readily to the more overtly nationalized industry. Most of its customers, the majority of the public, and even many of its own employees may not be aware that the organization is ultimately owned by the state.

In theory, the agency is likely to be bound by the same two conventional objectives as more overtly nationalized industries. The first and most important is to enable the state to gain control of key sectors of industry, and by so doing, to enable the government consciously to plan the economic development of the nation. Not surprisingly therefore the parastatal agency tends to take over from the private sector those industries which are deemed to be the most significant. The second objective however is liable to involve the organization in day to day political difficulties and infighting. This is a commitment which may exist explicitly in the agency's terms of reference or may be thrust upon it by events, principally by the government in a political crisis trying to compel it to pursue social ends quite different from that implied in the first. Specifically there may be a requirement to bale out or take over private companies whose collapse would not represent any particular setback to the overall national economy but would cause political embarrassment to the government, for example employment in a minister's constituency or bailiwick. One particular untoward result is that the management and employees of an ailing private company may see absorption into one of those organizations as a form of pensioning off from the necessity of paying their way. The political patronage implied in the operation of a parastatal agency is therefore considerable. Although the problems appear simply to duplicate those encountered in the normal straightforward nationalized industries, they are often more acute because the parastatal character of the organization implies more flexibility, so that even a small private enterprise can be bought over without the elaborate legal procedures which are usually a prerequisite of nationalization, and the consequent embarrassing publicity avoided.

It would be intellectually elegant if one could say that the parastatal agency as a device of increasing state ownership or of participation in industry is characteristic of the political left – a means of 'owning or controlling socialism', whether marxist or non-marxist. In reality it is to be found in corporate societies whether of the left or right: in the present form it is in fact fascist rather than marxist in origin and is a characteristic as much of right wing dictatorships as of left. The first objective of control and planning of the economy is non-political in the conventional left–right dichotomy.

In the second sense of 'social objectives', the parastatal agency is at best an instrument of welfare economics, at worst a form of patronage or bribery. The agency thus described is not a familiar pattern in the USA, for example (apart, perhaps, from the Tennessee Valley Authority and similar institutions dating from New Deal days). But the necessity to placate local interests at the expense of the community at large is universal. In this sense the parastatal approach is an institutionalized 'pork barrel' familiar enough in American politics, but adapted to west European, and even more, Third World countries' practices.

Last, in this general comment, it is important to note the ratchet effect of parastatal activities. Whenever a parastatal agency takes over an existing private company or creates a new one, it creates a powerful vested interest which will resist attempts to restore a company to the private sector where life is more competitive and inefficiencies or failure carry sharper penalties: efforts to privatize such institutions by successor governments are often economically messy, and politically inconclusive, as the British conservative government found to its cost or more than one occasion.

The origin of the modern parastatal organization, as has been suggested, was a fascist one, in the 1930s Italy of Mussolini. The IRI (Istituto per la Riconstruzione Industriale) founded then was an attempt by a corporate state to recover from the slump by the takeover of moribund private industry. That particular agency survived the fall of fascist Italy. There was a need for industrial reconstruction in the late 1940s far exceeding anything needed in the early 1930s, and the IRI proved to be an effective instrument. So much so, in fact, that the pattern was duplicated in other industries to the point where IRI and similar agencies now control about 1000 companies and are responsible for about 40 per cent of the Italian industrial sector. The implications of this multiplication and the problems and opportunities this created for the international enterprise will be considered in detail later.

It was not surprising in the circumstances that similar agencies appeared in other authoritarian or corporate states, e.g. INI (Instituto Nacional de Industria) in Spain in the early 1940s and IDI (Institut de Développement Industriel) in France. Rather surprisingly however the pattern was also being copied in social democratic countries in western Europe, though their advocates in countries like Britain and Sweden would probably challenge this ancestry. The first attempt in Britain was half-hearted and shortlived, the IRC (Industrial Reconstruction Corporation) which was intended to finance rationalized industry by takeovers of smaller companies by more efficient larger ones – in some respects securing some of the alleged benefits of nationalization at a time when the performance of the more formally nationalized industries raised little public enthusiasm for more on the same lines. The IRC, a social democratic concept was allowed to run down by a successor conservative government but re-appeared in a more radical form in the 1970s as the NEB (National Enterprise Board) which sought not merely industrial nationalization but state ownership. The NEB was in turn eclipsed on the return of a strongly right wing government in 1979. Significantly the pattern was also adopted in a more stable social democratic state, Sweden, as the Statsforetag, a public holding company with state funds subsequently increased by bond issues.

By the middle 1970s the parastatal agency was strongly established in western Europe, albeit in a variety of forms and therefore, to varying degrees capable of influencing or being influenced by international business.

The system can usefully be subdivided into two groups of nations, in the first of which there is only one such agency (or only one of any significance); the second being those nations where several agencies have been created for different industries or regions.

i.   Examples of states with a single important parastatal agency are to be found in Spain, France, Sweden and Ireland.

The Spanish INI is an autonomous body which implements national development plans on behalf of the Ministry of Industry particularly during the Franco period. It has evolved through three states. From its foundation in 1941 to the early 1960s it developed what might be described as the basic industries of a modern industrial estate: mining, public utilities, heavy engineering and so on. The second stage, comprising the remainder of the 1960s, was the period of Spain's so-called 'economic miracle' of rapid and sustained growth in more and more industries of relatively high technology. Significantly in the present context, the third stage in the 1970s and 1980s has been a 'supranational' phase when the Spanish government has attempted to attract foreign investment, most noticeably in vehicle manufacturing. INI was made to sell off some of its more important assets in this field, to the German multinational Volkswagen in the case of SEAT, and on a smaller scale commercial vehicle manufacturing plant to the Japanese company, Nissan, through the sale of a majority holding in Motor Iberica.

The French equivalent IDI is in practice very much less important as a state instrument for economic control, largely because the very close-knit relationship which already exists between the French civil service, banking and industry alluded to elsewhere. Collaboration between the public and private sectors of French industry is close, the nationalized Régie Renault, for example, sharing some research facilities with erstwhile rivals in the private sector. But collaboration takes place between French companies and the state, not with foreign companies, and it is in practice very difficult for an international enterprise to get access to key sectors of French industry, through the IDI or directly, if there is any resistance from French companies, who in this event get very substantial political aid from the government in resisting approaches by foreigners.

The Swedish Statsforetag is possibly the best known of these single-unit parastatal agencies because in the more open Swedish society it has been seen as a testing bed for many of the issues arising between public sector investment and private companies. The Statsforetag illustrates in a relatively small and homogeneous society, the issues of commercial viability vs social responsibility which so bedevil public sector organizations of this nature. In theory, at least, the dilemma has been resolved in Sweden. It has been accepted that the agency must be allowed to operate on a commercial basis, i.e. it will invest in a private company only if there appears reasonable prospects of a satisfactory return on capital. Its management on that basis has refused offers to take over ailing private companies: it appears, however, to have difficulty in shedding any of its operations which are not proving commercially viable. Some of its own white elephants may prove to be as expensive to feed as any less efficiently organized state enterprise anywhere in the world. In this sense economy is not a universal characteristic of all the Statsforetag's dealings.

Notwithstanding what has been said about commercial viability the state can require the agency to implement projects which could not be justified in commercial terms, but provision is then made for negotiations between the Statsforetag and the government for the payment of an appropriate subsidy. Fairly clear guidelines have been laid down and no serious clash has arisen between commercial criteria and state policy. In one sense the Swedes were fortunate in their timing when the Statsforetag began to operate in the early 1970s. The government responsible for the concept had at the time been in power for a generation and did not expect to lose a general election in the near future: and, most important, the agency came into operation during a period of prosperity. More commonly such organizations begin life as stopgap emergency measures in periods of political or economic uncertainty and are therefore the centre of political controversy from the outset. In this context it is significant that the growing uneasiness in relations between the Statsforetag and the Swedish government arose during the recession of the mid 1970s when more overt pressure was put on the agency to accept ailing enterprises about whose future prospects it had serious doubts.

The Statsforetag, almost inevitably in the light of what has been said about the Swedish government's attitude to international enterprises, has thus far kept the latter at arm's length, and does not seriously appear to be considering any partnership arrangements with foreign enterprises. The relative success of a single unit parastatal agency, well run and remarkably insulated thus far from political pressures, represents a formidable problem for an international enterprise. A cynic might argue that on the basis of its past record of success the Statsforetag is not the sort of organization which is likely to be regarded with any enthusiasm by foreign international enterprises. They have no particular reason to wish it well.

Finally in this group of single-unit parastatal agencies is the Irish Republic's Industrial Development Agency (IDA) which, in the light of the small industrial base existing in the Republic, has perforce to deal with international enterprises on a very large scale in order to build up industry – although it has a role in reviving local industries in difficulties, most modern technology is being introduced through international enterprise. At present, however, the IDA aims mainly to attract investment through grants and publicizing the favourable tax policies of the Irish government to exporting firms and has been successful in attracting European and Japanese enterprises. It could build up significant minority equity holdings in some of the foreign enterprises. In fact the major advantages of export tax holidays have been run down since the European Community ultimately brought pressure to bear on the Irish government to limit the concessions it makes to foreign companies, in order to bring Ireland's practices more into line with the other Community members. However, as and when the Irish advantages disappear, the situation, as has been noted earlier, may repeat itself with Spain and Portugal which, through parastatal and direct government subsidy, are attracting foreign investment by methods which might prove to be unacceptable to EC members.

ii. The situation where multiple parastatal agencies exist is at once more confused and offers more room for manoeuvre for the international enterprise. Again it may be useful to distinguish two subcategories: namely, parastatal agencies which operate ostensibly on an industrial sector basis, and those which operate on a geographical/regional basis. The qualification 'ostensibly' is prudent however because, whatever the principle, there are likely to be a number of compromise arrangements in practice. The Italian system is the best example of an industrial sector structure, the British of a geographical/regional.

The Italian agencies are grouped under the Ministry of State Participation. Three of the agencies can usefully be commented upon either because of their scale of operation or because they illustrate some of the political implications. These are:

IRI   (Istituto per la Riconstruzione Industriale);
ENI   (Ente Nazionale Idrocarburi);
EFIM   (Ente Participazione e Finanziento Industria Manifatturiera).

There are other public sector industries which do not come directly under the Ministry of State Participation, e.g. the state railway, electricity and the tobacco monopoly whose interests are more revenue raising than industrial developments.

Simply to list the parastatal agencies with their areas of interest shows the bewildering confusion which arises and gives some clue to the *raison d'être* behind many of them. They represent, in a sense, centres of power with, in many instances, recognized political allegiances among the top executives. IRI is the largest and possibly the least criticized, most closely approaching a nationalized attempt to control key industries. It controls the state airline, Alitalia; through its subsidiary Finsider, steel products; through Finmeccanica, most mechanical engineering companies, as well as the Alfa Romeo complex; through Italstar, much of the civil engineering and public works industry. The Alfa Romeo holding represents a significant holding in the Italian vehicle industry and through its foreign holdings in many parts of the world might reasonably claim to be a form of international enterprise itself: it is likely to be 'floated off', possibly as a joint venture partner with a foreign multinational enterprise.

ENI, the oil and natural gas monopoly, has achieved semi-autonomous power to the extent that it is a significant factor on the world oil scene, able to bargain at international level, and in the process involving the Italian government in a political crisis over its relationship with Saudi Arabian oil supplies, when allegations of bribery flew thick and fast.

Possibly the most curious mixture is to be found in EFIM: aluminium smelting, tourism, food and some types of aircraft, derived largely from a private group of Italian companies.

The most controversial of all the agencies in recent years has been a mining and metallurgy group, which was liquidated in the late 1970s and its assets absorbed by the larger IRI and ENI. There had been a degree of logic in its creation since Italy was short of refining processes in non-ferrous metals: its critics, however, would argue that its *raison d'être* was political rather than industrial and that it developed as a preserve of one group within the dominant political party at the time, the christian democrats. Certainly it quickly acquired a reputation for buying over commercially dubious but politically sensitive companies – and in the process overlapped into industries which might have been regarded as more appropriate to IRI or ENI, eventually, for example, sharing control with these agencies of the major Italian chemical complex Montedison.

In much the same way EGAM extended away from refining into transport and more politically sensitive areas. Some of these activities could be given at least a specious logic in terms of vertical integration, but the obscurity of the financial dealings and lack of factual information on these make it rather difficult to determine whether the logic was industrial, financial or simply political expediency.

The outside observer might perhaps be inclined to think of these agencies in terms of political fiefs rather reminiscent in their relations with one another of the political states of pre-unification Italy. In general, IRI is seen as christian democrat territory: ENI by contrast is dominated by the socialist party. To compound the confusion there are in some instances apparent competing groups within the organization, i.e. they may be semi-independent territories but come complete in some cases with their internal politics.

To a far greater degree than the Statsforetag, the Italian agencies individually and collectively are compelled to obey non-commercial state directives. The depressed areas in the Italian south, i.e. the Mezzogiorno, and the peripheral islands have probably the most acute economic problems of any part of western Europe; Italian state aid there has to a very large extent taken the form of requiring the agencies to build expensive and in many cases loss-making projects. The Alfasud, the Alfa Romeo operation in the south of Italy, the Gioia Tauro steel complex in Calabria, or a joint ENI/Montedison manmade textile plant in Sardinia could bring much needed employment to their localities: but whether the agencies would ever have contemplated them on a commercial basis is highly doubtful, particularly since most of the financing required has to be raised in the capital market, often through bond issues. By the 1980s the IRI subsidiary Alfa Romeo was actively pursuing the possibility of a joint venture with the Japanese Nissan company, on similar lines to the prospective joint venture deal between British Leyland, at the time an NEB subsidiary, and Honda. The Nissan deal was to have produced a Japanese designed vehicle, ultimately with some 80 per cent value of local components, but the negotiations were overtaken by alternative deals for hiving off the Alfa Romeo organization for sale or partnership to the Americans. The background to this was that by the middle 1980s the economic losses of IRI were so great that it became politically feasible for the first time in many decades to contemplate the privatization of some IRI holdings, including Alitalia and Alfa Romeo, with the steel group Italsider, a possible future candidate. In the present context it is the possibility of a Ford takeover which is of most interest. Alfa, as an IRI subsidiary, had been allowed to make staggering losses, simply because political rather than commercial factors prevailed. Ironically the major resistance came from the private sector company Fiat, Alfa's main competitor, which no doubt preferred the idea of a competitor cushioned from excessive efficiency by political control, to the prospect of a commercially operated Alfa Ford operation.

In contrast to the politicized parastatal agencies, the nationalized industries are relatively free from criticism. By their very nature, however, i.e. rail, electricity production and the tobacco monopoly, they are of little interest to an international enterprise.

Italy thus produces an interesting dilemma for international enterprises. The multiplicity of parastatal agencies and the power bases they represent might make them of interest to international enterprises as joint venture partners. But political instability, which helped to create the multiplicity and in turn increases it, makes the whole market a rather difficult one for the foreign enterprise to read.

iii. If Italy provides an example of parastatal agencies operating on an industrial sector basis, Britain provides an example of the geographical/regional basis. There were in this context three important agencies: the National Enterprise Board, the Scottish Development Agency (SDA) and the Welsh Development Agency (WDA). A similar Industrial Development Board still exists for Ulster but faces quite unique problems because of the political conditions existing there. The NEB was for a time by far the most significant, disposing as it did of very substantial sums and operating throughout Britain. In the event, the return of the conservatives under Mrs

Thatcher in effect killed off its *raison d'être* and the extensive privatization programme of the government accelerated its demise.

The fate of the regionally based groups was, however, different. The creation of the SDA and WDA was in part a response to political tensions between England, the major part of Great Britain, and the smaller highly nationalistic Scotland and Wales. The distinction in functions between these two agencies and the overall national NEB therefore owed as much to political pressures in Scotland and Wales as to economic logic. Both these institutions continued to flourish under the Thatcher government, perhaps a triumph of expediency over political conviction.

The relationship between parastatal agencies and international enterprises There are many aspects of the development of international agencies which must of necessity simply be ignored in a study of this nature; discussion is relevant only insofar as it relates to the possibility of competition or collaboration between such agencies and international enterprises. In competitive terms a domestic enterprise owned or financed by an agency is likely to be formidable, not because it is necessarily all that efficient but because it may be less inhibited by the necessity to make such a commercial return on capital than the privately owned international enterprise and incidentally may be able to drum up support of a non-marketing nature. If a domestic company supported by parastatal funds faces severe competition from a foreign competitor the state can and often does redress the balance by, for example, requiring public sector organizations to give preference to the domestic supplier.

In the case of possible collaboration, however, the most noticeable feature of the parastatal agency is its susceptibility to political pressure to make decisions which will be politically popular rather than commercially viable, particularly when short term political expediency is involved. A foreign enterprise in financial difficulties may simply be able to screw aid out of a parastatal agency by threatening to close down a local factory and create local unemployment. The Chrysler situation in Britian a decade back indicates the power of an enterprise in a politically sensitive area to extract aid as a condition of not closing down. Chrysler (UK) had been losing money for years but its continued existence guaranteed not only jobs but some foreign exchange earnings from exports. The British government in the event gave Chrysler an open ended cheque to stay in business for a few years more. Manifestly it did not want to nationalize an enterprise which might never break even, but appeared to be searching around frantically for some method of getting off a political hook. The reaction of the embryo parastatal agencies which were just being set up, namely the NEB and SDA, was a barely concealed relief that they were not yet ready to be activated in this situation. Almost inevitably they would have been pressured into giving a gloss of commercial respectability to a piece of political expediency. As it was, the car plants involved steadily declined to a rump assembly operation for a French multinational.

In other circumstances, however, the NEB made it very clear that it would welcome any form of joint venture with a foreign enterprise, particularly in areas of high unemployment.

When a rather similar but smaller scale incident occurred in Italy several years before, the American parent company decided to close down its Italian Raytheon plant. IRI was forced to take over, and though this was a politically popular decision in the regions where jobs were being threatened, it was at least arguable that IRI had been compelled to invest in a project which had already proved a commercial failure.

Parastatal agencies as political entities   It has been argued above that where there exists more than one parastatal agency in a country, whether the ostensible logic is industry sectoral or geographical regional, overlap may occur between agencies and so competition arise. In a very real sense separate political fiefs may be created with their own interests either against their parent ministries or each other, rather like territorial states. One English writer has compared corporations with such states and (not altogether tongue in cheek) suggested the study of the writings of Machiavelli on the politics of fifteenth-century Italy as a relevant authority. Arguably the analogy applies even more forcibly to the parastatal agencies as political entities.

This situation of conflict between power centres in the public sector is not new or by any means exclusive to the European examples thus far cited. The application of an earlier Canadian government's guide on the control of foreign investment discussed in Chapter 8 can be circumscribed by the provincial governments, or even municipal authorities, offering attractive inducements to the foreign enterprise if they wished to secure employment opportunities and did not share the federal government's concern over foreign domination of Canadian industry.

There are more overtly political disputes involving territorial jurisdiction where the frontiers of the parastatal cannot be clearly defined. Nevertheless, if a foreign enterprise regards these agencies as having much the same administrative discretion as state authorities and interests which differ from the overall national interest, they may be able to conclude bargains on co-operation or joint ventures which seemed unpromising when regarded only in terms of national policy and legislation.

Parastatals in the Third World   The examples of parastatals thus far quoted are European because it is there the principle may be said to have developed most systematically. But in numbers, if not in effectiveness, parastatals are much more widespread in the Third World, where governments so often tend to be officially socialist or *étatiste*. Such governments are constitutionally inclined to the concept of the parastatal which can generally be staffed by men and women whose major qualification is party loyalty or family connection. It has to be said that in many instances the organization which develops is highly inefficient, loss making and a political embarrassment, save as a source of political patronage.

There is a tendency among Western businessmen and writers in the field of international business to ignore the existence of the parastatals of the Third World, even where they dominate the industrial sector of an economy. There is an implicit assumption that they will be phased out in favour of more efficient methods, once their frequent manifest mediocrity of performance is exposed.

The truth, however, is probably the reverse. Technological or commercial incompetence are rarely, if ever, likely to be seen by their proponents as reason for dispensing with them. The faults must lie elsewhere, preferably with foreign imperialists, certainly with the private sector of industry. Parastatals in the Third World survive and flourish because too many people of influence have an interest in their existence, if not their success. They are, as has been remarked, perceived initially as a means of direction of industry by *étatiste* planners: by the time they have failed to live up to initial expectations, they have frequently become that institutionalized form of bribery for functionaries and the party faithful.

International parastatals   There is a comparatively recent development in the parastatal form to cover organizations designed to produce plans for regional groupings like the Andean Pact, rather than single national economies. It is too early as yet to form an opinion on their long term effectiveness, but insofar as the personnel concerned are dispensing money outside the political territories of potential patrons, there is hope that they will not become centres of political patronage to the same extent. Certainly such institutions as the Andean Development Corporation will have to be taken seriously by international enterprises hoping to operate within their territories.

Part III

Production Methods and Standards in the Multinational Enterprise

Introduction

The advent of the multinational enterprise has modified a good deal of the received wisdom on traditional economics, production methods and marketing policy. The qualifications to economic theory have been alluded to in the previous section, namely the extent in terms of intra-company transactions across national frontiers. The modifications which have to be made in considering production and marketing arise from two factors. First, the distribution of the factors of production and also the market size which normally determine in a market, i.e. how goods are produced and on what scale, can be altered by strategic decisions of a multinational company. It can introduce new production methods, not so much in response to conditions in a particular market, but because it has introduced new production facilities elsewhere and has phased out equipment from there which can be usefully employed in another plant in another country. Second, by allocating international markets to particular plants the multinational can change the size of the market available and so the appropriate production methods.

Finally, this section looks at the threat which arises from unauthorized copying or pirating of products or technology, and the extent to which the multinational can protect itself.

4 Product Policy for the International Enterprise

This chapter deals with the problems of production methods and product policy on a global scale, both as it affects the international enterprise and the host government. What follows applies particularly to the situation where the international enterprise intends to set up foreign based production facilities which are either wholly owned or subject to a joint venture or indigenization situation: but it also largely applies to the situation where the enterprise is supplying technology by licensing or the sale of a turnkey operation.

The chapter is divided into four main parts:

(a) the appropriate product policy to be followed, on the assumption that it is unrealistic to follow the same product policy through the world;
(b) the appropriate production methods which the enterprise might choose to operate in various parts of the world;
(c) the appropriate response of the host government, particularly on the issue of technology transfer;
(d) the concept of intellectual property rights and the threat to them posed by current thinking in the Third World.

PRODUCTION METHODS ON A GLOBAL SCALE

The international enterprise cannot expect to replicate the same production methods in all its production plants, if for no other reason than that the resources available to it, even in terms of the conventional economic factors of land, labour and capital, will vary from one part of the world to another. As a first approximation one can say that the production methods are determined by three elements: the size of the market; the level of local technology; and the local distribution of the factors of production. In the case of an international enterprise as opposed to a purely domestic enterprise, however, there is room for some manoeuvre, according to the perceived interests of the enterprise and the host government.

It is easy to see why the size of the market plays a role in the production methods available. The techniques of mass production depend on the ability to break down technical processes to more and more stages from which the benefits of specialization can be attained. The limit to the level of technology is the size of the market. It would be theoretically possible to design a brand new popular model of car to be produced at a level of 1000 cars per year. In fact, such a car would virtually have to be a mixture of jobbing operations and building by hand, far more so even than the exclusive Rolls Royce, and each car would be at least as costly to produce as the latter. A modern popular car is designed to be produced on a scale at least a hundred times as great so that capital intensive mass production techniques can be applied. If the local market is only 1000 vehicles, then the most that can be achieved is local assembly of components mass-produced elsewhere.

An important element, therefore, for the international enterprise is that it may have some choice in the market size. A local market which is too small to sustain any serious degree of new technology might be expanded by allocating to the plant an export market hitherto served by a plant elsewhere; or the small market may be absorbed into another. The enterprise has the choice of bringing in more advanced technology, if it chooses, simply because it has this option on market size.

The second element is the local level of technology available or readily absorbed. The level available represents a 'takeoff' point at which it is reasonable to suppose that improvements and innovations can be developed: the level which can be absorbed represents a technology which can be mastered if introduced from abroad, but which could not have been generated locally. It may be important to distinguish between these two levels, for there is a tendency in designing production facilities to incorporate all the most up to date features, and produce a situation where a subsidiary plant may be more sophisticated than that plant back in the more technologically advanced country in which the headquarters is based. The result can be that the new plant cannot be operated efficiently because the experience is not there, and the prospects of improving production still further are undetermined.

The issue of the appropriate level of technology also affects the third element, namely the distribution of the factors of production. The most frequent situation for the international enterprise will be that it is moving into less developed areas than at home and the prospects are that labour will be relatively cheaper compared with capital. It may make more sense therefore to bring in more labour intensive methods.

This is probably most easily achieved if the obsolescent techniques are being used in the manufacture of obsolescent products ('obsolescence' being used in relation to the most up to date methods used in the home plants). It may be necessary however to retool and change production methods significantly if the product is to be identical to that currently being produced at home. It may also be expedient to find the opinion of the host government or the desirability of more technology vs more jobs, if for no other reason than to ensure that if at the government's behest it creates jobs rather than the higher level of technology, it does not suffer by having royalty payments for the technology it uses vetoed by the host government because the technology is not new. It is not unknown in some countries for the institution concerned with human resource development, and more specifically job creation, to be operating quite independently, or even at cross purposes with institutions such as technology boards which are monitoring the type and level of technology being introduced.

PRODUCT POLICY AND MARKET INTELLIGENCE

At the micro level, the fact of being an international enterprise with production facilities scattered throughout the world has very profound significance, both in terms of product policy and market intelligence. Market orientation is not nearly so important as academic textbooks might suggest, once one gets beyond the first, and presumably the most important, market for a new product. It is a self-evident proposition that if a product designed for one market can be imposed on all other markets, rather than an individual product tailor-made for each market, then the potential savings are enormous. What is condemned in the inexperienced exporter, namely expecting a new foreign market to buy the product even when that has been specifically designed for the domestic market, makes sense for many international enterprises. This product orientation takes at least three forms. First, there is a policy of designing a 'universal' product which, however, is universal only in the sense that the design takes account of conditions in economies similar to that of the major market. This phenomenon is seen as the most common. Second, there is the policy of introducing the product into markets for which it is not very obviously designed, if this is going to be cheaper than giving the market what it would prefer. Third, and most controversially of all, there is the policy of phasing out the product as and when it becomes obsolescent in the major market, and only then manufacturing in the less important market – and incidentally satisfying any remaining demand for the product in the major market by exporting – a specialized but significant form of transferring industry across frontiers.

One consequence of this policy is that conventional market research or test marketing becomes irrelevant in the secondary market. The objective is no longer to determine the best product before the design stage is complete, but to find out what is the minimum adaptation to an existing product which will be necessary to gain market acceptance. Even questions of deciding on an appropriate time to launch the new product in the secondary market become subordinate to the question of when the production facilities can be made available, and this is as likely to be determined by the question of when they are no longer required elsewhere in more important markets. International productive capacity is combined with the existence of separate and disparate markets. These markets may be persuaded to accept products which are relatively cheap to supply into the new markets precisely because they do not have to be designed for these markets. This situation turns a good deal of conventional marketing wisdom on its head. In a very special sense the international enterprise can gain either from economic progress in less developed countries, or lack of it. The more standards of living and tastes in these markets converge towards those of the affluent West, the more the enterprise stands to gain from mass production and marketing of a standardized product designed for no one market but acceptable in all. On the other hand, the larger a continuation of a gap in the standard of living, the more the possibility of extending the life of plant capacity and products as and when they become obsolescent in the markets for which they were designed.

If product policy and orthodox market research and test marketing are downgraded or at least simplified in these smaller markets by the necessities of the major markets which determine product development and set the pace of introduction everywhere, then other factors become more important. These might be defined as political and technological intelligence. Political intelligence may be necessary to anticipate changes in what the host government will permit; technological intelligence to ensure that any new product can be phased in to its manufacturing phase with a minimum of problems.

WHAT PRODUCTS CAN BE TRANSFERRED ACROSS NATIONAL AND CULTURAL FRONTIERS?

The international enterprise, rather more than a domestic enterprise, has the facility of exploiting its expertise in new markets in that it can develop products for one market and subsequently bring them into other markets where they were not likely to have originated spontaneously to meet a perceived need. Clearly, however, the wider the gap both in material and cultural terms, between one society and another, the greater the potential problem of choosing which products can be transferred. Ultimately, the issue of product suitability is one aspect of a very large question, namely whether cultures and tastes are converging or diverging, and this is an issue which it will be necessary to look at again in due course. For the moment, however, the discussion will be confined to the specific issue of product acceptability.

THE MACRO APPROACH: THE INTERNATIONAL PRODUCT LIFE CYCLE CONCEPT

The concept of the international product life cycle is well enough known to require little comment. Briefly, however, it derives from research on the diffusion of technology from the United States, and the consequent loss on occasion of the 'technological edge' which that country has had on so many occasions. In general terms, the product life cycle can probably be applied to a number of industrialized countries. The concept in its generalized form suggests that a significant technological breakthrough is likely to come in one of a small number of Western technologically advanced economies. It may almost be an accident in which particular country the breakthrough comes: often the deciding factor may simply be that the crisis or opportunity for a new product was particularly obvious in one of these societies in which the technological level was appropriate for the new development.

Once the breakthrough comes, wherever it comes in this relatively small group of societies, it will spread rapidly to those others which were in the race, i.e. which have also the technological infrastructure. The enterprise which developed the concept may itself introduce it elsewhere by export or local production. It may be licensed, pirated or simply so adapted as to avoid patent protection by other advanced countries. This is the second stage, the equivalent of the rapid acceptance and growth of demand phenomenon in the conventional product life cycle.

The product then becomes available in other less developed countries, i.e. those countries which did not possess the technological infrastructure to develop the process *ab initio*, but which can simply reproduce a process developed elsewhere. Such a tendency is likely to be encouraged by government action to cut imports and build up home industries, so that imports are replaced by local production in subsidiaries or under licence. At first, and particularly in small societies, the quality and sophistication of these local versions simply do not compare with the products of the more advanced societies, but in some countries at least, as time goes on, and incidentally as the product technology reaches maturity in terms of the conventional life cycle, these countries which were technologically less advanced may begin to produce a product which stands comparison with that produced in the developed economies.

The last stage, if it happens, is that the tide of exports is turned, and these countries begin to export the products back to the countries of origin – a process which is likely to be encouraged if access to the existing markets in the developed world is guaranteed by the trade mark or brand name of a multinational company already well established in this market. This phenomenon has been remarked upon, namely that in many products the brand name rather than the country of origin is what sells the product – the fact that a vehicle is a Volkswagen is more important that the fact it was built in Mexico or Brazil, and so on. This fact goes far to explain the fear that Europe, the cradle of the motor vehicle and one of the major industrial complexes of the world, may become a net importer of motor vehicles by the mid 1990s.

The international product life cycle is an attractive explanation of the transfer of innovation, and a useful tool, but it has its limitations in explaining what happens to individual products. Its weakness is twofold; it is a macro approach, i.e. it describes the transfer of industries rather than products, and it is an analogy which can be stretched too far, confusing species with individual creatures.

PRODUCT STANDARDIZATION AS A CHECK ON THE PRODUCT LIFE CYCLE

Market orientation has placed increasing emphasis on the concept that individual markets require tailormade products, and that can be readily reconciled with the international product life cycle concept. The concept of product orientation and the standardization of consumer durables, however, poses an interesting alternative, in that if the level of technology is such that it will be difficult for the underdeveloped countries represented at stages 3 and 4 to master constantly changing technology, then the process of moving from exporting from developed countries to local production and export from the less developed country may be delayed, or even reversed. The advantages arising from mass production employing every available refinement of technology may outweigh cheaper local labour and trade barriers elsewhere. In a sense, the Japanese producers of consumer durables are very reluctant international enterprises, preferring low cost production at home, based on a high technological input into the manufacturing process, to all the incentives for local production abroad. They go international only when they see no alternative, and this reluctance has paid off handsomely. It may well be that the Americans, for example, will eventually revert to the same policy in consumer durables, and revert to exporting rather than international production, e.g. in compact motor vehicles. The lesson is that if some products can be transferred across national and cultural frontiers, the process is not always inevitable, let alone, one-way. Products and production can be transferred back if technology and politics dictate.

THE 'DOUGHNUT' EFFECT

The international life cycle concept is one which can be accepted with more equanimity by the international enterprise which can follow or take technology, and so industry, across the frontiers, than by the shopfloor worker in the developed country who sees his or her job disappear – or by his or her government. The concept is a comfortable one if one can be sure of constant innovation in the countries which have the industries in stages one and two. As long as new technology based industries are replacing those which are being exported, the dynamism of change is presumably acceptable there. The concept of the post-industrial society is one where traditional heavy industries have disappeared to less developed parts of the world and been replaced by high technology and service industries which leave the national environment a good deal more unpolluted.

There are, however, some snags to this idyllic picture of a better and better world. First, while new industries may grow up to replace the old in the developed world, they may not be developed by the same enterprise as is exporting the older technology – and any new industry which is creating jobs may not feel the same pressure to secure job continuity for those in the obsolescent industries whose jobs have been exported. Unemployment is likely to be created faster than new employment, and different people are involved. Second, there is the strong possibility that new industry will not appear on a scale to avoid de-industrialization on a large scale. This is what has been termed 'the doughnut effect' – a ring of plant capacity is created abroad, possibly by the international company, but there is a hole in the centre, with nothing to replace the lost industry, at any rate on the same scale. In this situation resistance to the transfer of industry, by workers, trade unions and governments, may not be a simple blind refusal to accept change, but a well founded fear of the consequences of the erosion of a technological lead to less developed parts of the world. The lesson is that if some products can be transferred across national and cultural frontiers, the process is not always inevitable, let alone, one-way. Products and production can be transferred back, if technology and politics dictate.

The implications of the doughnut effect, magnified on occasion by the actions of international companies, can be profoundly worrying for the industrialized West. Not only, for example, has much American and European 'smoke stack' industry been 'scooped out' by Third World countries; its high level technology is threatened by the Japanese, and even its middle level technology is being bettered by the newly industrializing countries (NICs) on the Pacific Rim, and it is difficult to see this process being reversed. Relatively sophisticated electronic, including domestic, computer manufactures are still expanding. But while the brand names may be the familiar Western ones, the production lines are increasingly in Malaysia, Hong Kong, Taiwan and Korea.

Salvation for Western production lines may lie in the increasing automation of the process which, by reducing the labour content, removes the advantages of cheap labour enjoyed at present by the NICs. But the race may be close, and there is a danger that while the Western multinationals will survive, their role in their traditional markets will be to distribute the products which they manufacture in the East.

THE IMPLICATIONS ON HOST GOVERNMENT POLICY OF PRODUCT POLICY

What a host government might want from a foreign international enterprise operating within its territories is the subject of the last part of this book, and will not therefore be dealt with in detail here. Nevertheless, even at which might be termed the micro level of decision taking, of how and what the enterprise chooses to produce in its local plant, overall national policy can play its part.

It must be said initially that many Third World host governments do not have any clear initial idea of what interests they have in the methods of production to be employed; and even when they do begin to take an interest, their first instincts may well be wrong. At the outset the individuals who have made the decision to permit the enterprise to operate locally, are likely to have little or no idea of what problems arise from production. Relatively few engineers or technicians come to the top in the political struggles of developing countries, nor are their party functionaries likely to have the appropriate knowledge. They tend initially to advance no opinions. If and when the authorities begin to take an interest in production methods, national pride and a wildly optimistic underassessment of the practical difficulties of moving towards the first rank of industrial powers prevail. The government is likely to want the most up to date methods of production, regardless of their relevance to local conditions.

The appropriate methods of production from the enterprise's viewpoint, as has been remarked, are determined by the three factors already discussed, namely market size, the local level of technology and the distribution of factors of production. The first of these, market size, may in some instances be a negotiable point if the international enterprise is in a position to offer to supply foreign markets from a local plant, i.e. markets already developed by the enterprise and supplied by other plants. The bargaining issues involved here in terms of protection from nationalization or indigenization have already been discussed. The second is almost inevitably a source of dispute based on differing perceptions of the technical competence of local personnel. The third factor, namely the factors of production available, is in practice connected with the second, for the issue most difficult to assess is the labour force available. Ought a host government have a manpower policy, and if so, how does this affect production methods to be employed locally?

There are broadly two policies which may be followed, depending on the population structure of the host nation. In most instances Third World governments face problems of a rapidly rising population and a flood of new job seekers entering the labour market in ever growing numbers, year after year. Some governments attempt drastic action to hold down population growth, and have the political will to do so: a developing state like Singapore is an obvious example. Others may have neither the will nor the power to change the situation. Political or religious considerations forbid birth control.

In the former situation, the logic of limiting population is to attempt to upgrade the individual skills of workers, even to the extent of encouraging wage rises in economies whose initial impetus comes from cheap labour. In such countries Western methods of production which concentrate on the saving of labour and more intensive use of capital equipment have an increasing place.

By contrast, Third World countries with large and rapidly growing populations might be better advised to encourage labour intensive industries, and within particular industries, labour intensive, rather than capital intensive, production techniques. This may mean using older fashioned production methods (and from the international enterprise viewpoint, plant equipment phased out as obsolescent elsewhere in its operation) or a conscious effort to redesign production methods in a quite different direction from that applying in the West or in areas of stable and aging population. The full implications of these developments have not yet been worked out by host governments, let alone individual companies.

THE DIFFUSION OF MANUFACTURING PROCESSES

The diffusion of many manufacturing processes throughout the Third World can in part be explained by the policies of Third World governments aimed at attracting direct inward investment. This movement of manufacturing plant into new areas (implicitly at the expense of manufacturing capacity and jobs in export oriented industry in the traditional areas) could be defined as secondary industry, which uses the products of the primary industries, i.e. the processing of the extracted raw materials. In time, a logical next step for the foreign company which has been forced to move production capacity, may be to look for other markets which it can supply from the new foreign based plant, and it may do what the traditional extractive type industry of the first group has done, namely supply manufactured products to its own home market and run down its original plant, if labour costs and financial considerations make this more economical. In effect these 'runaway' industries are the modern form of extractive industry, but with the raw material in this instance being the cheap labour available in parts of the Third World. In passing, it is worth noting that the ability of the multinational corporation to bargain with potential host governments can be considerable, even where the enterprise has no real alternative to a particular location, simply because of the degree of ignorance existing in individual countries both about what other countries are prepared to offer by way of concessions, and also lack of knowledge of any internal constraints on the enterprise from within or from its own home government. Governments do not appear to exchange information on this basis nor do they supply confidential information to any international organization which might exist to advise governments on their dealings with the multinational enterprise.

CRITERIA FOR TECHNOLOGY TRANSFER

Technology transfer is today seen by many as the almost instant, almost painless instrument whereby the prospects of the Third World can be transformed. The reality, however, may be somewhat different.

Technology is a concept which is remarkably hard to define, but which may include, or at least require, the existence of certain attributes in a culture before it can be transplanted. Arguably what is involved as much as anything else is attitude to change and its desirability. This is a factor which may apply in developed as well as developing countries. There appears to be no fundamental difference in allocation of resources or skills, between, say, the United Kingdom and West Germany, yet the ability of the former to match the industrial growth of the latter is embarrassingly low, for no other reason apparently than the resistance of institutions bedded in British culture. If this is true of a Western society, how much more may be the problem of the non-Western culture, with quite alien institutions.

INTELLECTUAL PROPERTY RIGHTS

Almost by definition, any multinational company is likely to be a leader in product design and technology – of what in legal terms might be termed 'intellectual property'. One obvious problem for such companies is that of unauthorized copying of their designs and knowledge – which is more popularly known as 'pirating' – which may occur in any products from books to computers.

A useful distinction is that between activities carried out by local individuals or companies without the consent either of the company or their government on the one hand, and infringements of intellectual property rights as a national policy approved by governments in the Third World on the other. This section will consider the first of these.

There are varying stages of copying. The most blatant is simply forgery, where for example a book is reproduced bearing the imprint of the original Western publisher, or a product such as a watch or microcomputer is copied and put out on the market with the name or trade mark of the original producer. Sometimes marginal changes may be made: in the latter case a minor change in spelling of a brand name, which is likely to deceive the local buyer, but the intent is the same. A variant on this, which however is deception rather than strictly pirating, is to produce textiles or garments with a Western name, with washing or cleaning instructions printed only in English, even though there is no possibility of the products being sold anywhere else than in the Third World country of production.

A second stage may be the slavish copying of a Western original, in theory protected by patents or trade marks, which however are sold with neither. The politer term for this practice is 'reverse engineering'. This may be defined as a product policy of development by imitation, and appears to be practised in many parts of the Third World, including China, where, for many product ranges, research and development consists of acquiring a Western or Japanese product, taking it to pieces and copying every component.

A variant of this may be the reproduction of components spares etc. by a local manufacturer. These then are offered as cheap substitutes for the original – almost certainly without the copies having to meet any quality or stress factors, e.g. ordinary steel or plated cast iron being used instead of specialist steels which may be required by the conditions under which products are intended to operate.

Few governments will openly defend outright copying which is intended to deceive, i.e. forgeries; they may however implicitly accept similar practices by refusing to sign the Universal Copyright Convention or intellectual copyright conventions. The legal basis for protecting intellectual property rights, the Paris Convention, has to some extent been eroded by the activities of the UN World Intellectual Property Organization, which has been used by some of the less developed countries to press for limitations of such property rights. Such countries are likely to be extremely reluctant to take action against their own nationals unless pressed hard at government level to do so. Increasingly, however, copying or unauthorized use of Western knowhow has become in some countries an instrument of government policy. The chief culprits are not the really underdeveloped world, but the NICs, such as Korea, Taiwan or Singapore.

THE ATTACK ON INTELLECTUAL PROPERTY RIGHTS BY HOST GOVERNMENTS

The treatment of foreign international enterprises in the underdeveloped world, and what is seen as the 'pirating' of their costly technology knowhow, arouses a good deal of resentment and concern both at company and national level in the developed world. Before discussing how the host governments operate against the interests of these foreign companies, it may be useful to consider objectively the burden of the complaints laid by host governments as a justification for their action.

Briefly, they argue that any domestic enterprise is placed at a permanent disadvantage *vis-à-vis* a foreign enterprise because of the virtual monopoly effect that the possession of vital patents give. Such a monopoly effect, it is argued, is not really removed in a simple negotiating situation even where legislation exists to require the foreign companies to lease out knowhow. Patents, as they run out, can be replaced by the development of new technology so that the permanent benefits anticipated by buying over existing knowhow simply do not appear. Insistence by foreign companies on the use of trademarks, which do not normally expire in a limited time, prevents any prestige or consumer loyalty developing to a domestic company even where the quality of the product matches that of the originating foreign enterprise. Moreover trademarks ensure perpetual royalties long after any benefits to be derived from their local use have disappeared. In this situation, a unilateral decision by the foreign enterprise to withdraw use of its trademark has very serious and, it can be argued, quite unjustified negative effects on the domestic company which used the trademark and, by association, acquired prestige. The situation may be worsened by the fact that the use of the foreign trademark limits the market for the domestic enterprise, by preventing its products penetrating areas where the trademark is still used by the foreign company, is effectively protected by the foreign company and acts as a barrier to competition. The very payment of royalties, it is argued, releases sums of money for publicity which further strengthen the prestige of the foreign company at the literal expense of the domestic licensee. Any or all of these arguments can be marshalled by host governments or local interests as the basis of attempts to limit what can be called property rights of foreign enterprises.

The concept of intellectual property has been extended by some developing countries to describe a bundle of assets, tangible and intangible, possessed by enterprises in the developed world, which they are able to deploy in the underdeveloped world, and whose possession gives them almost an insuperable advantage over domestic industry there. The whole thrust of legislation therefore is to limit such property rights and enable them to be transferred at minimum cost to the domestic enterprises.

What, then, is intellectual property under this wider definition? It comprises not only technology, but its appurtenances, even its prestige. These include patents, trademarks, slogans and the whole apparatus of publicity which not only represents technology superior to that available locally, but reinforces the belief among local customers that the foreign enterprise is superior to the domestic, that the foreign import is superior to the local product.

Because it is relatively hard to define and even harder to quantify, the problem of forcing a transfer, not only of what might be termed 'hard knowledge' but also of prestige, is remarkably hard to achieve by legislation. Nevertheless, and increasingly, the attempt is being made. There are several lines of approach. The most obvious, particularly in Latin America and the Philippines, is the existence, already noted, of Technology Transfer Boards, which are intended to monitor the quality of technology being imported, and regulate therefore royalty payments for its use.

Another approach is an attack on the concept of the international patent. Some areas of industrial development may be declared to be excluded from patent rights, so that any developments elsewhere in the world become an automatic public right of any domestic enterprise. Second, the life of patents may be reduced to a figure substantially less than applies in a developed society. A life of 15 to 17 years for a patent is probably normal in a developed society. It may be cut, say, to 10 in a developing country, so that a patent in such countries may have passed into public domain long before the patent rights have expired in the country of origin. Third, there may be a requirement for compulsory licensing of patents at a royalty rate determined by the host government possibly through its technology board, so that a domestically owned enterprise may be able to have access to the same imported technology as the subsidiary of a foreign multinational, and at very favourable royalty terms. And finally, attempts are being made to force the patent holders to begin production within a specific time, perhaps 30 months, in a particular territory or have the patent allocated to a local firm. Such foreign subsidiaries may in fact be banned.

The problem of trademarks is as complex, for reasons which have already been discussed. Basically, however, there are two approaches which may be followed by the host government. First, it may in effect 'nationalize' a foreign trademark so that after a given period of time a local company may use the trademark internally to the country without the consent of the foreign enterprise or the payment of further royalties to it. Less drastically perhaps there is the requirement of 'association', i.e. the foreign trademark must be used in conjunction with a locally owned trademark. A minor advantage may be that the double trademark may provide an excuse for halving any foreign royalty payment: more profoundly there is a hope that the prestige will, over time, apply as much to the domestic trademark as to the foreign, so that if the latter is phased out, the prestige will remain. The sceptic might detect an element of sympathetic magic in the process. However, if the technical standards of the domestic enterprise really reach the level of the imported product then the humiliating assumption by the man or woman in the street that the foreign product must be superior to the local could be eliminated.

A measure of protection may be given to the foreign enterprise and its intellectual property rights by international conventions on the treatment of foreigner's rights within a country. There is little doubt however that in political terms discrimination exercised by a Third World government and some communist countries, not merely a maverick like Yugoslavia but a rigidly orthodox one like Czechoslovakia, against the property rights of enterprise originating in developed countries is going to increase. The real protection of the foreign multinational is not to be found in appeals to equity or any other legal concept, but in the continuing difficulty of transferring 'knowhow' and attitudes by legal statute, and by the ability to innovate as fast as existing technology can be absorbed.

Much of the limitations on intellectual property rights discussed above have now been given legal force, for example by Brazil and Mexico. Insofar as such measures are successful they will probably be imitated elsewhere.

Part IV

Cultural Values at the National and Company Level

Introduction

The internationalization of business began in a substantial way by transactions between Western industrialized nations with broadly similar cultural backgrounds, or in a situation where a Western nature was politically or economically so dominant that it could impose its cultural values on any non-Western host nation. The multinational enterprise in this situation followed Western rules.

Today the situation is much more complex. International business now operates between cultures whose values are not necessarily similar or even compatible, and where even an economically powerful state could not, even if it chose, readily impose its values elsewhere. The obverse side of this issue is whether all cultures can successfully adapt to industrialization and the internationalization of business without transforming their own cultural norms to what they might regard as an unacceptable extent.

The problems of transferring cultural values desired by a multinational business into a profoundly different culture are therefore a good deal more subtle and complex than simply recognizing ideological differences. They raise issues of the status of individuals and professions, and of differing ideas of what constitutes acceptable behaviour, particularly for executives of a company, who may be recruited locally but are required to conform to values which are the norm elsewhere, rather than in their own society.

5 Cultural Values and the Internationalization of Business

INTRODUCTION

The point has been made that the international enterprise is largely a creation of Western culture, subscribing to Western cultural values, the only substantial exception thus far being the Japanese version, and marginally the Taiwanese and Korean counterparts. Increasingly however such enterprises are moving into non-Western cultures (or non-Japanese cultures), and it is useful at this stage to consider some of the implications of this move.

To what extent is success for the international enterprise dependent on Western or Japanese cultural aspects or, in a more limited context, their management style? Must other cultures adopt their values substantially; must local management and shop floor discipline operate to these imported patterns?

These questions are implicit in the internationalization of business in most parts of the world; at the moment however they are seen at their most acute in the newly industrializing countries, which have moved furthest along the path of industrialization. These are sometimes small, sometimes multicultural, and may have uncomfortable decisions to make on how they can adopt new styles without destroying local culture.

This chapter therefore discusses the problems of inducing changes within commercial or industrial organizations, first in Western, then in non-Western cultures, particularly the newly industrializing countries, in order to accommodate these organizations to the growing opportunities and threats being presented by current economic and political developments: what is discussed here is largely as applicable to the locally owned companies serving the international market as to the subsidiaries of the foreign enterprise. Such a study is particularly apposite, not only because of the growing importance of these economies, the 'new Japans', but also because it is by no means obvious how much current organizational and management theory developed for Western societies or Japan is relevant. Some of these societies, for example Hong Kong, Singapore and the Philippines, are

153

unique in that they represent bicultural or multicultural societies, drawing heavily both on the West and on Japan but being uniquely different both from the older industrial societies and from each other. The problems of adapting which such countries face are, arguably, more complex than the other newly industrializing countries, like Korea or Taiwan where there is more obviously a single dominant culture.

IMPLEMENTING CHANGE

First, however, it is desirable to clarify what is being changed or adopted by countries aspiring to Western or Japanese economic standards. The introduction of modern commercial and industrial techniques requires organizational change whatever techniques have been used locally to supply basically a domestic market. What, however, does change mean in the context of a foreign innovative company operating in a society with a reasonable degree of technological sophistication?

It can mean *technical change* – whether the introduction of a new machine or even of a whole new technology, which poses serious problems of recruiting or retraining a labour force.

Second, it can mean *social change*, basically in the balance of responsibility and power of the people involved in the company and the problem of motivating them to accept change. This is a problem which came into existence first two centuries ago at the time of the Industrial Revolution in England. Then, the introduction of a new technology into a long established and highly skilled weaving industry provoked rioting and the physical destruction of the new weaving machines by the traditional weavers, the so-called Luddites. The pattern has been repeated not only in England, but in many other parts of the world ever since. The real problem in cultures like the newly industrializing economies, therefore, is likely to be rarely if ever the technical one: it is the social one. To give an example of the persistence and possibly the universality of the Luddite phenomenon: in Britain today there is a substantial apprehension about the implications of micro circuitry based on the silicon chip, which is supposed to revolutionize production. If one examines the basis of the apprehension, however, it is not technological. No one really doubts the technical competence of British society to master the new technology: it is the social consequences, the implication for the relative status of trade unions and managers who at present command badly needed skills which are going to be by-passed, which creates the problem. Examples are to be found in the printing industry where attempts to introduce the technology now available have led at times to horrendous industrial confrontation. Groups adversely affected may try either to frustrate, or to channel – some would say distort – the adoption of new technology into an existing industrial or social framework which was evolved for an entirely different technology. They are not likely entirely to succeed or entirely to fail. But the political and social compromises which will emerge may appear extraordinary to another culture which will adopt exactly the same technology and come up with a quite different compromise solution. In this sense there are really three themes of change, and international managers faced with the problem of introducing new technology into a culture find themselves in difficulties if they think only of the first or at most the first two themes. These themes are first *technical change*, second the consequent *organizational change*. The deepest, and most neglected theme however is *attitudinal change*. It is really about this third theme that organizational writers in the West are now most concerned, but they are not always succeeding in making their point with the practising managers, operating in their own cultures, let alone contemplating changes in other cultures.

This problem of social change rather than technological change occurs in every culture which is capable of absorbing modern technology. It is probable that the initial success of any of the newly industrializing countries depended on a particular combination of technical competence with a workforce which was willing to work harder, for longer hours, and with less concern about preserving traditional skills than longer established Western industry. As long as the major cost of production was labour cost, and as long as labour was cheap and plentiful, there were no particular organizational problems. But as these societies move, as they inevitably must, into a more capital intensive means of production, the balance of power changes, and the problem of motivating the personnel involved changes also. How exactly does one motivate a workforce to accept change as the amount of equipment and technical knowhow per shop floor worker grows? Particularly if they believe they will lose out from change?

A fairly specific example may illustrate the point. A factory may have been set up originally on the basis of using cheap labour and minimum capital equipment. The overhead capital costs per production worker amounts to say 50000 dollars. Because of the new technology becoming available, management re-equips but this time has equipment worth 1 million dollars per production worker, and achieves a *pro rata* or more increase in output. The real problem, after the initial teething problems, are no longer technological, but organizational and motivational. More supervision of output is needed and the factory finishes up with as many supervisors as actual production workers. In financial terms, this may not matter all that much. Wage costs are a much smaller proportion of the total, and the enterprise can afford to employ more supervisors, even double or quadruple the wages of production workers. But what has been done has simply increased the ability of a relatively small number of people in the workforce to disrupt the whole system: and it is no longer going to be easy simply to sack these rebellious individuals and pick up an unemployed person off the street to replace the malcontent as the operator of a million dollars worth of equipment.

This might seem an exaggerated situation. Consider however some of the implications. Millions of dollars or a contract hang on the balance if a contract is not completed in time. Or a strike in one small section of a plant involves a handful of men and has a 'knock-on' effect, affecting thousands. That social or political problem, not the new technology is the problem, namely how to motivate people to act reasonably and not blackmail the management at a critical point – short of forced labour or a firing squad to impose military discipline. And even this solution has its own limitations.

In summary, then, experience of Western cultures suggests that there are two possible problems facing the newly industrializing nations as they move into the status of industrial society. First, the resistance to change among managers, some professionally qualified individuals and some shopfloor workers, who perceive they have something to lose from change. Second, and more generally, how to motivate personnel when the threat of real hardship no longer applies, and where the whole economy, under pressure from the government, is moving away from low technology, labour intensive industries to more sophisticated high technology ones.

In non-Western societies the immediate problems may appear to be different from those facing the developed countries of the West, but they exist and will have to be resolved. What is the appropriate response to change in organizational and social terms? All that can be said as a first approximation is that it will not necessarily be the same for these societies as for Western societies.

While the problems of organizational change and the relative ease or difficulty of persuading a particular culture are by themselves an interesting sociological study, they are subjects of vital importance to the multinational company. Inevitably the multinational is becoming multicultural and even multi-ideological, with all the implications which follow from this. What complicates the situation is uncertainty about the pitfalls of inducing change in cultures far removed from Western practices and, more profoundly, uncertainty about the direction along which cultural change is proceeding. These two issues will be discussed in some detail in this chapter.

THE PITFALLS OF ORGANIZATIONAL CHANGE IN DIFFERENT CULTURES

It would be both presumptuous and impractical to attempt an extensive review of organizational theory, particularly when almost all of what is available is Western and particularly American oriented. Such theory has to be applied with caution by anyone who is not an uncritical adherent of American methods. Even the most convinced enthusiast for these would probably find it highly desirable to water down their doctrine if only on the grounds that it is too strong medicine for relatively underdeveloped societies.

But whether or not there is agreement on what organizational change is best for all circumstances, some commonsense assumptions can be made about the problems of inducing change.

There are *ab initio* two pitfalls to be avoided in organizational change. The first is the transient fad: it is unfortunately true that organizational theory is like fashion in clothes and new ideas tend to be short-lived in most instances. In this sense it is very unwise to consider any theory of organizational change which is less than 10 years old and has stood the test of time. After all, if organizational change really bites deep, it will have a traumatic effect on the organization – and it is well to ensure that any trauma inflicted is not merely for the sake of transient fashion.

The second danger is the superficial change. As an example, one of the more common aspects to be seen in the British experience over the past 30 years has been in the adoption of the marketing concept. To put this at its simplest, this means ensuring that in the long run the enterprise would be producing what the market required, rather than simply producing in the area where the company's knowhow was greatest, and by so doing ensuring that new technology, as it was built up, followed existing developments even if the market demand was moving in a different direction. At first sight, then, the move was successful in Britain in that the number of marketing departments and marketing managers multiplied. All that was happening in many cases, however, was that departments and managers were being renamed without their function really changing or their effective authority being increased – the logical step, one would have imagined.

The same sort of situation is liable to happen in non-Western societies especially where young executives have been trained in Western management concepts, either in Western business schools or in business schools using Western concepts. As it happens, these may be the very people recruited by a foreign international enterprise as local managers. They and their employers may be happy to see the familiar titles and Western concepts being quoted. But they cannot readily be assured that the fashionable titles and concepts mean a fundamental acceptance of the Western culture which underlies them: or even worse, that the titles and concepts are appropriate in vastly different cultures.

Arguably, then, the problem which faces advocates of organizational change may be to decide between radical or selective change. It is easier in the context of the multinational to preach the radical, because the foreign models are there to be admired at a distance. What people do not always reckon on is that the cost of radical change may be enormous in social and cultural terms. Most of the ideas on organizational change, in which newly industrializing societies are interested, emanate, as we have seen, from Western societies and implicitly therefore depend on Western concepts of what is acceptable practice. Before looking at specific examples of societies which have evolved successful organizational practices, it is worth considering whether the implicit assumptions of these societies really apply to the newly industrializing, non-Western societies of areas like South-East Asia.

What is acceptable practice and behaviour in Western societies might appear a good deal less attractive in other societies. Among Western concepts one might, for example, consider a sense of responsibility to society as a whole, combined with what would appear to the non-Western as a callous disregard for the welfare of one's family. It is perhaps worth considering to which members of one's own family a good Britain feels any responsibility (or for that matter a good Frenchman, German or American). When all the sentiment is stripped away, a welfare state means that an adult has responsibilities to his young family, but not to a grown family; not even to elderly parents who might be put into an institution rather than be cared for with the family. No responsibility for brother, sister, uncle, aunt and so on. This is not to say that total neglect of one's extended family is universal in the West, but such behaviour is acceptable so that no unfavourable comment is raised by an adult shrugging off the responsibility for members of his own family. The state will provide – and to be fair the state does – in that no one dies of physical hunger or neglect because he or she is old and has no family. The obverse of this is that efficiency is supposed to rule the workplace. This means that the inefficient must go, that the individual is not guaranteed a place by the good reputation of a relative in the organization, who in a sense, would be responsible for the behaviour of any newcomer who was a relative.

If one analyses the situation, what may have been destroyed in the West, but not, significantly, in Japan, is the concept of reciprocity of rights and duties. Before and even in the early days of the Industrial Revolution, one spoke of master and servant, rather than employer or employee. The earlier term would now be regarded as totally unacceptable in the West, but it implied a personal two-way relationship. The link was broken by the employer initially in terms of hourly paid manual workers, the only relationship being concerned with the buying and selling of labour, with the employer denying any responsibility to his worker beyond paying for his labour. This break encouraged and was encouraged by, in many Western societies, trade unionism, whose very survival depended on a monopoly of workers' loyalty and an emphasis on conflict of interest between employer and worker. This applied initially to situations where large amounts of manual labour were employed. In some cultures a reciprocal relationship did persist in the relationship between employers and their white collar staff, with whom they remained in closer day to day contact. White collar workers received pensions and fringe benefits such as sick pay: in other words the employers' obligations extended far beyond the simple payment of labour. In return the white collar worker retained, and was expected to retain, a counter-obligation to the employer and employer's interests. This can be seen in the reluctance of white collar workers to join trade unions, knowing that such action would adversely affect this traditional relationship with employers.

This erosion of the employer–employee relationship to the point where it is simply concerned with the cash, inevitably leads to a situation of potential conflict over economic interests, to a far greater extent than occurs in countries which have not followed the process, i.e. Japan. It is not apparently inevitable that industrialization implies alienation. Developing countries have the opportunity to choose selectively any aspects of the Western system. They can learn what is relevant to their background rather than uncritically accepting all the Western patterns in the hope of achieving a Western standard of living.

Imitative change

One of the most fascinating examples of an imitative organizational change is now appearing in Asia. This is the imitation of the Japanese trading company, the so-called shosha. Of the hundreds which exist only nine or ten, the Sogo Shoshas, are of worldwide significance, but they dominate Japanese export success. It has already been remarked that, apart from Singapore, efforts are being made in Korea, Taiwan and the Philippines to model trading companies on this pattern. The legislation is pretty similar in all countries: if an organization has a certain annual turnover in foreign exchange earnings, it may be accepted for such status, which will bring considerable tax advantages.

A number of points can be made: there is an implicit assumption that Japanese success is a matter of organizational pattern and that it is enough simply to adopt the structure to ensure that success will follow.

The logic behind this is not all that clear. The Japanese shosha are not in existence because of the tax advantages. They grew out of the total relationship in the Japanese economy between the banks, industry and the merchants, and imply a degree of overlapping, interest and a common will which simply does not exist anywhere else. It may be a cause of some unease, but the trading house relationship with banking and industry evolved in a monolithic culture, and may be unique to it. The strength and the weakness of some of the newly industrializing countries are their multicultural backgrounds. Would any cultural heritage have to be sacrificed to ensure success? Would all the existing cultures? Would their 'new Japan' have to become 'new synthetic Japans'?

It is worth concentrating on the trading house syndrome because it is a prime example of an assumption that somehow to imitate means to become. The phrase 'sympathetic magic' has been used, i.e. the idea that if one performs certain rituals which are important for their symbolism rather than their rationality, certain natural events will follow: the rains will come, the crops will grow. There may indeed be an element of the cargo cult, i.e. the phenomenon noted shortly before, and particularly during, World War II in parts of New Guinea where primitive stone age tribes saw Western technology for the first time and by simple observation drew quite logical but nonsensical conclusions about appropriate organizational change and behaviour. What they saw was that the white man built harbours, levelled fields and put in the appurtenances of a modern airport; great ships and birds would descend from the heavens with rich gifts. The origin of the heavenly gifts was not clear: it might even be that they were being sent by the ancestral gods of the tribes and misappropriated by the newcomers. The solution was simple: imitate the airfields, prepare models of the great birds; the gifts would arrive for their rightful recipients, and so the cargo cult began.

The phenomenon had its humorous, as well as its pathetic side. But when the new activities meant that traditional agricultural and hunting activities, on which the community's very existence depended, were neglected, the implications were much more dangerous.

To suggest that much of the imitation of Japanese success is a form of cargo cult might appear to be both offensive and mistaken. But it is at least worth considering that, to achieve success in the American, German or Japanese style it may not be enough to transplant a part, but to consider the whole ambience within which the organization operates, and to consider whether it is (a) possible, (b) relevant or (c) worthwhile to accept the radical changes to values in society which may be involved.

Selective change

What is clear is that non-Western and non-Japanese societies have to be selective about what they import from these countries in terms of organizational change. And even more important in the present context may be the appropriate attitude of the foreign international enterprise which wishes to operate in a culture vastly different from that at home. In one sense they have a limited choice, in that policy is to a very large extent dictated by the host government which may choose, with its eyes open, to make a cultural sacrifice in order to attract foreign interest and is willing to pay the price. Thus, for example, the Singapore government has deliberately placed a heavy emphasis on the use of English and is willing to accept the cultural price, presumably because it regards this choice as offering the best opportunity of survival in a highly competitive world and because such a choice avoids the dangers of favouring one indigenous culture at the expense of another. It is not too difficult for the foreign multinational's subsidiary to go along with this policy, particularly if the multinational company is American or English in origin. The problem, paradoxically, is more difficult for a Singapore company. It is very difficult to tear up roots, and arguably very unwise. Discrimination is needed in the techniques to be adopted.

WESTERN MANAGEMENT STYLE AND COMMUNITY ASPIRATIONS

The 1950s and 1960s represented the high tide of American prestige in technological development and management style, and in American society, a material standard of living which was aspired to by western Europeans, and dreamed of by the rest of the world. In the light of the proven success of the American system, it is not surprising that American management style, as much as their technological prowess, was seen as the model for much of the rest of the world.

What, then, is or was the American philosophy of management? It will be useful to look at two of the better known propositions of the time, one relating to management style, the other to community aspirations. The propositions, in the event, have been overtaken both by events and the fresh theory derived from them, but, as will be illustrated, still have relevance.

The two schools of thought were expressed by Harbison and Myers on management style, and Farmer and Richman on community aspirations.

a.   The Harbison and Myers model

The writings of Harbison and Myers on the subject of management practice contained two elements which are particularly important in the present context. These might be defined as the style of management and the source of managers.

They distinguished four relatively self-explanatory styles of management which they defined as dictatorial, paternalistic, constitutional and democratic; there is implicitly a progression in the desirability of these stages.

The dictatorial style implied absolute authority on the part of management, with no rights being available to the workforce. The paternalistic might be seen as similar to a feudal system with both managers and managed having reciprocal rights and duties: the former's duties would appear, however, to owe more to a sense of obligation – *noblesse oblige*, one might instance.

The constitutional style turned on the proposition that management's rights are only part of the overall picture, that other groups have rights which are constitutionally as legitimate: trade unions, for example, or the state itself have the right to impose conditions in certain areas. Finally there was the somewhat vague concept of democratic management where the legitimate authority of management is subject to the rights of others to express their views freely in an attempt to influence management thinking and action.

The source of management elite is threefold, depending on the state of society and its progression along desirable lines, as accepted implicitly. The three sources are the patrimonial, the political and the professional.

A patrimonial source is one which derives directly from ownership. The managers are the owners or the family connections of the owners. A patrimonial style is present in any non-marxist society. In the West, the most obvious example is to be found in small family owned concerns. In the less developed world, however, family connections may remain highly relevant, being in this concept an aspect of the extended family system. At management level, the extended family enables the owners to find trustworthy executives among relatives, where they might hesitate to bring in strangers who owed no family loyalty. Although Harbison and Myers do not discuss the role of the shopfloor worker in this context, the same argument applies for employing relatives of good workers, in the knowledge that creditable or discreditable behaviour by one reflects on all the family and is a powerful discipline.

In some cultures another aspect of patrimonial management, again not touched upon by the two writers, but relevant in this context, is the presence of the extended family, both as a provider of wealth for an individual, or conversely as a consumer of wealth. Western observers are probably most aware of the phenomenon, when, for example, a West African student is financed to a Western education by the combined sacrifice of relatives and the local community. The obverse of this admirable trait is his/her duty to meet the needs of that family, even distant relatives, if he/she returns to the community a relatively wealthy person in terms of that community. This wealth can quickly be used up to meet the needs of all who have a claim on his/her largesse.

A rather similar but more efficient system exists in a more discreet form in the clan system among overseas Chinese. Wealth might be mobilized from many parts of South-East Asia or even scattered family members in the West, to enable an aspiring entrepreneur to launch their business. But this would only be one aspect of a cultural pattern where a wealthy family member would have a moral obligation to help another member who had fallen on hard times. The difference between the West African and Chinese moral obligation is that the latter culture has probably a more business-like approach to what constitutes genuine hardship. Arguably, a patrimonial management style could depend on wealth for an initial investment being painfully accumulated: the converse, the need to support the needy or importunate might limit the accumulation of wealth for expansion.

The second source of management authority is the political, and this would presumably lay emphasis on the political acceptability of a manager who would be expected to conform to the political orthodoxy of the culture in which he/she operated. In the USA one would therefore expect a manager to be in favour of a free enterprise and suspicious of government intervention. Certainly they would be highly unlikely to be overtly social democratic, far less marxist. In the UK and parts of western Europe, a social democratic colouring would be acceptable – indeed, if one were to be cynical in the UK context, a social democratic colouring would be expedient in that there is no disadvantage in being so, but, on occasion, a danger of being right wing even when a right wing government is in power. On the other hand, an overtly marxist manager in the private sector would be a rarity, and their career prospects would scarcely be enhanced. In totalitarian states such as the USSR or pre-war nazi Germany, party membership of the ruling authority might well be a *sine qua non* of higher management, and political orthodoxy could count for a good deal more than technical competence. This situation of course applies in many parts of the developed world where party or religious loyalty can count for a good deal more than anything else. Certainly in totalitarian regimes and highly ideologized economies in the Third World the survival prospects of a manager overtly hostile to the ruling orthodoxy would be remote.

The whole aspect of the political legitimacy of management is one which troubles most countries, but in different ways and to different degrees. The American caricature is of the man in the grey flannel suit as representing the unexceptionable but uninspired manager, although the maverick genius might be uneasily recognized as valuable. There has been in the USA no serious questioning, however, of management's right to manage. By contrast, in some parts of western Europe, most notably perhaps in the UK, there seems on occasion to have been a managerial loss of nerve, as though managers no longer believed in their own right to make decisions – a process encouraged by the tendency throughout much of the post-war period, for governments, whatever their political complexion, to defer to trade union opinion. This situation was changing by the mid 1980s with the emergence of a conservative government which explicitly repudiated much of what even its own previous governments had granted. Only time will tell whether the reversal of attitude towards the legitimacy of management will be permanent.

In other parts of the world, from the totalitarian marxist and ideologically committed Third World governments, as well as the more corporate minded societies among which Japan, France or the technocrats of some Latin American societies are numbered, the political legitimacy of management is less obviously challenged. Part of the price of this may be a relatively rigid political structure, which may not bend easily, but which perhaps could more readily shatter under pressure.

Finally, there is the professional background source of management, the concept that competence acquired by training is the sole criterion for legitimacy in management. The self-evident justification of this proposition, at least in Western terms, requires little illustration, and management is seen as a profession to be practised in a non-ownership situation (i.e. salaried) and with personal political allegiances being irrelevant provided that they fell within a broad spectrum of acceptable attitudes broadly conforming to the existing establishment.

In much the same way the Harbison and Myer analysis implies an upward progress in management style towards the professionally qualified manager. The American trained engineer with an MBA might be seen as a typical example.

b. The Farmer and Richman model

An alternative model of community aspirations which had a good deal of relevance to management style was that developed by Farmer and Richman also in the early 1960s. The original concept developed by these writers was an attempt to weigh in importance factors which would determine the relative rate of progression and indeed the overall prospects of a community. Management style and sources are only two factors in this culture mix.

The writers have divided the relevant characteristics of a society into four main groups which are, in turn, subdivided. The relevant characteristics are defined as educational, sociological, political and legal, each of which is allocated a weighting of one hundred, and economic characteristics with a weighting of double that. Within each group further subdivisions are made; thus, for example, in the educational group, a total of up to 50 is allocated according to the level of literacy, 20 for the percentage of the population with higher education, and so on.

There are, in this system, no absolute measures, nor can there be any. In making a subjective judgement about what marks are to be allocated to one subcharacteristic, the individual can only 'rank' mark in terms of other cultures with which he/she is familiar, and, of course, judgements both in ranking and absolute marks can vary enormously according to the opinions of the individual.

In this mixture of objective and subjective judgement, it is not too surprising that almost invariably a ranking by any individual is likely to give the highest rating to a society like the United States, and it is therefore not certain whether the case of US superiority on community aspirations and, therefore, realizable potential has been proved, or whether the weighting is in fact determined by the characteristics of the society with which the researchers are most familiar. There is probably an element of both conditions operating.

Again, as in the case of the Harbison and Myers model, the passage of time has not wholly substantiated the hypothesis behind the model, in that one or two communities which would probably achieve a lower score on the existing weights have done rather better in relative terms than the USA since the measure was devised. It is perhaps worth remarking, however, that although there have been criticisms of the approach, it is difficult to point to any which have demonstrated their superiority. It might well be that a new version might change the weighting, or introduce new elements, but the model remains a useful tool which might enable an international enterprise to make a decision on where and how to direct its efforts in the world marketplace.

RECENT DEVELOPMENTS IN WESTERN MANAGEMENT THEORY

What follows in this section is a very broad and rather superficial sweep over recent research and writings on organizational change in the West since the material produced in the 1960s. Japan will be discussed in a later section. The intention is not to review in any detail what individual writers, particularly American writers have to say, but rather to concentrate on what are the values or shortcomings of this work to managers operating in a different culture, on behalf of a Western based multinational.

Earlier it was argued that there were in effect three themes to the research, namely technical change, the consequent organizational change as it affects manangement and finally attitudinal change as it affects the workforce.

The first deals with basically non-human aspects, i.e. technology and the organization of management structures on the analogy of a machine, the so-called 'scientific management' concept. The other two are very much concerned with the human and the sociological aspects of working in the organization. In passing, it should be said that although these three broad themes were developed in a chronological order, the second did not replace the first, nor the third the second. Although the emphasis of research has changed, the research itself tended to overlap. Considerable traces, even in the earliest theories of scientific management, are still very much applicable to the industrial scene in most countries.

The first in chronological terms can be said to relate very broadly to the so-called scientific management. This consists of the use of quantitative techniques, like work study, on the one hand, and on the other the attempts to perfect managerial organization as a machine. To take an example of this last, there is the concept of functional management, with each management office highly specialized and with a narrowly defined field of action. Functional management, in effect, represents the perfect organizational machine. The study of organisations in order to discover how the machine works and how it can be imporved has a long and respectable history.

The second broad theme or group consists of the writing of researchers who believe that the study of management as a bureaucratic machine is simply not enough. Put very simply, these point out that the various managerial posts are filled by human beings, that management cannot be studied merely as the interrelation of offices like cogs in a machine, but must be seen as social interactions between human beings.

What all the studies in both the United States and various parts of Europe have in common is that they are studies of social behaviour within the management hierarchy, they are less concerned with relations between management and the shopfloor. And they are all sociological studies of behaviour. Their subject matter is very much social and socio-psychological, being concerned with the effects on interaction between managers caused by differences in age group, social class, education, training, etc. These factors identified in the various studies relate to particular cultures within Western society and would not necessarily make sense outside these cultures, or even, as cultures change, at a different time within the same culture. The studies are of general interest and usefulness to anyone studying management but it must always be remembered that there is no way in which they can be translated exactly into the terms of another culture. A Samurai is not the equivalent of a mediaeval European knight, nor a mandarin of a modern British civil servant. Such slick analogies are convenient but dangerously misleading.

The third and very broad theme of management studies is that concerned with the relations of management with the rank and file employee, the shopfloor worker, and the relations of the latter with his/her organization. This research has been concerned largely with the complex issue of motivating a workforce to accept the objectives of the enterprise and, from time to time, the necessity to change established practices. The most crudely authoritarian approach of doing exactly what you are told, or be sacked, is no longer a practical or appropriate style of management. One can say that since the end of the depression of the 1930s this third theme has been the primary interest of students in the West. There are basic underlying themes – e.g. that of trying to reconcile the employee to the organization; that of enabling the individual employee to achieve a greater degree of 'self-realization' (whatever that phrase might mean); of predicting whether, or by how much, organizations will have to be modified towards, for example, more democratic, person oriented structures as tasks become more complex and require more and more personal initiative and discretion on the part of the individual within the organization. Although, as has been remarked, these are Western studies, all of these themes are primarily sound and relevant in any culture, and imply a study of societies, of cultures, not merely of technology, for their implementation.

As already stated above, of these three themes or subjects of study the first, the so-called scientific, is comparatively straightforward, and much of the concepts which have been developed are arguably relevant outside the Western societies on which their observations are based. The application of management technology is universal and applicable in any society. The second and third, however, are very much dependent on social and socio-psychological factors of the societies in which the studies took place. Now these social factors are not, and are never likely to be, universally applicable. Social classes and systems, trade unions, industrial traditions, especially of relations between employers and workers, vary very considerably from society to society.

There is a tendency to assume first that the only differences in industrial behaviour which are significant are those between the people in technically advanced societies and those in less advanced societies, and second that as a society progresses technically, so will the social attitudes and behaviour approximate to those in the advanced societies. This is possibly a rather superficial judgement.

No other country has exactly the same social and cultural background, so no other can have quite the same social/industrial problems. There are similarities between Western countries, for example between Britain and the USA, but no two are identical, nor can they be as, although the technology of certain industries may be identical, they are operating in different social systems. Any study of management problems therefore must also be a social study, as management cannot be studied in a vacuum but only as it operates within a social context.

This may seem obvious, but it is, like many obvious facts, something that is frequently ignored. There is a tendency among Western writers and Western industrialists concerned in international business to assume to a greater or lesser degree that other countries will, in fact ought to, adopt the social values and systems of their own particular society, and that therefore their socio-managerial problems will and should become the same. This characteristic is probably most often to be seen in American enterprises, particularly those which have gone international only recently. The implicit ethnocentric approach is rather disturbing when one considers the implications behind it.

Different societies present different problems for managers, but they offer advantages as well as disadvantages for those who know how to adapt management to that society. They offer only disadvantages to those who seek to change a whole society to meet an alien and inflexible management approach.

THE LIMITED RELEVANCE OF WESTERN EXPERIENCE

A major problem of all the Western, and particularly the American, advocates of organizational change is that their conclusions end up mirroring the ideal conditions perceived by their own society, e.g. a pattern of relaxed discipline and individual initiative rather than overt authoritarianism. Implicitly most, if not all, of the recent writers are arguing that as far as possible organizations should be democratized or even, more specifically, Americanized.

There are at least two qualifications which have to be made before an uncritical acceptance of any of the theories could be justified as applicable outside the country of which the individual writer has most experience. First, that many of the ideas reflect peculiarly American answers to peculiarly American conditions, where, for example, conventional authority and status are more likely to be questioned than in most other countries. Second, if the American pattern remained the sole and unqualified success then one could have more confidence in their implicit claims to universal application. Manifestly however this is not the case even in the West. Arguably the Germans, with their mixture of authoritarianism and codetermination, are simultaneously less and more democratic, and are at least as successful as the Americans.

It is useful to know what has happened in more advanced societies, but the knowledge is only useful if it can be translated from one cultural context to the other. Because of the importance of social aspects, the Western international enterprise which is trying to create change needs to have an intimate knowledge of the society in which it proposes to operate. Management knowledge is not enough, tried management techniques evolved in one context, i.e. of Western developed societies, may be of little value in quite another social context.

AMERICAN CONCEPTS

America is clearly regarded as the source of most developments in organizational change as well as other aspects of management development for two obvious reasons. First, it has been, at least until fairly recently, the most economically successful of the Western economies and a model therefore to be admired and imitated. Second, the research carried out in the American context is available in English and therefore more readily accessible than work done elsewhere.

As has been noted, it is dangerous to imitate uncritically the American or any other Western countries because the problems with which mature industrial societies are concerned are very different from those in rapidly industrializing non-Western societies. At the risk of being misunderstood, American writers are ethnocentric and understandably so. American practices have until fairly recently been seen as the best and American concepts of democracy should apply to industry – this is the theme of virtually all the writers. This is neither necessarily true, nor even necessarily arrogant, but has to be understood in the whole context of American education and training until very recent times.

The job of the American education system was to take vast numbers of immigrants from quite different cultures, and to Americanize them, indeed to democratize them, by suppressing their original cultures. It was necessary to do this if America were not to blow apart, as immigrants perpetuated their inherited cultures, prejudices, hatreds and so on. In this sense education and training was an enormous success. The characteristic of the second generation immigrant family was a rejection of the original culture, a refusal even to retain the original language in the family. In a sense, the recent trend to rediscover ancestral roots is a triumphant vindication of the policy. The people who try to trace their ancestors back to Europe and Africa especially, are, in reality, playing with a sentimental and harmless hobby. The second generation Americans were reacting vigorously against their original culture and its values, to prove themselves good Americans. The third and subsequent generations feel no such inhibitions in studying what has become a remote and exotic culture, rather than something which threatens their American identity.

The effect of this pressure to conformity has therefore been that both the teachers and the taught have been willing to participate in the process. This has served American society well. The problems arise when the same attitude is applied outside the United States, where both the cultural situation, and the objectives of imposing what amounts to a new ideology, do not apply.

One of the American values inculcated was the enormous prestige attached to business and the business executive. There was no obvious rival elite, no hereditary aristocracy, established religious leaders, no military or mandarin class civil service such as might have been preeminent in the culture from which the immigrant had emerged.

Is this a model which should be followed in other cultures seeking to industrialize, and possibly using the international enterprise from America or elsewhere to achieve this goal?

HOW RELEVANT IS THE AMERICAN MANAGEMENT CULTURE TO INTERNATIONAL BUSINESS?

The Americans for most of the two centuries of independence have had abundant resources relative to the working population available and in a great number of instances pioneered not only technological but appropriate management techniques to exploit the market. US writings in the area thus dominated the field of management culture and were widely imitated elsewhere, with significant success in western Europe, but with less obvious success elsewhere. In a sense the problem of relevance was not immediately obvious, until the techniques had to be applied in cultures which were very different from that of the American heartland. What, then, has tended to emerge is that in the American situation, vastness sometimes equalled provincialism on a massive scale: what was appropriate and highly successful in the huge domestic American market was simply and unthinkingly applied elsewhere, regardless of local conditions.

What is perhaps surprising in the situation is that American techniques were seen as the solution for any part of the world and any culture, not only by the executives of the American multinationals, but in many instances by businessmen in the Third World seeking the American secret. American management techniques designed to solve American management problems in specifically American situations are still enthusiastically sold, and even more enthusiastically bought, in many parts of the world where their applications are, to say the least, doubtful.

Thus we have the situation that American management techniques were still almost at the peak of their prestige at a moment when the reality of American economic performance showed a relative decline compared with some of its European counterparts, but above all with Japan. It is highly probable that within a few years, if the inappropriateness of much American practice in the Third World becomes apparent, then there may be a spectacular decline in the prestige of American management practices, just at the time when the American economy and political ambience work out a successful response to their current difficulties, and the realities of the US situation begin to improve.

This then is a paradox of American culture which affects profoundly both the American multinational operating abroad, and the non-American operating in the American market. The paradox is that the United States is at once the most sophisticated and the most provincial of all societies. It is sophisticated in the sense of being a technologically advanced, high consumption society, whose products and to a large extent, mores, are familiar throughout the world. But it is provincial because of its vast scale. For the average American, and even the great majority of senior American executives, the USA is the whole world, in that one need make no significant contact with foreigners or foreign cultures, save perhaps on holidays abroad.

When therefore an American executive, particularly one who does not come from one of the more cosmopolitan melting areas of the country, is exposed to another culture he/she is likely to suffer culture shock, far more perhaps than a European counterpart living cheek by jowl with other cultures. It is perhaps significant, then, that it is the Americans who are most concerned with culture shock as a phenomenon, rather than the Europeans, and who tend to create their own enclaves abroad.

THE ALTERNATIVE WESTERN NON-AMERICAN MODELS

Earlier in the chapter the studies of Harbison and Myers and of Farmer and Richman were cited as examples of American management thought. It might perhaps appear to be unfair or simply arbitrary to have selected two studies at a particular period, some three decades back, and sketch briefly the developments which have taken place in the society which produced the concepts, let alone acknowledge any amendments which the originators of the concepts might have wished to add or modify. But the authority of these propositions in their context is important in that, as has been remarked, they were evolved at a peak of American technological and managerial prestige and were therefore given a degree of authority in that they provided some sort of generalized framework into which American success might be fitted.

What has tended to happen, particularly in the case of the multinationals since these concepts have evolved, is not that they have been disproved, let alone discredited, but that alternative management styles and sources have been at least as successful. In this context it is perhaps necessary only to look at two cultures which have produced at least as good results, albeit by very different routes. These are the German and Japanese models.

The German model is by no means vastly different from the American, but there are at least two very significant differences. In terms of style it can be argued that the German management is scarcely democratic in the American style, but that it is rather constitutional in style, in that a very specific attempt was made by the Allies after World War II to promote trade union interests and dilute the authority of the patrimonial owners by the adoption of codetermination, which gave shopfloor workers and salaried managers a say in the overall control of large enterprises and which effectively limited the interests of owners. The implications of codetermination may impose limitations on the freedom of action of an international enterprise even outside this area where codetermination is possible. It would be a bold individual who cast aspersions on the professionalism of German management, but the type of management training which is typified in the USA by the MBA approach, indeed the whole standing and prestige of management schools, is lacking in the German system.

The community aspirations have been similar to those of the American model; in the Japanese example as will be noted in the next few pages, the differences are considerable.

THE BRITISH EXAMPLE

Britain can scarcely be cited as an example of a successful alternative to the American management pattern, but even its relative lack of success has some lessons. It has been argued by some that a reason for the relatively weak performance over the last century has been the adoption of a set of cultural values which failed to give appropriate status to the businessman and the industrialist. Unlike the USA in the eighteenth century, there had been no successful revolution to discredit the established elite: a process which was to be repeated in the twentieth century in Germany and Japan by military defeat, which replaced the traditional elite and thrust the business executive into this position by default. The Industrial Revolution two centuries ago produced technocrats and entrepreneurs whose values might appear remarkably similar to those of the new industrialists of Singapore or Hong Kong. Unfortunately, in England the ambition of the newly rich, newly successful class was acceptance into the existing social system, not a change in the system. They were not 'gentlemen', and a public school system grew up which catered for this demand – a process which incidentally may have helped to take some of the best intellects out of the commercial world and endowed them with different values.

Britain did not make the transition in the way that America, Germany and Japan have done: in part, because it has not been subjected to a traumatic revolution or military defeat sufficient to destroy the established elites, commerce and industry have not achieved the prestige of becoming the new field for the elite.

The major advantage which may be available to Britain is possibly more familiarity with other cultures as a result of its colonial past. Even where the British company may react inappropriately to a cultural problem, it is probably at least aware that there is a problem – a point which may not always occur to an American enterprise making the assumption that what is American is universal.

THE COMMON FACTORS IN WESTERN ATTITUDES

Although there are substantial differences between management styles between, say, the Americans and the Germans or the Germans and the French, there are, nevertheless, a number of conventions which apply universally in the West, but which may not be present in the case of Japan or some other non-Western culture.

The first of these might be to re-emphasize that an impersonal relationship is acceptable in management. By this is meant that it is possible for managers to work together without particularly liking each other. Personal compatibility and friendship probably make a relationship more effective, but are not a *sine qua non*. Total dislike would be deleterious to effective working but the convention is that so long as an individual works competently, their personal opinions, interests etc. are irrelevant. Respect in most Western societies depends ultimately on qualification and achievement measured by promotion. People ought to be promoted, in most instances, not because they are likable, but because they are efficient, in Western terms. This is not to say that the qualities are not reversed in practice, but no one would attempt to justify nepotism, i.e. promotion by family connections.

Increasingly, in an overtly democratic society, family or social background are being challenged as qualifications for promotion. They have not disappeared by any means, but their significance is diminishing.

One of the more significant factors is the Western attitude to age. There is, effectively no longer much respect accorded to age. A young senior manager may be seen as a dislikable whizzkid, but he/she is accorded respect for his/her achievement. An elderly manager, at the same level, is not automatically seen as the senior – any more, indeed, than any shopfloor worker in Western society would be paid more than a newly qualified journeyman with the same skill.

The point can be illustrated by what might seem a ludicrous instance of human folly: a manager might decide that his appearance militated against him, dye his hair to get rid of a white or grey effect; at the extreme it is not unknown for a manager to have a surreptitious facelift during a vacation in order to look younger. It is difficult in the West to envisage a situation where a manager would deliberately take substantial cosmetic action to appear older, on the theory that he would thereby command more respect.

In a sense, attitudes to management, respect for qualifications and individual achievement and lack of respect for family background or age can be seen as one facet of the move away from the extended family concept of relatively primitive societies, but also extant in many relatively advanced non-Western cultures, over to a welfare state concept, where the individual's responsibility towards the family diminishes, while the state's responsibilities increase accordingly.

As in so many other aspects, there are significant differences to be observed in the Japanese organization and cultural pattern and these will now have to be considered.

THE JAPANESE MANAGERIAL PATTERN

From what has been said so far, it is very difficult to draw meaningful comparisons between management theory and practice in the West, on the one hand, and the situation in Japan on the other, because the cultural background is so different. By an extension of the same argument it may be difficult for non-Japanese cultures to adopt the very successful Japanese practices because of this different background: and this is as true of non-Western as of Western cultures. This difficulty of cultural adoption and adaptation is a two-way barrier, as can be illustrated by examples of the relatively rare Japanese failures. In some parts, for example, of South-East Asia, Japanese practices have made Japanese companies unpopular, rather because of mutual incomprehension than ill will on the part of the companies.

To illustrate some of the problems it may be helpful to take concepts of organizational change already discussed in Western terms, and consider how far they are appropriate to Japan.

First, so far as technical change is concerned, Japanese history since the 1850s has been one of the successful importation and improvement of new technology. In many cases the Japanese licensee has resolved the technical problem of adaptation even before the foreign originator.

Social change in the West has been considered under the broad themes of scientific management, and the subsequent recognition of the human needs of the individual participant, whether manager or shopfloor worker.

Scientific management, it can be argued, emphasized the impersonality of interpersonal relationships: individuals in the organization derived their powers from their status. In that sense the question of whether one personally liked or disliked a colleague was irrelevant to the issue of finding the best organizational pattern for a particular situation. It is possibly in the area of impersonality of interpersonal relations that the distinction between Western and Japanese organizational approach is most different, in that the latter places far greater emphasis on harmonious relationships, indeed emotional bonds, between superior and subordinate or between equals. In a sense one would be no more likely to find a family whose members actively disliked each other, and yet who remained together, than a Japanese organizational group which adhered in a situation where the individual members disliked or even were indifferent to each other.

CAREER ADVANCEMENT: DIFFERENT CRITERIA IN DIFFERENT CULTURES

The Japanese career pattern for executives has some significant differences from those in the West. In the latter case promotion can be seen as a ladder up which a professionally qualified person may rise initially in his own particular speciality, with an occasional move perhaps from a line to a staff job, and at the higher reaches into general management. In a sense the development of the concept of an MBA is an attempt to prepare the specialist for a move into general management by giving the student a working knowledge of other disciplines. The Japanese executive's progression has been likened to a spiral staircase, via job rotation through the range of corporate functions, accounting, manufacturing, marketing, personnel, etc. The effect ultimately is to produce a very experienced generalist, although the initial contribution of the junior manager is likely to be small. The functional specialization aspect of organization has less meaning in Japan.

There is clearly a hierarchy in the Japanese organizational system which is significantly different from that in the West: most importantly, the concept of seniority by years of service with the organization counts for a great deal. Graduates entering in the same year with the same general qualifications tend to be promoted upwards at about the same rate. In a curious way, premature promotion above one's peers would be as unacceptable as no promotion.

Initially the status of a new entrant into a company depends on his/her educational standard: thereafter to a very high degree promotion becomes a matter of seniority. It is highly improbable that technical incompetents would be admitted to a Japanese company; if they were, they would probably be shielded and receive promotions about the same time as their peers, in terms of year of entry. The Japanese company in fact has achieved a situation where individual ambition is subordinated to the interest of the organization, and where competitiveness is directed outside to the marketplace.

Allied to this phenomenon is a highly effective two-way communication rather than instructions simply being passed down the hierarchy for implementation lower down. The ease of communication, which in no way weakens respect and status for one's senior, enables relatively junior executives to suggest lines of action, which after discussion will be adopted by consensus rather than in the strict hierarchical sense of decisions taken at the top.

The most recent theme in Western writing on organizational change has touched upon the issue of motivating the workforce. The situation is seen rather differently in Japan.

The Japanese organization system has been rather loosely described as a feudal pattern of rights and duties in the Western sense: equally it has parallels with the concepts of the extended family or a tribal loyalty in other cultures. The point, however, is that the Japanese worker is likely to see himself as a life-time member of a company which in turn becomes a type of surrogate family, to which he owes working life, companionship, even company housing, health care for the worker and his family – virtually a complete environment, rather than simply an organization for which he works for a fixed number of hours daily. This is a condition which once operated in Western society also but was dropped, in the belief that it was a barrier to industrialization.

The system facilitates a relatively painless redistribution of personnel to a work situation. This fact too is combined with an emphasis on group performance which places rather more importance on the environmental context, e.g. a work team, than on professional qualification or training, and a team performance rather than individual excellence. Indeed it has been argued that the Japanese simply do not accept the concept of specific competence and a job description as being a prerequisite in choosing an individual to do a job: rather they would amend the job description to the competence and abilities of the man chosen in some other way to fill the job.

From what has been said it is clear that many of the problems which preoccupy Western researchers, namely the need to reconcile the desire of the individual to achieve self-fulfilment in spite of the demands of the organization, simply do not exist in the Japanese context or at least do not loom as large in Japan as in the West. The Japanese appear to have avoided most of the Western complexes, by an emphasis on emotional sensitivity, consensus and a group spirit, a paternalistic approach by the whole organization. These principles are at least as successful as the Western alternatives, but less easily imitated. They might represent a better approach even for Western multinationals or other non-Western societies.

A by-product of the Japanese system is the generation of loyalty both upwards and downwards in the managerial hierarchy, and incidentally outwards and inwards in relation to the world outside. The Japanese organization expects loyalty from its suppliers and distributors, but can be expected to provide it in turn. In the same way whole societies may be affected: in western Europe the fact that some areas have attracted Japanese investment (in the UK an area like Wales is an obvious example, or in the Republic of Ireland): this gives such an area an edge in further development. An environment which is regarded as conducive to success by one Japanese company will be seen in much the same light by others, and this applies whether it is an area where aggressive marketing is seen to work, or an area where production facilities might be envisaged.

There appear to be relatively few critics of the Japanese system, at least available outside Japan, although non-Japanese managers in a Japanese multinational enterprise are likely to be aware of their limited prospects of promotion to corporate headquarters. And it is not unknown for younger Japanese executives in the USA, to yearn for the less formal hierarchy and relationships which they see in US corporations. Such critics as there are tend to concentrate on four main areas, where they suggest Japanese organizations have something to learn from the West.

There is firstly the profit orientation of most Western businesses, which contrasts with the Japanese tendency to operate on other constraints than maximum profitability in the short run, and on a co-operative basis of team responsibility and credit. There is therefore in the West, a need for built-in checks on the individual manager's performance and accountability, to allocate praise or blame.

This is allied to a second Western tendency often to select for early promotion over their year's 'peers', young executives who might be described as 'high flyers'. The exceptional individual in a Western concern is more likely to have more responsibility and authority at a younger age than their Japanese counterpart, whose promotion tends to match that of their year 'peers'. The Japanese system arguably, therefore, encourages individuals to 'play safe' rather than to seek to excel.

Third, there is a tendency among many Western firms to delegate responsibility downwards in the hierarchy, a policy which, if successful, probably simplifies the organizational structure and makes for quicker decision taking than on the 'consensus' approach in Japan.

Finally in this list of criticisms of the Japanese organizational system by a Japanese is the greater freedom which is observed among top executives in the West to plan their own time: Japanese senior executives, it is claimed, have more and more ceremonial tasks pressed upon them by their very status.

It is perhaps a characteristic of any society to believe on occasion that the grass is greener somewhere else. Certainly some Western critics of the pursuit of the profit motive to the alleged exclusion of all else, or the application of scientific management techniques at the expense of the individual, would esteem Japanese methods to be more humane on occasion than the Western approach. The concept of lifetime employment rather than a ruthless 'hire and fire' approach might leave a middle-aged, intelligent but not brilliant executive in the West rather more secure and perhaps therefore rather more efficient in the long run. Moreover, a number of Western enterprises appear to be open to persuasion that a move away from the strict cash nexus, hierarchical approach, with its emphasis on efficiency, may be even more efficient than the Western systems overtly directed to this objective. Certainly they might see merits in the workforce regarding themselves in some respects as family members of the enterprise, as Japanese workers do. The point, however, is that both Western and

Japanese executives are beginning to see merits in the other's system, and look critically at the assumptions on which their own is based. In view of the enormous imbalance between Japanese who speak English or another European language, and the number of Westerners who speak Japanese, the former may find the tasks of comparison and assimilation easier.

COUNTERVAILING POWERS AS A CULTURAL FACTOR

Thus far this chapter has considered some of the cultural problems which may face the Western or Japanese multinational which is contemplating a move into alien cultures. And what has been emphasized are the difficulties in motivating personnel, particularly locally recruited executives. In another respect, however, the move into relatively underdeveloped societies may be less prone to difficulties in terms of employing people as well as the growth of consumerism increasingly being experienced in the West particularly.

It is usual to discuss the movement of manufacturing plant by the international enterprises from their original bases in Western economies into new areas, particularly in the Third World, either in terms of market opportunities which cannot conveniently be met by exporting, or in terms of the cheaper labour available. This was the area discussed in Chapter 2 and of course these factors remain the most important. But apart from particular opportunities or threats, there are long term cultural factors, which do not appear to be working in favour of the present Western societies remaining unchallenged as the workshops of the world. These can be called 'countervailing powers' in the Galbraithian sense, and indicate some of the factors particularly in Western cultures which may be turning the cultural climate hostile to the industrialist. If the latter is a domestically based operator, and cannot 'go international' he/she has to accept the situation, but may have the choice to move out, and this is why we must consider these cultural countervailing powers as they affect the Western industrialist, not only in the home country but anywhere else he/she might decide to go.

COUNTERVAILING POWERS IN WESTERN CULTURES

The related series of phenomena which increasingly affects multinationals (and indeed all industrial and commercial units) are those which place more and more restrictions on what enterprises, or executives in enterprises, may do. Allied with these phenomena are the appearance and apparently inexorable growth of regulatory bodies to enforce them, and a whole body of legal expertise and legal precedent to enable individuals or power groups to attack any activities by enterprises which they see as inimical to their interest. These can conveniently be grouped under three main headings.

a.   Environmental controls

Environmental controls, which lay down regulations on where and how enterprises may operate and the degree to which they will be allowed to affect the social and physical atmosphere through pollution (which is now an all-embracing term for activities which some groups would oppose). The limitations may affect whole industries: the siting of individual plants, what and how products can be promoted; or at the micro level the imposition of quality and safety standards on individual products. Pressure groups attacking specific industrial projects, consumerism and product liability legislation are all examples of this.

It would be foolish to claim that the results of these controls are all negative; and certainly the enterprises themselves are hardly always the best judge of what is in the community interest. At the same time it is difficult to avoid the conclusion that the jungle of legislation and penalties, including criminal liability on individual executives, has got to the point where new developments may simply be abandoned in many Western economies. It could take too long and be too expensive for a company to develop what appeared to be a perfectly safe product. Yet the company might still face a disastrous pitfall in terms of product liability years later. There are few legal risks in not innovating, of doing nothing until directed to by government. One curious result is that it is, for example, likely to take only about a third as long to build an atomic power plant in a developing country, with an authoritarian government, than it would be in the country where it was designed. In the latter, clearing the legal obstacles is likely to be more time consuming than the actual design and construction times: and every Three Mile Island incident, let alone the far more disastrous Chernobyl one, probably adds on another five years to the time scale.

For its supporters, consumerism and product liability are seen as countervailing powers defending the community against ever more powerful commercial and industrial interests. But when a society gets to the stage where there is more individual prestige and reward in attacking industrial innovation than in designing for and producing such innovation, then such environmental controls, the bureaucratization which is needed to enforce them and the power of disruption given to individuals and groups, may be the symptoms of a disease in that society as serious as the abuses or irresponsibilities of the industries which first produced the reaction.

b. Anti-discriminating controls

The second set of controls are those which are intended to pursue desirable social objectives, but which have an immediate effect in limiting the freedom of action of the enterprise to conduct its business as it sees best. This group of legislative moves can broadly be described as anti-discriminatory, in terms of colour, sex, religion and age as well as legislation protective of the individual in terms of job security. In the long run the results are likely to be beneficial to the individual company as well as the community if they release the potential of groups which have effectively been prevented from doing so. But the immediate complications of quota allocations, positive action and positive discrimination, with a backlash of changes of reverse discrimination can put the company into a 'can't win' situation where it may seek to minimize risk by doing as little novel as possible and employing someone only if they can find no other way of doing the job. Jobs rapidly become property rights and only machines have no legal powers.

c. Property rights

The third groups follow on from the concept mentioned above, as jobs in developed societies rapidly becoming property rights of their holders. Property rights imply power, and this can be seen as the obverse side of the growth towards industrial democracy, in the social democratic countries of western Europe. Industrial democracy, in the form of codetermination, has been discussed in more detail, and there is no doubt that it has served its communities well in terms of social place. But again the immediate effects, as perceived by the enterprise, are more complications, more restrictions on actions, and a desire to see a way out.

Before discussing these countervailing powers, it is worth looking at the Western marxist world, which is having the same problem, with different emphasis and conceivably more parlous results on their rigid political structures. Within these societies, bureaucracy is almost certainly considerably more powerful than anything experienced in the West, and the result has been the creation of vested interests and functionaries, 'apparatchiks' might be a more appropriate word, whose power lies in the existence of the bureaucracy. They have no incentive therefore to support reform, even if this is a condition of technological advance. The result is that, unless there is a direct and sustained drive from the political top to achieve a breakthrough in particular industries and technologies, the bureaucracy rather than the technological problems may become the major obstacles. It is still far from clear whether the Gorbachev reforms will have any lasting impact on this state of affairs. There are several other highly undesirable results. Overmanning, particularly at the highly non-competitive parts of the system: an inability to respond quickly to a new situation; and commercially the most disastrous of all, the apparent inability to diffuse any technological breakthroughs into other areas which were not specifically foreseen as using such information. It is conceivable that the same technological breakthroughs are being made more than once in the Eastern Bloc system because society prevents the original information being widely known and applied.

The countervailing power in the Soviet system tends to be even more overtly political than in the West, and criticism or opposition, even when made by those who implicitly accept the ideology of the system, very rapidly becomes illegal. Any attack on a rigid system has to be resisted lest the monolith cracks. The strike weapon, almost unknown a few years before, has begun to operate successfully, but only where it can obtain powerful nationalist or religious sentiments as allies, as has happened in Poland. The other form of countervailing power is the tacit acceptance of time-serving conformity to a system and an avoidance of risk taking, i.e. the acceptance of a considerable degree of entrepreneurial stagnation.

The multinationals of the West and Japan can, and do, co-operate to a limited extent with the marxist bureaucracies. Their power in the situation is official approval from the top, and the prospect for the participants of enjoying some of the half-forbidden fruits of the Western world through hard currency earning. The limitations remain, however: a fear of the consequence of change on the position of the apparatchiks, and fear of too close and too fruitful co-operation on the part of the Eastern bloc executives, who may be on the chopping block if the party line changes.

LARGE STRATEGIC DECISIONS AND THEIR IMPLEMENTATION

In many instances the intervention of a multinational in a new territory will result from, and pose, substantial policy decisions on the part of the host government. The decisions may in effect be to create a new industry, destroy long established ones, break long established cultural patterns, bring substantial rewards in terms of increased wealth and local employment and substantial disadvantages, varying from environmental pollution to displacement of whole communities, etc. What lessons can be drawn from the past about the ease or difficulty with which such strategic decisions can be initiated, accepted or implemented by host governments?

As a generalization one can say that in advanced industrial societies of a democratic persuasion, the quality and quantity of resistance to changes which might threaten a sectional interest is already large, and growing apace. It is a safe assumption that the major part of any lead in time between planning and production can be ascribed to planning and obtaining planning permission to go ahead. By contrast, in spite of the existence of bureaucracies in less developed countries, the problems of getting planning permission can more readily be short circuited.

THE TEMPTATION TO MOVE INTO THE UNDERDEVELOPED WORLD TO ESCAPE COUNTERVAILING POWERS

The temptation for the multinational to move into the Third World is that the countervailing powers experienced in the West have not *yet* happened there, and rich markets may be captured, either in their domestic markets or by exports, before they do.

Many Third World countries in theory are as regulated, or even more so than the Western world; but in general, since they do not take the appurtenances of the Western world for granted, they are still likely to be more concerned with the prospect of creating wealth than in controlling its creation. Some of the more dubious consequences may include atmospheric pollution on a scale which would not be tolerated in a developed country; lower safety standards and workplace conditions; and, in general, acceptance of a lower quality of product. But limitations on what the company does or does not do are largely self-determined. The rules are laid down by local cultural susceptibilities, not law. The major way is that already discussed, namely that what is done locally may offend against susceptibilities of consumer groups back home, and they may raise adverse publicity there.

In the long term a successful market will probably develop the same consumer restrictions as the existing developed world. But as Lord Keynes once remarked, 'In the long run, we are all dead', and the consequences of such developments are going to have to be handled by another generation of shareholders.

WHAT WILL HAPPEN TO THE INTERNATIONAL ENTERPRISE?

The future prospects of the international enterprise are shrouded in uncertainty, because while its growth continues and international co-operation involving its activities grows, so too does hostility to the concept. It is impossible, therefore, to prophesy with any certainty, whether the international enterprise will persist and even grow in the next few decades: one's judgement of its fate depends largely on how one interprets changes in society worldwide.

It is convenient at this stage to draw together some tendencies which have been implicit in much of what has been examined earlier, and make some sort of assessment about where the multifaceted multicultural societies, which represent markets for the multinationals, are moving.

There are two fundamentally opposed tendencies to be observed in operation throughout the world which have far-reaching implications for the strategy, indeed the future of the international enterprise, and in particular the multinational corporation. These can be summarized, perhaps in terms of converging and diverging trends in societies throughout the world.

Convergence is a phenomenon which can be seen in the tendency towards standardization of products and homogeneity of tastes; this is something which can be observed at the macro level in societies and at the micro level in individual products. The argument, insofar as it applies to societies, is that all societies are basically desirous of a high material standard of living, a style of life of which the USA, or more precisely the USA as portrayed in much of its TV and film material, is deemed to be. Arising from this is the assumption that the great majority of products which have been developed for the American market will have a market in other parts of the world and when disposable income in these societies rises to the point where there is a significant market. Even in societies which have not reached this point, being 'well-to-do' largely means enjoying the appurtenances and, as important, the tastes of the middle class of north America or western Europe.

Some of the implications of this have already been seen in terms of product policy and most specifically in the tendency of the international enterprise to produce standard products, the 'universal' car, etc., designed for one particular advanced economy or region and subsequently produced throughout the world – a tendency at odds with the current dogmas of market orientation and market segmentation.

Divergence is a phenomenon which can be seen in the tendency towards loss of control by multinationals, both in terms of cultural differences, particularly as these emerge in terms of differing management styles, and also in terms of political action, at national, regional or international level, to restrict the freedom of action of the enterprises.

These then are the issues which will be discussed in this section, schematically as in Diagram 5a.

Insofar, however, as many of the issues have already been touched upon, albeit in a different context earlier, the treatment of the issues will not be equal. Some issues already discussed will be mentioned simply in passing, while new areas will be dealt with in detail. It cannot be assumed, however, that reference to issues already adequately covered implies that they are of less consequence than the new material.

The issues of convergence and divergence can conveniently be illustrated by chronological development. Thus in the 1950s and early 1960s, for reasons to be examined, there was a fairly widespread assumption that much of the world was developing along American lines of materialist prosperity, if not American ideals. It was fairly logical then that the 1970s could be seen as the application of these assumptions to fairly specific product development, namely the widespread adoption of American styles, not only in other Western industrialized societies and Japan but even among the more prosperous younger generation of the marxist bloc and the Third World. This

CONVERGENCE ◄──────────────   ──────────────► DIVERGENCE

(1) *In terms of consumer tastes*   *Diversification and loss of control*

    1950s/1960s Assumption of American model   (1) 1970s/1980s cultural reaction
                 of cultural development   Loss of confidence in American model

    1970s/1980s Standardized products   (2) Greater efforts at control of MNCs

                                       (a) National Level (indigenization, etc.)
                                       (b) By regional groupings (e.g. EEC, Andean
                                           Pact provisions)
                                       (c) International (UN, ICC and OECD codes
                                       of conduct)

Diagram 5a   *What is Happening to the International Enterprise in Terms of Cultural Developments?*

was seen in the enthusiastic acceptance of Western fashions, from pop music to jeans (with American products having a cachet over local imitations), and to the ill-concealed anger of the more conservative establishment of many of these cultures, who saw in it blatant imitation of American norms and as marking a challenge to the ideological and cultural purity of their societies. Covergence on the American pattern was a powerful factor. But from the late 1970s and certainly for much of the 1980s, the prospects have been for the increase of divergence tendencies. In part this has risen from a loss of certainty that the American pattern is the most desirable or successful, in part from a reaction to American cultural influences. It will be necessary to examine some of the reasons for this uncertainty about the 'American' future in more detail, but it is worth noting that the challenge has not come from the most obvious source, namely marxist socialism, but from other Western societies and management styles, as well as the Third World.

In the Third World this reaction has been more confused and diffused, but is seen at its most extreme in, for example, Islamic fundamentalism in Iran and elsewhere, or the challenge to American political dominance in its own backyard of Central and South America.

These might be seen as general, cultural or ideological challenges: in more specific terms, the multinational corporations are being increasingly subject to constraints designed to give national governments greater control over the operations of multinationals, particularly foreign multinationals, within their own territory. This major challenge incidentally, in its more thoughtful and effective form, may come from societies which are not ideologically opposed to free enterprise, but which nevertheless see the freedom of action of international companies as a threat to national or even regional interests.

Finally, it is worth emphasizing in this introduction that the chronological approach has its dangers as well as its advantages, in that it is easy to assume that while many of the 'convergence' trends became more evident in the 1950s, 1960s and the early 1970s while the 'divergence' trends became stronger towards the end of the period, divergence is replacing convergence in the 1980s. It would be more accurate to say that divergence trends have been added to rather than replacing convergence, and it is by no means clear whether divergence concepts are transient, inevitable, or even that in some form of hegelian or marxist dialectic a synthesis will emerge.

AN ASIDE ON CONDITIONS WHICH MAY BE PRESENT IN DEVELOPING COUNTRIES

It is highly dangerous to generalize about conditions in developing societies which now contain over half the world's population. Nevertheless, it is fairly safe to assume that most of the following conditions will apply in the average underdeveloped society.

There will exist a degree of inefficiency in the administrative machinery, particularly at the middle and lower levels which will have the effect of holding up decisions, most of which will be trivial in themselves but whose effects may be cumulative in delaying decisions involving the foreign businessman. A civil service post carries status and security in a relatively poor society, and the attitude of officials to the general public as much as to the foreign industrialist may be indifferent, arbitrary and arrogant to a degree which would be intolerable in a developed society. This may be allied to an unwillingness to accept responsibility, so that the businessman can find that the most minor decisions have to be relayed up the hierarchy with an interminable delay. Even more difficult to assess is the role of the minor bribe to encourage action. In some societies where the civil local government official is poorly paid, tips may be a normal part of his/her income and he/she will not take action without some sort of financial incentive.

While the attitude towards the foreign businessman (and even more to the local businessman) may be cavalier, the attitude towards superiors in the bureaucracy can only be described as obsequious. Often it will happen that the key posts in a bureaucratic structure are filled by political nominees, or even worse, by family relations of political nominees. Their qualifications for the post may be minimal, far lower indeed than their subordinates. But the latter are still likely to make decisions or delay decisions affecting the foreign businessman until they have decided what is in the personal interest of their superior, rather than in the national interest.

To some extent the same problems apply at the lower level of commercial enterprise, with delay, an unwillingness to take responsibility and bribery as normal hazards. A heartening, if unquantifiable, phenomenon which is reported in parts of the world is what might be termed the 'freemasonry of the MBA', i.e. graduates in this area, particularly from foreign universities, tend to be more helpful to foreigners with the same sort of academic qualification.

A low level of efficiency in administration, however, does not mean a correspondingly low level of expectation about the results to be achieved by collaboration with the foreigner bringing in new technology and production techniques. Almost inevitably both government official and private business partner or licensee will have an exaggerated estimate of the ease with which technology can be imparted. There is almost a mystic belief in the ability to transfer experience and practices, developed in one culture, into another. Murphy's law, namely 'Anything which can possibly go wrong will go wrong', and O'Riley's law, namely that Murphy is an incurable optimist, have cross-cultural application. The fact that difficulties arise, that production targets and dates are very easily missed in purely domestic planning, does not always prevent local interests entertaining suspicions about bad faith on the part of the foreign business partner when the same phenomena involve the foreigner.

BRIBERY AND EXTORTION IN INTERNATIONAL BUSINESS

The issue of bribery is one which has attracted worldwide attention and condemnation, some of the latter being of a rather hypocritical variety. Bribery is such a semantically loaded word that few people, if any, would justify the practice in unqualified terms though many would regard it as inevitable in many parts of the world. It would be useful in discussing the subject to define shades of meaning in what can be an ambiguous term.

There is at least one situation which is unambiguous. This is the covert payment of money to a functionary or politician not on the official payroll of the company, with payment being made into a foreign bank account. How widespread this practice is can only be guessed at – such information as is available arises mainly from the American congressional hearings on the issue. Other industrialized countries, where it is reasonable to suppose that bribery would be accepted as a normal part of an international transaction, are a good deal more discreet. In general it is not a legal offence in the home country of the foreign enterprise to pay a bribe in a foreign country. The tax authorities in the home country have the means and the legal powers to acquire details of payments, at least as far as any 'front man' in the deal: but insofar as the bribery is creating jobs and foreign earnings, the immediate harm is not being done in the home country and there is therefore no *prima facie* legal basis for instituting legal action.

The main loser in such a bribery situation is likely to be another company or the economy on whose behalf the recipient of the bribe is supposed to be acting. Virtually by definition, the government or the tax authorities of that country are not likely to be able to prove bribery especially if the payment takes place outside its territories. The numbered Swiss bank account or its equivalent elsewhere can defy the most rigorous investigation by a foreign government.

A more ambivalent situation is that where excessive commission is being paid to an agent. The problem here is that of defining 'excessive'. An acceptable percentage in a bribery-free market might range from a fraction of 1 per cent on a large capital transaction to a double figure percentage on a small order for consumer goods. What is acceptable here depends on the scale of the order and the conventional markup in a competitive situation. Where, however, a foreign contract involving large sums includes commission figures in excess, say, of 10 per cent, where in fact the commission on one deal amounts to a fortune for an individual, and where the ultimate payer is kept in the dark about how much commission is to be paid and to whom, it is difficult to avoid the conclusion that an element of bribery exists. Payment in this situation is likely to be to an officially appointed agent with the implication being that he/she in turn will make the necessary payoffs.

The only conceivable test of whether bribery takes place is that the level of commission paid should be known, be comparable with that offered by other companies in the market and that the recipient of the commission should not be passing on part of his/her emoluments to another person who has such a connection with the purchaser as to make it reasonable to suppose they had influenced the decision in favour of their paymaster. The application of such a test, however, in the context of a Third World society is virtually inconceivable.

What might be termed a 'light grey situation' is the payment of small sums or the giving of gifts to minor functionaries, not so much to obtain a favourable decision, as to obtain faster service, e.g. a tip to an official who is supposed to issue a permit or to a telephone operator to ensure prompt service in an inefficient society. One begins to arrive at the hazy situation where payment for a specific service is bribery but a Christmas present for more unspecific services, or expensive meals or evenings out are apparently acceptable even in Western societies where standards of personal honesty are generally reckoned to be higher.

It is an interesting comment on the current state of international morality that it is apparently a good deal more wicked to offer a bribe than to accept it. While a few prominent or unlucky individuals are now and then pilloried as recipients of largesse, the great majority of bribe takers are never identified let alone punished. However, as one international businessman pertinently remarked: 'What you call bribery, we call extortion!' It is reasonable to suppose that the initiative for corrupt practices comes from the recipients of the bribes not the payers: in a society where corruption is endemic it takes far more effort for the foreigner to opt out of the system, even if they can, than to go along with it. It is arguable that the greatest impact of the so-called Lockheed scandal of 1976 was not the allegation of bribes in general, but the thought that bribes had been paid in Western societies and at a social level where corruption was regarded as unthinkable. An allegation of bribery at the level of the Dutch royal family was much more shocking than similar allegations would be against premiers or princes in most parts of Africa or Asia – the whole affair was in a sense a backhanded compliment to the expected integrity of the political and commercial standards of the Dutch.

For the foreign businessman who is in a genuine dilemma about whether to go along with local practice in a foreign society where he believes commercial practices are different from his own, there are three courses open, one of which is blameless, the second defensible and the third indefensible. The first is simply to refuse to compromise his principle of no corruption – and incidentally ensure that his local agents know and follow this policy, even if it means that the order is lost. This in practice may be an impossible ideal at the minor functionary level: the tip to expedite paper work etc. The second is to respond to approaches, but not to initiate them – at worst to submit to a degree of extortion, if he is convinced that this is normal practice and is likely to be indulged in by competitors. There is little if any moral basis for this rather inglorious stance, but at least the businessman can argue that he is contributing to, rather than initiating, a situation of corruption. The third choice is to take the initiative in a situation where there is no reason to suppose that corruption is practised. It is a highly dangerous policy and the instigator has no one to blame but himself if things go wrong.

In an absolute sense, bribery of any form, from the Christmas gift to the lowest functionary, to the creation of a numbered bank account in Switzerland for a politician, is wrong. It would in the last analysis be casuistic to pretend otherwise. As a working rule, however, there are two situations when it changes from the venial to something a good deal worse. The first is when it moves away from an attempt to accelerate the implementation of a decision already made, to an attempt to affect that decision. If a contract has already been awarded, it is morally more defensible to tip a functionary to hurry along an import licence, than to pay someone to get the contract in the first place. The second is simply scale: a small present which can be interpreted as a sign of individual appreciation is one thing; the large payment in hard cash of the type described earlier is another, and rather different situation.

Bribery, in short, is something the international enterprise may have to live with in many parts of the world, if it wants to operate them. What it cannot justify is creating the condition where it did not exist previously, or raising its level by a significant degree.

NATIONAL LEGISLATION ON BRIBERY

It is highly probable that acceptance of a bribe from a foreign multinational could be deemed a criminal offence under virtually any legal code operating in any country anywhere in the world. In practice, where bribery is endemic, persecution of the takers of bribes is rare.

Even rarer, however, is legislation sponsored by a government to make bribery illegal abroad. This is an area where most governments prefer to turn a blind eye, unless the activities of their nationals or local representatives of companies having corporate headquarters within their territories, become too blatant in their operations in the foreign marketplace.

To be fair to governments which choose to ignore the issue, there are serious legal and political problems involved. What may be involved is a criminal act which takes place in a foreign country, where in fact the person who actually pays the bribe and the person who receives it are foreign nationals. Any country which passes this sort of legislation relating to foreign nationals in their own country can be accused of trying to impose its writ within the territory of a foreign sovereign power, and the fact that the legislation is supposed to be in the interest of that power will scarcely diminish national resentment there.

The power which is most often accused of attempting to impose its legislation outside its own territory is the USA. It is not perhaps surprising to find, then, that it is the only country which has introduced very specific legislation against such practices abroad, whether individuals or legal personalities, such as companies, registered in the USA.

The Foreign Corrupt Practices Act of 1977 was passed following the revelation of the extent to which American companies were prepared to use bribery as and when it appeared necessary to secure foreign sales etc. The Act requires companies to keep books and records of payments in detail, and to introduce controls which in effect ensure that individuals in the field cannot use company expenses in such a way that their purposes would remain unexplained and unaccountable. Bribes, after all, have to show up in bookkeeping transactions, and the intention of the legislation is to prevent such activities being disguised as more acceptable expenses. There are also criminal penalties for the making of payments to foreign officials, politicians or political candidates for favours.

The Act is highly controversial, and that not merely because of any implicit claim to political jurisdiction outside the USA. American enterprises tend to be highly critical, not merely because they are apparently subject to restraints which are not imposed on any foreign rivals, but because of what they regard as ambiguities within the legislation. Thus it may be permissible to pay clerks or industry officials in a foreign country, but not an official with executive power where it could be argued that the payment was to obtain favours rather than facilitating administrative procedures. The Act also attempts to distinguish between bribery, which is illegal, and extortion, i.e. payment to avert a threat – a distinction which arguably is largely meaningless.

THE ICC CODE OF CONDUCT

In the light of the very real problems of enforcing by legal, indeed penal, means a code of business practice which would eliminate bribery, it is not surprising to find that the alternative codes are recommendations rather than enforceable practices. There are, basically, three major sources of anti-bribery codes, namely the International Chamber of Commerce (ICC), the Organization for Economic Co-operation and Development (OECD) and the United Nations. Of these the ICC code is perhaps the most specific to the issue of bribery. The other two go into details of good conduct for the international enterprise to an extent which tends to render them somewhat platitudinous.

The ICC has over 50 national interests among its members, including representatives from all the major Western industrial nations. Its code on financial practice arose from the creation by it of a Commission on Ethical Practice, under Lord Shawcross. The Shaw-cross Commission Report was the basis of the code issued in 1977 to which has been added a review panel provision.

The ICC is directly making the point, both to businesses and to governments, that bribery, as perceived by one side, is bribery as perceived by the other. As in the case of the American legislation, the ICC code attempts to draw a distinction between 'facilitating' payments intended to encourage a lethargic and possibly underpaid functionary to expedite any paperwork. Otherwise the remaining provisions are much what would be expected, namely prohibition of bribery, extortion, etc. Provision is to be made for details of agents who receive more than the specific sum annually in terms of remuneration and who are likely to be dealing with government organizations. Other expenses and proceedings, etc., are to be in accordance with local law. The intention of the review panel is to review the operation of the rules of conduct.

CORRUPTION AND THE MARXIST CHALLENGE

Conventional wisdom in Western circles is that implicitly, and uneasily, it is acceptable to go along with local practice, but not to worsen a morally indefensible practice by raising the stakes, so to speak, or extending the practice into hitherto uncontaminated areas of public and commercial life. There is however another political factor in the background which has implications for the West as a whole if not for the individual company. This is the presence of the marxist model: in the areas where bribery is most endemic, i.e. the Third World, the marxist alternative is very obvious.

It would be reasonably accurate to say that the Western democracies have been winning the material battle, but losing the moral one. Manifestly free style economies are out-performing marxist ones and, in a sense, much of the marxist and broadly socialist economy is parasitic on the West, drawing heavily on it for technology and loans. And yet, though the evidence is of the inadequacy of the marxist model in matching Western production techniques, marxist practices exercise a profound attraction to the deprived of the Third World. Arguably one of the most attractive features of marxism in opposition is that it has had many of the personal qualities of puritanism, which makes its advocates a marked contrast to the venality of public and commercial life which characterizes so much of the non-communist Third World. In this sense, every Western or Japanese enterprise which goes along with the system provides ammunition for these groups in society, which are determined to relegate capitalist practices to the dustbin of history.

This personal honesty of the communist in opposition does not, however, always carry over to the communist in power. Marxist societies, with their vast bureaucracies and large numbers of apparatchiks with power to grant or withhold favours, are national breeding grounds for corruption. Indeed corruption, 'blat', the fixer may be a necessary lubricant to make the vast machine turn over smoothly. A supply of hard Western currency eases many problems in the communist countries. In a sense, corruption has been institutionalized by the double standards of the hard currency shops, where high quality goods are available only to those with foreign currency or high political connections. The non-institutionalized corruption, when exposed, is punished in a draconian form. But it exists, and is probably growing as more and more of the citizens of these countries have access to Western contacts.

APPENDIX

Rights and responsibilities of the international enterprise

It is customary to think of personnel issues in terms of job selection, training and industrial relations, and these issues are of considerable importance to any enterprise. But for the international enterprise which is contemplating entry into the Third World, the issues are at once more general and more profound. The enterprise faces first the fact of a permanent and growing job crisis, where the government of any developing nation may have to find new jobs by the million or tens of million as the population grows; and second the fact that even the most primitive infrastructure of educational facilities, medical facilities and all the other adjuncts of a modern state may simply not exist. The enterprise may have to provide these and much more, and in the process find itself engaged in activities, and accepting what amounts to seignorial authority, of a type quite alien to its operations elsewhere. Before discussing what might be termed the more conventional aspects of personnel issues, it is important to look at the much wider range of rights and duties which may fall into the foreign enterprise in the Third World, first in terms of jobs and training, and second in the more subtle issue of findings its cultural niche in an alien society.

The concept of human resource development and the implications for the multinational company

The difference between a problem and an opportunity is, in many instances, simply a matter of attitude, and this may be true, not least in terms of those Third World countries which have a rapidly rising population, and are normally regarded as being overpopulated. Without straining reality too much, the situation might be redefined to assert that their major, indeed only major, resources are human resources, and that the most important issue is to transfer this vast potential for wealth into the reality of wealth.

What these countries need, according to this argument, is a mechanism to train their growing population into more efficient agricultural and industrial producers. This almost certainly means accelerating the movement off the land, where primitive agricultural methods create underemployment, and at the same time dealing with the displaced masses huddled together into cities, by creating an industrial workforce. It is no accident that the really huge cities of the late twentieth century are developing in the Third World in Calcutta, Mexico City, Sao Paulo and Jakarta, where the choice may be to industrialize or to starve. This is a situation where the foreign enterprise may be a major source of new industry and supporter of the spin-off local service industry.

The need is for skilled manpower – and womanpower – but not to any great extent highly educated to conventional university or technical college standard. There is in many Third World countries already a surplus of highly educated personnel with educational backgrounds irrelevant to the real needs of an industrializing society, of men and women with what in theory are appropriate skills, who are inhibited by an ingrained cultural distaste for certain types of jobs, e.g. manual labour, even of a skilled variety. What most of these countries need *en masse* are the skilled technicians which keep the machines, indeed the whole infrastructure of modern society, going.

The tendency in the more farsighted of the Third World countries is therefore to legislate for training facilities at the technician level. The problem however is that the legislation may be difficult to apply, if the training organizations cannot be created, or if the companies cannot or will not supply adequate training. The training is needed both for the youngster emerging from childhood and also the dispossessed agricultural labourer or peasant who drifts into the cities seeking a livelihood. This is an area fraught with problems, but one in which the international enterprise may be able to bring in its experience from training elsewhere in the world. At the very least the foreign enterprise is going to ensure that industrial training for its plant is at an appropriate level, just as it is likely to ensure that the technology it employs is at an appropriate level. In passing, it may be noted that one of the more significant shortcomings of industrial planners in developing countries is their failure to ensure that, where there are technology boards monitoring that the technology which is being imported to foreign enterprises is appropriate, these boards seem to have little or no connection with the government inspired industrial training boards producing the skilled workers appropriate to the technology. Technology boards and training boards often represent quite distinct political fiefs.

The background to human resource development

The situation in the Third World

The conditions in all the hundred or more countries which could be loosely categorized as the Third World vary enormously, but they have one factor in common, namely rapidly rising populations. The pattern of change in the age distribution of a nation's population, as Western techniques, and particularly Western medical knowledge, become available, can be summed up as follows. First, a dramatic fall in the death rate, particularly the death rate at birth or in childhood; then a rapidly rising population, the potential effects of which may be concealed for some time by the age structure. In many of the Third World countries half of the population may be under 15 years of age, and still below childbearing age. No matter how rapidly population growth were to be checked, the impact would take 30 or 40 years to work its way through the existing population.

In the fortunate countries the rapidly growing population can still be fed, but, at what amounts to an exponential rate of growth, even the richest and emptiest lands are going to reach saturation point in terms of their ability to feed the population by existing techniques. Most Third World countries have already reached the point where it is difficult to feed the population, i.e. they are already overpopulated in terms of available resources and production techniques. Since the population cannot be reduced except by catastrophic events, the techniques of production have to be raised to match growing demands, and this in a nutshell is the case for industrialization, whether through the foreign enterprise or by other methods.

Increased output in the agricultural and industrial sectors merely buy time unless and until exponential population growth is slowed down. The next stage, if catastrophe is to be avoided in the long run, is to reduce the birth rate to something like replacement level.

There are enormous implications to the problem of reducing the birth rate, in many cases in religious or cultural terms and in all cases in purely economic terms. As has been pointed out, whatever may be the national interest, a large family is the only security parents have for their old age in a poor society with no welfare infrastructure. Two factors are likely to be necessary, if not always sufficient, conditions for a check in population growth. The first is that national wealth must be growing significantly faster than population, so that the individual can perceive his or her conditions materially improving and can hope for more material goods even without a large family: at the extreme, to see the price of a large family as a diminution of living standards rather than the only guarantee for the future. The second condition appears to be education, and particularly education for women. Educated women as a whole have smaller families than uneducated in the Third World, and their families are likely to be healthier and better able to secure a living. For some cultures, however, Western oriented education is seen as a threat to the established cultural or religious order; in others it may be a challenge to male supremacy in a society where machismo is the only form of status a poor man may have.

In most Third World countries the situation is stark because population growth is uncontrollable by political action, and the international enterprise must take this factor into account. Such a rapidly rising population represents two factors in its calculations. First, a potential growth market unless and until exponential population growth destroys the existing social fabric: second, a source of labour whose employment would go some way to create wealth and so a domestic market, but where the workforce characteristics may pose problems unknown in Westernized industrial societies.

It is with population growth as a source of labour we are concerned here. The point was made that in a few instances the speed of population growth can be reduced by political action. A government may have the political will, allied with an appropriate cultural and religious background in its community, to press successfully for family limitation, and in the process move towards the more capital and technologically intensive type of industry typical of Western societies. Singapore is perhaps the most obvious example. In other societies (and these are probably more typical) religious and cultural sentiment is likely to be hostile, in part for the reasons adduced above. Here the prospects of voluntary limitation of population growth are small, at least in the short to medium term, and labour intensive industrial methods with a lower technological content may be more appropriate.

A later part of this book, Chapter 7, will attempt to make explicit some of the implicit problems faced by host governments in deciding what they should seek from foreign enterprises in terms of job creation, the transfer of technology and industrial 'knowhow' and the earning or saving of foreign currency. But, whatever may be the desirable objectives for developed Western or marxist states, the overwhelming need of the Third World is likely to be jobs – and the international enterprise may have to take account of that in presenting its proposals to any host government in the Third World facing cultural or religious constraints on policies of limiting population growth. And not the least problem for that company may be to persuade a government, even when facing a rapidly growing population, and even more rapidly growing unemployment, that the best production method is not the capital investment model of the developed world to which the government aspires.

The situation in the developed world

The general situation in the developed world *vis-à-vis* population structure is substantially different. Here the general tendency, with few exceptions, is of a stable population, which incidentally implies an ageing population. The implications of this situation are fourfold: first, that industry is likely to be more and more capital intensive, rather than labour intensive; second, that there will be a premium on educated and skilled labour rather than cheap labour; third, that there will be a greater incentive and possibility of employing female labour, if for no other reason than scarcity of trained labour; and finally, that it may be necessary to retrain existing skilled labour in new technology, rather than training a new generation every time a new skill has evolved. A similar pattern is to be found in Japan.

By and large the same situation is happening in the European marxist countries where the population is, if anything, ageing more rapidly than in the Western democracies.

It would be rash to assume that the population structure of the West and parts of the communist world will continue on the same pattern indefinitely. Nevertheless, the assumption on present evidence is that the real growth in population, labour supplies and ultimately markets will lie outside the major industrial nations of today. That is a factor with which the international enterprise based in the West or Japan will have to reckon in planning future developments.

Part V

Financial Aspects of International Business

Introduction

The theme of this short section might be described as the political implications of taxation for the multinational enterprise. The enterprise may have considerable freedom of action in deciding in which country to make its profits (or losses) appear, by regulating the price of cross-frontier transactions with its own local companies. At the same time different nation states levy different levels of taxation and possess different levels of competence in exacting taxes. These two facts put together mean that the enterprise, if it intends to minimize its tax burdens overall, may need a global policy towards taxation rather than simply responding to local tax demands. The political implications of this ability to move profits, and therefore tax liability around the world causes resentment at the local level, where there is a suspicion that a foreign company is not paying its 'fair share'.

6 Finance and Taxation

INTRODUCTION

The financial objectives of the international enterprise can be summarized simply – the attainment of the objectives is considerably more difficult.

The objectives are:

(a) at least to preserve, if possible to enhance, the financial assets of the enterprise, where these may be denominated in various currencies, any or all of which are liable to fluctuate violently in relation to the rest;

(b) to apply the financial assets of the enterprise to the most profitable projects available to the enterprise anywhere in the world, subject to the constraints on investments of capital which may be applied by national governments. The fact that the interest of any government may be in ensuring that funds available locally to the enterprise are to be used within its own territories and may legislate to prevent the free movement of capital.

It is not difficult to formulate a number of principles to enable a company to direct its investment, its new product development and its markets: unfortunately the effects of political uncertainties and, in recent years, of exchange rate fluctuations may have the effect of raising doubts about the efficiency of financially sophisticated methods in a highly unsophisticated political jungle, which might be a fair description of much of the Third World. Even in the developed world the relationships between countries and then foreign exchange rates has been such as to make sophisticated financial decisions almost as hazardous as intuitive judgements.

PROTECTING OR ENHANCING FINANCIAL ASSETS

A number of techniques have been developed to enable an international enterprise, holding financial reserves in a number of currencies, to protect itself against variations in one or more. Basically these techniques follow the commonsense assumption that when one currency is weakening relative to another, it is expedient to move mobile funds into the stronger currency, to have outstanding debts expressed in that currency and liabilities in the weaker currency. *Mutatis mutandis*, it is desirable to have all assets, fixed or liquid, expressed in the strong currency insofar as this is practical and meaningful. In theory this redisposition of assets and liabilities is a temporary move planning a relatively shortlived foreign exchange crisis.

The problems of such a strategy are political. First, action to protect the interests of the enterprise by moving assets out of another currency under pressure worsens the crisis for that currency and so is likely to arouse the hostility of the government concerned. To make matters worse, insofar as most international enterprises are American and the US dollar is no longer the hardest world currency, it may be that American international enterprises can and will protect themselves by actions which weaken their own currency and attack the interests of their home economy. All international enterprises have this implicit conflict of interests even with their own government.

The second problem is that in an era of fluctuating currencies it is difficult to devise a defensive posture that can be held for only the period of a short term crisis. In fact crises tend to be long drawn out. The pound sterling lost value against the dollar for two years or more in the middle 1980s without there being a decisive crisis. The dollar two years later followed the same pattern, losing value against sterling and more importantly the deutschmark and the yen. The only logical measure which could be taken by an international enterprise in such a situation was to pursue a policy inimical to the interests of the depreciating currency, for years if necessary, even where that currency was the one in which its assets were officially designated.

The third, and related, problem is that the original exposure techniques had been devised on the assumption that only one major currency was under threat at any one time. This was logical enough in a period of fixed currencies, when speculation against one currency required the purchase – and so the strengthening – of others. But it has become obvious that the fall of one currency will probably lead to defensive devaluations by others, and the situation has been much more complex; in a currency crisis today, several currencies move in relation to each other, and there is no easy defensive posture. Whatever the international enterprise does to protect itself probably exaggerates the instability of the current world monetary situation.

Initially the techniques which have been developed by the corporations have been designed simply to protect the financial assets of the corporation. From this point, however, it is but a short step to currency speculation, and the multinational corporation with access to substantial currency assets throughout the world is in a strong position to speculate, not merely from a defensive point of view, but in order to enhance its assets – and in the process it adds a further destabilizing element to the world financial scene.

PRICING IN THE INTERNATIONAL MARKET

In general terms the pricing policy for an international enterprise operating in foreign Western developed societies is not likely to be substantially different from those at home, or indeed those of a domestic enterprise. The policy is likely to be a cost-plus one, involving adding up all the costs and adding a mark-up, the 'plus': this 'plus' element of the cost-plus is likely to reflect the going rate in that particular industrial sector in that particular economy.

In the less developed world, different factors may apply, and that for three reasons. If an international enterprise operates a manufacturing assembly plant in a Third World economy, built on the proviso that imports will be excluded, then the enterprise will be operating in a seller's market. This does not mean, however, that the enterprise will necessarily be able to exploit something approaching a monopoly situation. What very often happens is the intervention of the second factor, namely government administered prices reached after negotiation. Almost inevitably, however, such prices are ludicrously low in terms of market demand and the result is a substantial black market where the real profit may be siphoned off to middlemen or corrupt officials. The third situation arises particularly in terms of imports, but may also be a response to the host government's awareness of pent-up demand creating a large market potential. The rate of tax level on the product may even be two or three times the actual cost of production and the price at which the consumer buys has only the remotest connection either with the cost structure of the enterprise or its profit objectives.

It is convenient, however, to look in more detail at some of the considerations affecting pricing policy. These can be listed as financial and political, which are intertwined, and marketing. It is not without significance that marketing tends, in many markets, to come last.

POLITICAL CONSIDERATIONS

The major factor here is the possibility of transfer pricing which a company may wish to practise either for tax or political purposes, in order, for example, to move funds into politically more acceptable areas. This may mean a multinational enterprise with its headquarters in an increasingly left wing dominated country moving funds abroad, in spite of official currency controls. Or more often a multinational company may discreetly reduce its commitments in a politically unstable host country by undervaluing the exports from that subsidiary to other subsidiaries in financially more sympathetic areas, or back to the home country of the enterprise.

FINANCIAL CONSIDERATIONS

There are three factors to be considered under this heading:

(a) the return on capital invested, particularly in terms of the cost of raising capital locally. This in turn is a function of the local rate of interest, the local rate of inflation and the foreign exchange rate. It is almost inevitable that for most of the time the rate of inflation in the countries where subsidiaries are located will be substantially different from that of the home country, and particularly when the capital has been raised abroad, e.g. either in the home country or on the European market there are problems of ensuring that the return is adequate.

(b) the contribution to overall overheads of the enterprise. This is an issue which goes to the heart of the financial operations of the international enterprise. If the subsidiary is to be anything but a marginal activity, it may be expected to contribute to general overheads, including research and development, wherever that may be taking place. This raises considerable political problems where, for example, the research and development produces technology or products which may not appear in the subsidiary for years. The technology being employed locally is not particularly novel and may have been phased out elsewhere. The host government, operating perhaps through a technology board as in Latin American countries, feels that the specific tariff is not worth paying for.

(c) the rate at which the capital investment is to be written off. This, in part at least, depends on the political judgement of the headquarters on political prospects within the marketplace. If the subsidiary is located in what is believed to be a politically unstable region, or nationalization is foreseen in the near future, the temptation will be to emphasize profits and profit repatriation at the expense of long term involvement. The situation may be complicated by limitations placed on profit repatriation, particularly by countries which have balance of payments problems. In this situation retained profits may be used to acquire more and more control of industry – a course which is likely to raise suspicions and local unpopularity, or the enterprise may be forced into ventures which are far away from its original interests. One of the more unusual examples of this is to be seen in Brazil, where the highly successful Volkswagen subsidiary, Volkswagen do Brazil, has been forced into the cattle raising business as a means of employing its blocked profits.

There is a further complication in the issue in that the rate at which capital investment is written off does not correspond to the technological situation or tax structure within the subsidiary, but is determined by the availability of equipment which is being phased out of an enterprise's operation somewhere else, e.g. at home, where the policy may be of scrapping equipment well before its physical life is ended, both because it is advantageous to do so and because of the intense competition prevailing in the market. The subsidiary may have to take over new equipment prematurely from its point of view, because its new equipment is the scrap of a more advanced plant elsewhere.

TAXATION ASPECTS OF INTERNATIONAL FINANCE

Taxation, and its avoidance or evasion, is one of the more contentious issues facing the international enterprise in its relationship with host governments. Although governments and public opinion may be sensitive to the issues of ensuring appropriate technology is being introduced into their society, or that a satisfying number of jobs are created locally, money is an issue that strikes home most readily, and an accusation that a foreign company is not paying its due share of taxation is more likely to arouse passion than more esoteric arguments about technology or jobs that might be created.

The situation is relatively simple when the international enterprise is operating very clearly within a simple domestic market with little or no export. Here the only basis for argument may be the issue of royalties for imported technology. But where the enterprise is engaged in cross-frontier activities on a large scale, in effect buying and selling to itself, in the form of components rather than complete products whose market price can be assessed independently, then the difficult problems about where potentially taxable value added occurs can give room for a good deal of argument between the international enterprise and the host government.

(a) From the viewpoint of the international enterprise, there are three steps open to it if it intends to maximize post-tax profits. First, it can choose the appropriate profit centre or centres on the basis of the relative tax structure of the countries in which it operates. The considerations which apply might be simply the low level of taxation in the profit centre country, or the existence of tax treaties with the enterprise's home country, which would ensure favourable treatment. Second, the enterprise then seeks to ensure that the products, or at least the invoicing of the sales, pass through that area at a point where the value added mark-up can be introduced.

There is sometimes an illogical but very human limitation to this process, namely the determination of executives in any part of the organization to present themselves as being highly efficient. The best measure of efficiency still remains the creation of profits, and there is a tendency for all managerial units to constitute themselves profit centres, if at all possible; to justify their existence and promotion. Consequently mark-ups may be insisted upon by any unit which is involved in the processing, even if it is only the processing of information, not the creation of anything physical, and this process takes place regardless of the overall interests of the enterprise on a worldwide scale.

The third step arises where there are practical limitations on the transfer of taxable value added, either because of the behaviour described above or because of resistance from the tax authorities, to the evasion of the tax base by these means. This consists of seeking out acceptable deductible expenses in terms of royalties, or interest charges.

To a large extent such manoeuvres imply the existence of a transfer price policy whereby the price being charged to the customer across the frontier varies, depending on whether the customer is an affiliate owned by the same enterprise or a completely independent company with no financial link.

(b) From the viewpoint of the government, whether host or home, the problem is to ascertain whether the pricing and value added policy of the enterprise appears to have been intended to lower the tax burden within its territory and, if so, to make its own estimate of what the taxation level ought to be on a domestic valuation. For the tax authorities in a developed society this is a difficult enough exercise. For the tax authorities in a less developed economy, it is an almost impossible task. The very suggestion that transfer pricing is being practised is in these circumstances a source of bitterness and ill will.

TAXATION PROBLEMS

In theory at least the principle of national taxation on the international enterprise is simple. There are a number of options open to the host government and the parent government in allocating taxation claims, but in the last resort, unless they have double taxation agreements, they can and will impose tax rates in exactly the same way as for a domestic enterprise.

The system would then work as follows. The host government would impose its taxation, and the bill would be met by the subsidiary of the multinational. The remaining profits might be retained in the host country or repatriated. The home government then has to decide whether to allow any tax paid in the host country as a tax credit, thereby reducing the tax burden, or simply as another deductible cost, before tax is assessed on the net profits. It would also have to decide whether to tax overseas profits in the year they were made, or the year in which they were repatriated: the particular set of rules applied by the home government would encourage or discourage foreign investment – e.g. the refusal of tax credits for overseas taxation or an insistence on profits being taxed whether they were repatriated or not would make overseas investment a much less attractive prospect.

The problem however is lack of knowledge by tax authorities of internal costing. Under a transfer price system, it is possible for an international enterprise to move goods across frontiers at fairly arbitrary prices unrelated to the real costs of their production, in order to reduce taxation in one country and pay it in another where the tax level is lower. There may be other reasons for transfer pricing, e.g. the evasion of capital movement controls, but the effect is the same anywhere in that, as has been remarked, a government, particularly if it is a Third World government with a relatively unsophisticated administrative machine to collect tax, feels it is being swindled of its due tax revenue.

One solution which is being canvassed is unitary taxation, i.e. the tax authorities in a country look at the overall global profits of the enterprise and demand what they would regard as their nation's *pro rata* share, regardless of where the profits officially have been made. Since countries are hardly likely to underestimate the contribution of their own nation, and since the countries which are effectively the profit centres are still likely to tax on declared profits in their own territory, an international enterprise may some day finish up with global tax demands exceeding its profits.

Unitary taxation as a concept was originally developed in California before World War II and became increasingly popular particularly in the 1970s. Political pressure from the federal government and multinationals both American and foreign brought about substantial changes amounting virtually to its abolition in California by the mid 1980s. But the principle remains an attractive one, the more so for companies lacking the sophisticated administrative machinery to undertake sophisticated tax assessment by other means.

TAXATION STRATEGY IN THE WIDER CONTEXT

It is, in theory at least, possible to conceive of an optimum taxation strategy which could be operated, so to speak, in a political vacuum to maximize the enterprise's profits. International enterprises, however, do not operate in a political vacuum. Quite apart from the hesitation an enterprise might feel at pushing its tax strategy against the national interests of a potentially hostile host government, there are other factors to be considered. The most obvious of these are those which relate to expected changes in the value of foreign based fixed assets or cash held in a particular currency. It may be desirable to liquidate assets in as short a time as possible in the face of official blocking action: the same surreptitious methods which might have a role in tax avoidance might equally be applied in this problem too – but with the flow being in a quite different direction from that which minimized taxation.

ACCOUNTANCY PRACTICES AND STANDARDS

In a curious sense accountancy practices and standards can be seen almost as an aspect of culture, with very profound implications for the structure of industry. The essential feature of an accounting practice might be said to be a culture's attitude towards its own government and the attitude towards meeting its tax demands. Some cultures appear to accept the legitimacy of government tax demands as unquestionable and have little difficulty in regarding deliberate attempts to withhold legal tax demands, not only as a crime, but a form of sin. This puritan attitude is not likely to be carried to an extreme. Some individuals will evade taxation, and the higher the level of taxation the more they will evade it, so that in any society a sufficiently high level of taxation will produce a 'black' non-taxed economy. But by and large it is assumed that while small companies and shops may be rather lax in their tax returns, large companies are expected to be honest, and the dishonest businessman who deliberately evades taxation is the exception, attracting little sympathy if he is caught and punished.

In other societies tax evasion is assumed to be the norm: there is no sense of wrongdoing in tax evasion, not only at the personal and small business level but also at the large corporate level. There are of course penalties if one is detected, but the crime is seen as technical rather than moral. There is in consequence a rule of conduct, unpublished but well understood, about bribery, tax evasion and how all the mechanics must be handled to ensure, for example, that the instigator of the tax evasion is not likely to put their signature to instructions which would leave them open to blackmail by their agents in the activity, and so on.

There is probably a fairly high correlation between the acceptance of tax evasion as a moral crime at one extreme and a technical offence like illegal parking of one's car at the other, and the standard of accounting practices. In some societies one can believe a company balance sheet; in other societies there may be two or three balance sheets, and their corresponding company accounts, depending on the use to which the information is to be put.

There are a number of important consequences of which two are of particular significance to the international enterprise. First, people will not invest in the equity shares if they have no confidence in the accuracy of the published figures. A flourishing stock exchange implies a high standard of accuracy and honesty in reporting. This incidentally is why, apart from other cultural inhibitions to the purchase of equity shares, it is not too easy to create a stock exchange as a means of funnelling savings into industry in a society where tax evasion, bribery and any other practice which cannot be presented openly in accounts is the norm. A number of the stock exchanges which are at present being opened in Third World countries are highly unlikely to have any great success because a potential investor without inside knowledge and access to the true state of the company's affairs would be unwise to invest. The only shares which are likely to be freely traded are subsidiaries of foreign enterprises with a reputation to maintain.

The second consequence is the considerable difficulty that international companies are likely to experience if they have to publish accounts in different parts of the world. To publish accurate figures in some countries would merely invite swingeing tax demands from tax authorities who automatically assume that any published figures are tactical bids in a bazaar bargaining process. To publish false figures in a society where tax evasion is regarded as a crime is to invite disaster.

The international enterprise has therefore every incentive to encourage standardization of tax accounts, and even the requirement for the divulging of more and more information. Within the European Economic Community, attempts are being made to raise the standards throughout to those of the highest, but the problems even in a relatively homogeneous area like western Europe are enormous. On a worldwide basis the problems are well-nigh insoluble in the foreseeable future, for what is implied is not merely a raising of standards, but a change in cultural values. Where both OECD and the UN are seeking standardization and a well respected body like the International Accounting Standards Committee set up standards, harmonization and standard practices on disclosure of financial information is very much a pipe dream.

The UN report on International Standards of Accounting and Reporting for Transnational Corporations, published in 1977, contains unexceptionable statements of ideals, but in the absence of universal and effective enforcement at national level, it is likely to remain an ideal rather than a sanction.

Part VI

Government Attitudes to Multinational Companies

Introduction

This section is written essentially from the point of view of national governments and particularly host governments which have to decide on what, if any, terms they will allow foreign companies to operate within their territories. In relation to the awesome power of a national government of even a medium sized economy like Britain, most international companies might appear relatively weak. But the evidence suggests that because companies have a clearer idea of what they want than do the national governments with which they deal, the companies often emerge as winners in any negotiations. Companies present a consistent policy; national governments may be riddled with conflicting interests and prone to short term expediences.

Finally, notwithstanding the growing attempts at the international level to present a common front in dealing with international enterprises, the evidence available thus far suggests that international organizations are even less successful than national governments in dealing with these companies. This section considers why this is so, and what, if anything, might be done about it.

7 The Pros and Cons of Direct Foreign Investment

INTRODUCTION

Hindsight is always a major problem in historical exposition. In the context of direct foreign investment in the United Kingdom or most other countries it is possible to impute a degree of rationality and planning both on the part of the foreign enterprises and the British government which simply did not exist at the time the key decisions were made.

It is possible to see the actions of many of the foreign enterprises which invested in the United Kingdom or elsewhere in western Europe after World War II as shortsighted. The decisions which were most significant in the long run were probably made as a response to short term problems, i.e. assembly or manufacturing locally were a means of overcoming currency restrictions which were in the event to disappear very quickly. The problems which dictated policy had in many instances disappeared even before the policy could be implemented, and manufacturing capacity came 'on stream' in a brand new situation.

In the same way it can be argued that most governments' policy on direct foreign investment was short term expediency in the late 1940s and early 1950s, which, until very recently, was never rethought. Direct foreign investment was a 'good thing' almost regardless of its nature or purpose. Obsessed initially with very acute foreign exchange problems and the memory of pre-war dole queues, post-war western European governments reacted uncritically to overtures from foreign companies: computers or candyfloss, it mattered little; the only problem was an internal political one of different parts of the country attempting to secure the new factories, so much of whose costs were in any event going to be borne by central government, not the local community. It is however necessary to consider the types of industry which in the event have been or are being attracted into western Europe, and analyse their pros and cons accordingly. A useful categorization of foreign investment in the present context might be in a fourfold grouping.

221

The first group comprises the highly technologically oriented industries whose rate of change and development can only be described as exponential, e.g. data processing, aerospace technology and the like. The prospects of new and substantial foreign investment in this area are limited. And, just as important, in any of this group of industries research and development, for example, is likely to be confined to the parent company or at the very least dovetailed into a research project whose overall results would be available only at headquarters in another country.

There is in this group a very real dilemma for the host government in deciding its attitude to foreign investment. If it wishes its industry to have available the latest technology, it ends up subsidizing very expensive and ultimately non-commercial research and development whose results cannot easily be applied – where indeed the product which is ultimately created is a national status symbol rather than a commercial proposition; or it permits foreign control and continuing dependence on an outside source for vital technology. There is probably no solution – certainly the problems of western European computer or aerospace technology are far from being solved even if they have been kept largely out of foreign ownership and control.

The second group of industries includes those which require large investment and mass production, but where technology is no particular problem in the sense that there are competing locally owned enterprises; moreover, the dynamism has largely gone out of the situation. Their characteristic is defined by this slowing down of technology – year by year designs and products are refined but no revolutionary breakthrough is likely. Examples are to be found in the car industry and sections of the engineering industry. The appearance of the Japanese car manufacturers in the UK and USA, for example, has not produced technologically pioneering models – only very high quality traditional models. These industries are not dependent on research and development from the headquarters company overseas – the subsidiary can and will, when necessary, produce to its own designs. The major threat of loss of technology comes, for example, from further delegation by an American headquarters towards increased Europeanization, so that a local subsidiary is only a part of a European operation, not a self-contained enterprise, i.e. cars are now being designed for a European market, perhaps designed in one country but produced wholly or partly elsewhere.

Overall, the contribution of foreign enterprises in this group is in terms of job creation not new technology or export earning. In practice, exports are becoming less significant in two ways. There is a tendency for production, e.g. of cars, to be set up in traditional export markets in the Third World; completed products are initially replaced by the export of kits to be assembled locally, and, as more and more components are fabricated locally, exports from the traditional suppliers are phased out. Second, a tendency to Europeanize production facilities implies that export markets can be gained by or lost to any of the national subsidiaries through a directive from the non-European headquarters which is seeking to maximize benefits from European production facilities as a whole, rather than from individual national units. It may in this situation be necessary for government policy to take counter-measures. In the present context however it is enough to note that foreign ownership is not too significant – although it is desirable from the host government viewpoint that a competitive locally owned segment remains.

The third group are the processed or convenience products, which originated mainly in the USA and were then produced locally by the foreign enterpriser. This includes processed foods, soft drinks, cleaners, cosmetics and traditional pharmaceuticals insofar as these are produced by companies which are not sufficiently pioneering to be included in the first group. In some instances the incomers also buy over traditional local companies in the same or related lines, which however continue to operate under their old brand names. Two characteristics may be noted about enterprises in this group. In spite of the advertising and promotional claims, research and development in a genuine sense is relatively unimportant and is related more to advertising needs than genuine improvement. Secondly, such research and development as exists has no real economic or political significance and in this respect there is no obvious requirement for a specific government policy unless, for example, health factors are involved.

Export earnings are in practice small. The characteristic of many products is that they reverse the normal pattern of value added output, i.e. the finished product may be bulkier and travel less well than the original raw materials – a characteristic which is exaggerated by the dubious packaging techniques often employed, intended to give the appearance of quantity rather than the reality.

The only major exception on exporting appears to arise in the case of the traditional local companies taken over by the foreign enterprise. They may have established small 'up market' segments in areas where for example British influence and tastes were once important.

Although on balance these industries contribute little to real wealth creation their objectionable features arise rather from their nature and promotion and distribution methods, than from ownership. The foreign control of such industries threatens no significant host government interest.

The final group of industries in this classification are those with a significant but not overwhelming pattern of technology which is developing, but is in the event unlikely to prove as inordinately expensive as in the first group. The characteristic of such an industry which is most likely to affect government policy is that there is effectively no domestic industry in this field largely because the markets for its products have not been readily accessible to local manufacturers. Few industries have developed spontaneously in countries which do not have an adequate domestic market or easy access to a substantial market, and a condition for the creation of these industries 'from scratch', so to speak, must be the appearance of a new market opportunity.

The most obvious examples in the United Kingdom or Norway are the 'spin-off' industries from North Sea oil. The only country with substantial experience of offshore exploration was the USA, and it is not surprising therefore that the American companies tended to predominate in the early stages and still, nearly two decades later, represent a significant factor in the industry.

It can be argued that if such opportunities ever arise again in the future, government policy might ensure that foreign technology was diffused rapidly to local companies, e.g. by requiring joint ventures or licensing rather than permitting wholly owned foreign companies to scoop the new market. In the event, for example, British companies have proved to be relatively successful in the offshore oil field, even in the absence of such a well defined policy. Within a few years British or Norwegian technology in these fields has matched American, and has in turn become a marketable commodity in world markets. Arguably, however, this process might have been quicker and more complete if government policy had been positively directed to achieving this end.

The adaptability of such technology however highlights a weakness. The technology involved amounts as much to operational experience as to scientific development. It can therefore equally well be absorbed from British or Norwegian companies by the next country to find itself with a new market.

In defining the aim of host government policy in this situation, it might be expressed baldly as accelerating the diffusion of knowledge and experience into their local industry via international companies but equally checking diffusion in the other direction. This is in very approximate terms what Japanese government policy has been achieving – with remarkable success.

THE REGULATION OF FOREIGN COMPANIES

The legal framework

Historically in most Western developed industrial countries there has been no distinction between domestic and foreign controlled companies. Much legislation which affects foreign companies can only be described as very oblique in its intentions. A major theme of this section will be that both government policy and legislation relating to international business either preceded current problems or was framed with other purposes in mind.

To take but one example of a Western country which is very subject to investment activities by foreign companies, namely the UK: the main relevant legislation for some 30 years after World War II derived from the need to control capital transfers out of the UK, in the immediate post-war years by putting wartime controls on a peacetime footing. The Exchange Control Act of 1947 contained the first relevant peacetime provisions on the regulation of foreign controlled enterprises. *Inter alia*, the Act limited the transfer of British owned enterprises to foreign control, and the right of foreign owned enterprises to borrow money within the United Kingdom or sterling area territories. In effect these provisions would ensure that if British companies were taken over the financial assets realized would still be subject to exchange control, and that foreign companies could be required to bring in more foreign exchange to finance their British operations. Additionally foreign takeovers of British companies, like any other takeovers, could result in a reference to the Monopolies Commission or similar bodies if the takeover appeared to limit competition substantially. By the time of the effective abolition of exchange controls in the late 1970s the political and economic scene had changed out of all recognition; but with the abolition of these controls went the major control on foreign companies.

In practice, even in the 30 years of its existence, the foreign exchange and monopoly legislation was liberally interpreted, since the British government was anxious to encourage foreign, particularly

American, investment. Very considerable foreign direct investment did in the event take place in the next quarter century. Its nature will be discussed later but the most significant feature of the investment was that a good deal was directed into the development of assisted regions where old industry was in decline and unemployment was high. Such investment attracted government finance under the various regional policy schemes, or through specific aid provisions.

A second major thread of government legislation was therefore to be found in regional incentive schemes, often appearing in finance bills at budget time, and in various Industry Acts. These had wide provisions to pump public money into schemes to assist industry in depressed regions. Other countries within the European Community had similar regional legislation; in the case of federal states, most obviously the USA, but also other federations or confederations like Canada and Australia, legislation tends to be passed at the state level.

The third thread has been legislation creating parastatal organizations intended in the British case by the Labour governments of the 1960s, but in other parts of Europe a generation earlier, as we have seen, to increase state control of the industrial sector.

The fourth major thread in western Europe has been the advent of EC policy. It is as yet too early to predict the precise effects, but two issues will probably loom large. It will in the long run be impossible to make any distinction between EC companies and companies incorporated in individual member countries. The distinction, if any, will be between EC and non-EC companies.

The other EC issue is the confusion which now exists on regional policies – not merely the EC regional policy, such as it is, but the continued readiness of national governments to compete against each other for foreign investment. As has been suggested, regional policy remains a potent instrument in host government policy towards foreign companies. If a comprehensive EC policy emerges it will affect the ability of member governments to use their traditional instruments to influence or control foreign companies and their operations in member states.

CONTROL OF THE INTERNATIONAL ENTERPRISE IN THE LESS DEVELOPED WORLD

The situation on regulation and control in the less developed countries is not so clear cut. It has already been argued in Chapter 3 that the drive for local ownership, partial or complete, indigenization, etc., can be seen as a recognition of the fact that the most practical method of control in less developed countries is through ownership. It is not necessary to re-examine this argument, but it is worth elaborating some issues raised earlier on a second method of control, namely the use of technology boards which evaluate the relevance of foreign technology being imported, and at the same time relating this phenomenon of the technology board with another, and apparently quite unrelated phenomenon, also already discussed, namely the growth of legislation in these countries, relating to training and institutes for translating such legislation into positive results.

It has been suggested that there seems to be a surprising lack of co-ordination between technology and training requirements in many less developed countries. Arguably to co-ordinate these activities would go far to bring a degree of national control on the foreign enterprises, in a relatively simple manner.

ADVANTAGES AND DISADVANTAGES OF DIRECT FOREIGN INVESTMENT

The remainder of this chapter will examine some of the conventional pros and cons of direct investment in a host government by foreign firms – in part at least by reference to the fourfold categorization already established earlier. It is necessary to examine the issues in a fairly rigid structure: in this case first the pros and then the cons. In real life, however, such a neat dichotomy scarcely exists: the same issues may have both advantages and disadvantages, with the net balance difficult to assess. It is virtually impossible to quantify and effectively evaluate political and national goals. In the last analysis a decision may have to start from a received political premise about how much private or public enterprise a nation should accept: whether foreign ownership of part of industry is intrinsically undesirable, and so on. What is rather surprising is the evidence that many governments in, for example, western Europe do not appear to have defined these political premises, let alone the consequences. The present situation, as has been suggested, is an aggregate of the consequences of particular situations – in some cases reactions to a particular crisis, in others inertia. A major theme of this chapter is that the unwillingness or inability of successive governments to decide what it is that they

wish from foreign enterprises has prevented them maximizing the pros
and minimizing the cons.

Advantages

Many of these have been implie in earlier comments: they can most
usefully be made explicit under three general headings, namely job
creation, transfer of knowledge and foreign exchange implications,
and will be examined in turn under these headings.

a.   Job creation

When direct investment involves a 'greenfield' operation, i.e. building
and operating a new plant as opposed to buying over an existing local
company, the job opportunities are immediate and obvious – first, in
the building operation, and in the longer term in the new employment
created by the factory.

As has been seen, direct foreign investment frequently is directed
into the regional areas suffering from industrial depression, ideally job
replacement being phased in as older traditional industries shed
labour. There are two aspects of regional policy: one negative, the
other positive. The negative aspect is simply the prohibition of new
plant or substantial extensions to existing plant in areas of relatively
high employment. The positive is the use of generous subsidies.

The net result is that, although a new foreign enterprise may provide
jobs, a significant part of the cost is still met by the local taxpayer if the
enterprise is sited in a development region: generally speaking,
governments encourage incomers to go into these regions of high
unemployment if there is no positive case for a site in the more
convenient, more dynamic industrial regions. Nevertheless, even if
the foreign enterprise is only partly the cause of new jobs, it is a
necessary part.

What is less clear about the establishment of the new enterprise is
whether it dovetails into government policy as neatly as is sometimes
assumed. Development areas are in economic difficulties because
traditional industries, which have shaped the infrastructure and
created the whole ambience of a region, are in decline, and this is very
clearly observed in the problems of the north of England, and Scotland
and Wales. Moreover, the traditional industries tend to have been
male dominated, involving highly specialized skills which may not be
easily adapted and which are also physically demanding. It is hard to

judge whether or not an ex-shipyard worker or miner can readily be fitted into a new industry where a prime qualification might be manual dexterity such as is more readily found in women, and where physical conditions are quite different. Some men will adapt quickly, others will be quite unable to make the adjustment. In many modern industries brought, for example, into Europe by American or Japanese enterprises, most of the jobs could be equally well done by women as by men. The tradition of time served skills and rigid demarcation may not be very appropriate to a new factory in a new industry using new technology. The newcomer may also give preference to skilled tradespeople, who could in any event more easily get jobs elsewhere, rather than the unskilled for whom no other jobs are available. A man or woman who has learned one skill, however irrelevant to the new job, is more obviously trainable, while a person who has never had any formal apprenticeship is a more uncertain quantity. This phenomenon of the trainable rather than the available manpower being employed goes a stage further. New foreign companies are rather more exotic and glamorous than the local establishments and may therefore be more attractive to the more adventurous – or those with the most initiative in the available labour force – who see the new jobs as having increased prospects. Thus the effect may be that while governments anticipate that the unemployed will be found jobs, it may in many instances be the already employed who will come forward. Such job hunters appear better prospects for the recruiting company precisely because these are so obviously employable. Given the choice between hiring someone already with a proved record of being able to hold a job and an unemployed person, the recruiting company will exercise common sense rather than consider whether this is really what the host government wants. Admittedly, in most instances, a job vacancy will be created a stage further back and an unemployed person may get a job in turn. It is, however, a fact of life that jobs are most easily abolished when vacant. The local company, losing personnel, may simply do with fewer, especially when it counts the cost of retraining a less skilled person, and fewer jobs are actually created than appeared likely. Indeed, bearing in mind the onerous conditions attached to shedding surplus labour under the employment protection legislation in various parts of Europe, the prospect of workers giving up their jobs voluntarily may be welcome to some employers.

There are other implications outside the scope of this study: a lowering of skills in the local companies; embarrassment to them in having to recruit and retrain; higher wage levels and expectations being created by the newcomers, which make life more difficult not only for the local companies but also the government, attempting to restrain wage demands based on the comparability argument.

Notwithstanding the qualifications which have to be made and the danger of oversimplifying what is really happening when new jobs are created, there can be little doubt that, as a means of creating new employment, the introduction of new industries by direct foreign investment can be very effective.

The situation in a greenfield operation, then, is reasonably clearcut. Either brand-new jobs are being created or at the very least productive functions and jobs at a second stage are being transferred into the economy by the foreign enterprise. The situation where the foreign enterprise enters the market by buying over a local firm is more complex. In the first instance, if the bought-over company is outside a designated area of high unemployment attracting government aid, the company is free from the constraints of having to settle in what it might regard as an unnecessarily remote region. It will not of course be able to secure the government grants and concessions available under regional policy, but by definition the advantage inherent in its location ought to be equal to the concessions given to locate in the regions.

Are new jobs likely to be created? There is no easy answer. Presumably the incoming enterprise hopes to do rather better than the existing company and would therefore anticipate expansion, unless the attraction has been the market rather than the production facilities available. Rationalization may follow and the new subsidiary might in fact be allowed to run down, so that its markets could be served by others; or it may simply become an assembly plant, with research and development and the core production facilities being based in another country. Conversely another subsidiary might have its markets increased at the expense of plants owned by the foreign enterprise elsewhere.

In summary, then, greenfield operations almost certainly on balance create new jobs, albeit at some cost to the local taxpayer; and the gain in jobs is net rather than gross. The musical chairs effect of people changing jobs may be that vacancies created in some other company may not be filled. When existing companies are bought over the situation is not so clearcut. It may well be that this is an area where government policy on foreign direct investment warrants reconsideration.

b. The generation and transfer of knowledge

The second major argument commonly advanced in favour of direct foreign investment is that of knowledge generation and transfer: namely that an international enterprise which has originated or at least applied a body of knowledge in one part of the world is almost uniquely endowed to apply it elsewhere. 'Knowledge transfer' in its normal context is largely what is popularly known as 'technology transfer', now regarded almost as the panacea which will close the technology and wealth gap between developed nations and underdeveloped. Knowledge transfer as used here, however, also applies more generally, from prestigious technologically based research and development to the more mundane areas of marketing techniques and less definable attitude change among managers and shopfloor workers. It is, nevertheless, convenient to treat technology as the more important issue before following on to what might roughly be defined as marketing knowhow and cultural change.

Technology Precisely because technology is something of which everyone is supposed to approve, it often happens that the context is rather ill defined, as has been illustrated earlier. Technology may include not only the dynamic new industries, data processing, space technology, new materials and drugs and the like, such as are outlined in the first group of industries listed at the beginning of the chapter, but more mundane details of new methods of production, labour saving devices which can be incorporated into existing production lines and so on, as suggested in the third group. In passing, it is worth noting that there is sometimes a problem for less technologically advanced societies in absorbing new industries or techniques. It can happen that a new industry or process is too advanced for a society in that, while personnel can be trained to apply the technique, the back-up infrastructure is not available: at the other extreme there is always the possibility that a government unfamiliar with the technology available may approve the payment of excessive royalties for what is in effect 'old hat' technology. It is to counter this problem that the investment and technology boards discussed earlier have been set up in some Third World countries.

In the case of most countries in western Europe, however, these problems do not exist to any serious degree. It is difficult to envisage a new technology being developed out of the blue in another industrially advanced country where the knowledge could not be readily absorbed and, if necessary, put to use in another advanced country. Where technology transfer has probably most advantage is in the areas of high research and development costs of the first group, where simply to keep a viable industry going might involve an annual expenditure of hundreds of millions of dollars or the local equivalent. In this sense, if the stakes are simply too high for a privately owned enterprise in a small to medium sized industrial country to keep up to date, and the government is unwilling to finance original research, then technological transfer is a second best, where the third best is progressive obsolescence.

How useful or necessary is foreign direct investment as a means of promoting technological knowhow in such countries? There is no ready answer but there are two alternatives to consider.

The first might be described as a polite variant on the pirating of ideas, discussed earlier in the book. Many new developments arise in one country more or less by chance, as has been instanced in the earlier discussion on the concept of the international product life cycle. A technological breakthrough depends on a particular level of technology already available, together with a perceived need. Enterprises in several countries are probably working independently to solve the problems. Even if the breakthrough had not come in the particular country when it did, it is certain that it would have come elsewhere within a very short time. No individual, national or company genius was the *sine qua non* of the aeroplane, car, jet engine, television, transistor, etc. In this situation it is a matter of pride simply to have been the first. It follows therefore that once a process is shown to be possible it can be repeated in another state with a similar level of technology, and that without simply pirating the process. Once a method has been achieved of accomplishing something, alternative methods can often be found which do not involve simply slavish duplication. Designing one's own product from scratch can be more expensive than simply copying: but it is infinitely less expensive than first establishing whether such a product can be developed in the first instance. The major barriers, technological and psychological, have been breached. Even simply buying a rival product, taking it to pieces and trying to improve rather than imitate is a vastly different business from researching the technological unknown. The only criterion here is expense. If it is cheaper to adapt and improve than originate, it may be cheaper still to let the original enterprise do the adaptation and improving as well.

More direct than adaptation is imitation by consent, i.e. licensing the right to manufacture. Any government is sovereign within its own frontiers and can lay down its own requirements about patent protection. Japan is a classic example *par excellence* on the exploitation of foreign technology, almost exclusively American, which was used to build up a very high quality of industrial output and a staggering rate of growth of GNP. In the early post-war years individual British enterprises which were farseeing enough to obtain technological knowhow from American companies which were not at that time interested in foreign investment have enjoyed a large measure of success: there are conversely a number of instances where American licensors subsequently lived to regret the decision to grant a licence instead of entering the market more directly.

With all those qualifications it has to be said that countries like the United Kingdom have absorbed very considerable amounts of technology, not only from foreign subsidiaries directly but as a spillover effect: manpower trained by the incoming company but available to local companies, skills in ancillary industries and the like. It must be recognized that there were alternative policies, although these are most easily perceived in hindsight, and no longer exist. It is too late for Britain to become another Japan, even if this were seen as desirable.

Marketing knowhow   An area where foreign controlled enterprises have substantially established themselves is where the problem is not so much of technology but of marketing and timing. The enterprise which has developed products and markets in different countries throughout the world is likely to have the ability to judge when a product which has been developed elsewhere can most usefully be brought on to a new market in a host country, and even to judge the extent to which it can force the pace in a market to the point that what had hitherto been a consumer luxury passes into a mass consumption stage. This is most obviously seen in consumer goods, but it may translate, in industrial terms, into the launching of a new technological development by creating, earlier than anticipated, a mass market.

The phenomenon is most obviously seen in the third group type of industry at present dominated by American companies: the convenience foods and many of the appurtenances of the so-called consumer society. The major criticism of these enterprises is contained in the phrase 'consumer society' which has become somewhat of a term of abuse.

In the last analysis, however, most of these products are marginal luxuries: the real problem is not the technology of the cornflake – it is in part at least the inability to apply the urgency of the marketing techniques of the comparatively trivial consumer goods to those industries which create a more solid industrial base for prosperity.

Cultural transfer   Finally in this issue there is the problem of cultural transfer, insofar as this can be considered an advantage. What is involved is the ability of the foreign enterprise to challenge and break set ways – to create, for example, a new relationship between management, workers and the community, nearer to the pattern of the home country – an issue discussed in part in Chapter 5. A new attitude would not necessarily diminish the inevitable sense of conflict between management and labour but could eliminate some of the irrelevances and mutual incomprehensions which can arise from a rather rigid class and educational background such as exists in some countries like the United Kingdom. This is not to say that American, German or Japanese styles of management are inevitably better than the British. Insofar, however, as the foreign enterprises operating in Britain are largely drawn from cultures whose economic successes are greater than that of the United Kingdom, there is at least a case for arguing that if the United Kingdom is to find a way out of the political and economic deadlock which bedevils so much of it, it could do far worse than consider the practices and attitudes of these foreign enterprises in their home territories.

A strong but largely unstated argument in the 1960s and early 1970s for Britain joining the European Common Market was an awareness of the painful contrast between the success of most EC economies compared with our own, and the assumption that almost by 'sympathetic magic', a phenomenon discussed earlier, success would rub off if Britain joined. It did not: the lesson is perhaps that it takes more than mere association, i.e. a willingness to learn by study and selective application of what is most usefully copied from foreign companies in our midst.

c.   *Foreign exchange implications*

The third advantage which is claimed for the introduction of direct foreign investment is its implications for foreign exchange earnings. At its simplest the argument runs thus: the initial direct investment will bring in an infusion of foreign capital; since it is highly probable that the foreign subsidiary will produce locally what had previously been imported, the import drain on foreign exchange will be correspondingly reduced; and finally a foreign owned enterprise, being by its nature internationally oriented, will in many cases rapidly become an exporter – in some instances even exporting back into the home market of the enterprise. There is some evidence that a number of American enterprises are now supplying their home markets in this way, reducing their home operations virtually to a marketing activity, backed up by research and development, but with sourcing of finished products from Britain and elsewhere.

As against this inflow of foreign exchange has to be set only the repatriation of profits and possibly the payment of royalties for research and development work carried out by the parent enterprise at home.

It will now be necessary to examine in rather more detail the various elements of advantage and disadvantage in the equation, and particularly the capital structure which may evolve. In general, a wholly foreign owned subsidiary will seek to establish as a long term situation that the fixed capital assets are clearly attributable in ownership to the parent company but that working capital will, where possible, be raised locally.

Import substitution   There has been a tendency in recent years to emphasize the distinction between an operation which is essentially an import saver and one which, from the outset, is intended for export: the difference is probably of kind rather than merely of degree.

On the surface the idea of local manufacture, if only for a domestic market, looks attractive to the host government, which sees an initial injection of capital followed by foreign exchange savings on replaced imports; to the local customer who prefers to deal with a producer who can offer on the spot advice and maintenance, and is readily available if things go wrong; and to the general public which, apart from the new job creation aspect, probably prefers the idea of a local product rather than a foreign import.

There are, however, likely to be a number of drawbacks. In some instances, particularly in the early stages of production when teething troubles may arise, the local product may not be as reliable as the longer established import: this however is a common enough experience for all new products, not those merely affecting foreign owned subsidiaries. More serious in the long run is that local production in the new subsidiary is likely to be on a smaller scale for a smaller local market, with a consequent rise in unit cost and price, even where production costs seemed likely to be lower. The customers find themselves paying more than they had before for the import and possibly also being offered a smaller choice. In some instances, and this may be part of the deal between enterprise and host government, there will be protection against competitors by tariffs or import licensing. Again, however, this is a problem of any infant industry, not merely production by a foreign owned subsidiary.

To what extent would or does local production work to the disadvantage of the individual customer in the host country? The answer is that he or she probably suffers fewer of the disadvantages in a developed country whose markets are open to foreign penetration, since in normal circumstances no post-war government, dependent on a high level of exports and, as has been noted earlier, with membership of GATT to consider, could impose tariffs or other controls simply as a device to attract local investment. Consumers may find their choice relatively limited but would almost certainly have the option of buying alternative products, including imports. In this sense, import saving investment of this sort will be the exception rather than the rule. If a government cannot or will not give increased protection to the local producer in a market which is in any event becoming steadily less and less promising, then investment, if it comes, is as likely to be export oriented as much as domestic market oriented.

Export earning   Compared with import savings projects, an investment which is intended from the outset to serve an overseas market is almost an unqualified benefit to the national economy as a whole and to domestic consumers as individuals.

There are two possibilities. More rarely, a plant will be set up by a foreign company simply to supply its factories or outlets elsewhere. Reference has already been made to this practice, and it may well be that recent purchases of British companies by some continental manufacturer when sterling was at its lowest were of this sort. In this situation the domestic British market is relatively unimportant or non-existent, save for 'export rejects'. In this context, and given a realistic exchange rate based on productive capacity rather than on artificially strong petro currency, Britain would be seen as on a par with Portugal or Finland – almost a European Hong Kong of sorts.

The foreign exchange earnings of this type of operation may not, however, be as great as might be supposed. This issue of transfer pricing is discussed in more detail elsewhere but in the meantime it can be noted that if the main sales outlet is the company's headquarters company, it is relatively easy to ensure that minimal prices are levied so as to ensure that the profits accrue at home.

More generally, however, an export oriented operation will take account of the remaining importance of the domestic market, if unit costs are to be lowered sufficiently to make exporting profitable. In this situation the local consumer almost certainly gains: almost by definition the quality of the product has to match the best of international standards, the price is kept comparatively low because of competition, real or potential, ensured by low tariffs. There are in fact only two qualifications to be made: first, that if exporting is based on any form of marginal costing local customers may have to bear more than a proportional share of overheads, with the point already noted that free competition gives them an alternative supplier if price is pitched too high; secondly, they may be offered a product designed essentially for foreign customers – which again they are not forced by lack of choice, to buy.

Notwithstanding these two qualifications, the presence of foreign export oriented subsidiaries confers substantial benefits. At the very least the consumer is not worse off for the additional choice in the marketplace which the subsidiary confers.

The advantages may in the future be increased by a significant change in government policy. This is the practice followed by the British government in dealing with Japanese investment, for example, of making permission to build and the payment of any government subvention conditional on export performance; although it has to be added that any implied bargain of this sort could hardly be enforced in a court of law, without the British government running the risk of flouting its EC commitments by, in effect, subsidizing exports.

Disadvantages

Because of the notoriety which has attached in recent years to international companies, particularly the multinationals, it is not hard to find a large number of sticks with which to beat these enterprises, some of which were outlined in the introduction. It is however more difficult to examine some of these charges dispassionately, largely because the assertions cannot be easily verified or disproved. Some of the major issues are laid out below in more detail.

a. *Loss of national sovereignty*

A point was made earlier about the growing significance of state intervention in industry, and in the establishment, if not the successful fulfilment, of national plans. Certainly anyone who believes in the importance of a social market economy cannot but be concerned about the degree of national planning, much of it divorced, in the event, from reality. There may therefore be an element of *Schadenfreude* in comments at the extent to which international companies can free themselves from the restraints of national planning. The basic arguments are well enough rehearsed to require little comment. If an overall strategy is laid down for an international company which has its headquarters outside the host country, it is not surprising that the role allocated to the subsidiary in a global strategy may not be what a national plan would like. Export markets might, as has been suggested, be re-allocated arbitrarily by an American headquarters which was not happy about the performance of a European or Asian subsidiary or which found the host government overly hostile.

Over and above broad issues of policy there are very practical issues of day by day behaviour. Some of these alluded to below will be dealt with in more detail later but the major problem revolves round the issue of transfer pricing. This arises from the fact that the international company not only has different branches or subsidiaries in different countries, but in many instances trades with itself, i.e. buying and selling between these branches. In other instances it may have production facilities in one country, but a marketing organization elsewhere, so that while the former actually fills foreign orders the revenues pass through the latter. Since such measures can be carried out by the so-called transfer price system already discussed, i.e. the book value of sales within the organization can be shown at a different price than would prevail 'at arm's length' if the products were being sold to an outsider, it is very difficult for a national government readily to detect whether transfer pricing is taking place, particularly if there is no independent check in the form of comparable products being offered in a free market. How does one value components or semi-processed materials? The national government may find such practices objectionable for a number of reasons. Some of which have been discussed in an earlier chapter. Three examples of these are:

i. Currency controls   Currency controls are now part and parcel of national planning in some areas of the world, and it was a significant example of the 1979 British conservative government's aversion to its predecessors' planning methods that it rapidly abolished exchange control after some 40 years of the practice. A blurring of the distinction between current and capital transactions means that an international company can to some extent evade controls, can move its capital out of a politically hostile or economically shaky country to a degree which would be impossible for a private individual or a domestic company.

ii. Tariffs   To a smaller degree the same problem arises with tariff valuation. The declared value of products being imported is not necessarily the sole means of valuation available to customs authority. But unfamiliar unidentifiable components being shipped in may have to be taken at the declared valuation, and transfer pricing together with the decision taken about the profit markup discussed next, gives room for some freedom of action by the enterprise.

iii. Taxation   The same device of transfer pricing may be applied to ensure that the profit in any transaction accrues to whichever of the branches of the international company bears the least tax burden. In real life, however, the international enterprise may have any machiavellian tendencies towards tax avoidance frustrated by the ambitions of management at branch level. Insofar as profit is possibly the only objective measure of efficiency, these managers will wish to show their own organization in the best light by accumulating profits, adding large markups even in inter-company transactions, regardless of whether it makes overall financial sense that the operation becomes a profit centre.

It is perhaps some consolation to the hard-pressed civil servant that these three considerations may point to different strategies, and that the international enterprise does not always act rationally as a global monolith. Nevertheless all of the practices limit national control which governments increasingly seek to impose and which they may successfully impose on domestic companies.

Finally in this preliminary survey of the problems posed by a degree of freedom from national government control, it is instructive to consider the operation of price controls imposed by British governments in the middle 1970s by the conservative Heath government in 1972/3 and reinforced by the labour government of 1974. In brief the Price Commission operated on the principle that price increases had to be justified by cost increases: only certain types of increased costs could be passed on as price increases and even then a proportion had to be absorbed by the company. There was no reference to whether the profits hitherto accruing had any social justification – although the labour government normally waxed strong on such issues. Moreover, there was a significant element of bluff in the whole operation in that the Price Commission simply had no means of examining the cost structure of most companies. But the vast gap in the whole system arose from exports and imports. Britain was not a nice bureaucratically tidy closed economy. Exports had to be exempted because it was clearly in the national interest that prices should be raised if at all possible to earn more foreign exchange: imports were exempt because these costs were outside the control of the importer, and the whole of these costs could be passed on to the purchaser in the form of increased prices. The result was, of course, that international companies, whether British based or foreign based, could ignore the controls if they chose. As long as the company could keep ownership while it passed goods over a frontier they were exempt. It mattered little whether the same goods flowed out as exports and back as imports or more discreetly that British supplies were diverted into a foreign market as exports while the customary supplies for that market become British imports.

It is fortunate for the more bureaucratic British governments that British managers were by and large law abiding, that they appear to have followed the spirit as well as the letter of the law. Suppose, however, that a left wing government took over in Britain in the early 1990s and decided to re-impose price controls. How would the foreign owned companies behave? There is no reason, however, to suppose that a foreign company would feel any great inhibition about seeking such loopholes in the bureaucratic walls which ill considered legislation creates. In the last analysis national planning of the sort that traditional labour governments attempt, cannot easily cope with the manoeuvrability of international companies, save in terms of a siege economy backed up by draconian legislation. Whether or not this is a cause for joy or sorrow depends, of course, on one's opinion of the efficiency of national planning as practised in the United Kingdom.

b.   Political aspects

Thus far the disadvantages of lack of control have been confined largely to the financial aspects, although the ability to evade price controls has important political implications as well. There may be more overtly political issues, however, in which subsidiaries of foreign companies follow policies of which the British government would disapprove.

An earlier chapter discussed in another context the political fallout of a number of well publicized incidents where a clash has arisen between the host government and a subsidiary of an American multinational over, for example, trade with communist countries. The embargo on Ford of Canada trading with communist China, and the angry reaction of the Canadian authorities to this intervention by American policy, was well publicized at the time, but faded away as American relations with China improved. Less well publicized were similar incidents involving other American owned subsidiaries elsewhere which were, for example, prohibited from trading with Cuba even where a mutual trade agreement existed between the host government and Cuba.

There is a very serious aspect to this whole issue, namely the extent to which it might be regarded as justifiable to evade legislation which is regarded as unjust by those affected. The issue, of course, did not start with international business, it is as old as law itself, and received its most recent boost in the British context in the efforts of trade unions and some local councillors to defy conservative government legislation which they regarded as unacceptable, even if legal. This is the sort of djinn which may be conjured out of a bottle by one political party, only to find it cannot be stuffed back in after it has fulfilled the political purpose for which it was released. The mixture of a sense of grievance, accentuated by the knowledge that extra legal tactics have been used in the recent past by the legislators themselves, is a potent one. It is not rendered any safer by the knowledge that much of the legislation is unenforceable, whether it is a bureaucratic price code or a pious resolution on the conduct of multinationals passed at an international level.

The problem of restoring respect for the law is wider than the issue of the foreign companies. In the latter context, however, there are at least three policies which any potential host government could contemplate.

(a) It could entirely prohibit the operation of international business, i.e. compel foreign companies to pull out or forbid its own companies to have any sort of operation abroad. This sort of solution is legally possible and enforceable, but would spell economic disaster for many economies.

(b) It could ensure that it does not pass legislation which is in practice unenforceable, or subscribe to declarations of intent which are in the last analysis meaningless, e.g. in negotiations with large multinationals on conditions for permitting them to operate subsidiaries; and treat some of the woollier pronouncements on international business issued by international agencies with the indifference they deserve.

(c) Finally, it could ensure that laws passed affecting international companies are both moderate and easily regulated so that at least the incentive to evade the law would have gone.

A BRANCH FACTORY ECONOMY

A complaint which is commonly made is that incentives intended to bring new industry into depressed regions often do not create brand-new enterprises or even cause companies to relocate themselves in their entirety. What normally happens is that a branch factory is established – what would in effect be an extension to the main factory if this had been permitted. The problem which then arises is that the branch factory is the one which has most often to bear the brunt of recession in order to safeguard the interests of the main plant. A mild recession then has no perceptible effects on the main factory but a multiple effect on the branch.

The same argument can be applied on an international scale. Generous regional grants, tax holidays or subventions may be paid out by a host government to attract foreign investment. But even the most successful drive to attract direct investment results only in the setting up of subsidiaries – few international enterprises will actually move their home base. The reasons are not hard to understand. Quite apart from requiring all the key headquarters staff to move to another country, the company would almost certainly have to change its nationality, and this is not likely to occur save in the most dire circumstances.

Over time, a branch factory may become more independent and integrated into its local market, it may even, again over time, become more important than the parent company. It is not unknown, as has been noted, for some American enterprises to become almost shell companies at home, moving more and more of their production facilities to low cost areas. The logical place for such 'runaway' industries is Mexico, Puerto Rico, Central America or South-East

Asia where assembly operations or subcontracting for the major industries of North America, Japan, or western Europe are becoming commonplace.

There is however a reaction in parent countries to the whole process of creating branch factories abroad, just as there is in the Midlands of England a reaction to the siphoning off of jobs to the development areas of the north, Scotland and Wales. In the main, as has been remarked, the pressure in America comes from trade unions which have had considerable success in recent years in bringing pressure to bear on the US government to discriminate against foreign operations by US corporations by tax measures. The same phenomenon is seen in the protests of trade unions against cheap imports from abroad: it is not surprising that British trade unions denouncing low cost foreign products as costing their members jobs are in turn being accused of much the same thing by the Americans – with perhaps more justification.

In summary, then, the problem is that any official policy by a potential host government of encouraging direct foreign investment cannot but attract branch factories with all the potential dangers of fluctuating employment this implies.

LIMITING THE BRANCH FACTORY EFFECT

There are several methods which a government may use to limit the branch factory effect. A branch factory's expendability depends on the fact that it will cost the parent company relatively little to run it down or even pull out entirely, i.e. most of the costs are variable rather than fixed. The plant may be characterized by the employment of a higher proportion of labour to capital equipment than would be the case in the main factory, and possibly the use of obsolescent equipment which had been originally used elsewhere and phased out there. There are relatively common characteristics: after all, part of the attraction of building a subsidiary in the first instance was the prospect of lower labour costs and the prospect of finding a use for equipment or designs which were becoming obsolescent in a more competitive home market.

An obvious way of reducing the dangers inherent in branch factory status might be for the host government to make it more profitable to invest in new heavy fixed capital equipment which would represent an ongoing cost which would not be reduced when production was being cut back. This is a policy issue which touches on the conflicts of aims already alluded to, between jobs, technology and foreign exchange earning capability: and as such it will have to be dealt with in more detail in the next chapter. Briefly, however, any government subvention by regional policy legislation could be tied to fixed capital equipment whose brand-new nature was beyond doubt – reconditioned equipment ought to be treated much less generously. Logically, of course, fixed costs are irrecoverable in any event and a decision to pull out entirely would still be a tolerable choice if the tax losses incurred could be put to good use in the parent company's accounts. But in most cases the complaint made is not that the branch factories are being closed down, but merely that they are reduced to a care and maintenance basis to be revitalized as and when demand picks up. Moreover, the pressure could be exerted only where the subsidiary was located in a development area where it was deriving some benefits from regional policy legislation.

A second way of reducing the branch factory effect would be to make it more costly to dispense with labour so that there was little profit in varying labour costs according to whether business was slack or not. This would be a rather controversial policy in the sense that chronic overmanning in British industry in most of the post-war years may well have been a root cause of many of the country's problems; and the tendency towards increased job protection in recent years may already have worsened the situation.

The two methods so far described are essentially fiscal. An alternative longer term method might be to require the subsidiary to take the form of a joint venture between the foreign and a local company. While this does not guarantee against a close down, it makes it more difficult to take action which could be judged as oppressive of local shareholders' interests. Insofar as the most probable source of new direct investment is likely to be Japanese, this might not be a particular obstacle to investment, since Japanese companies operating in different cultures from their own frequently prefer to have a local partner as a cultural shock absorber.

Unfortunately there is no ready way to deal with the situation of existing branch companies: a growing problem is that in a period of depression the tendency will be to allow branch factories to run down rather than re-invest, on the grounds that the economic and political future of the country does not warrant other treatment. This sort of tactic is very difficult to counter by the host government. In the last analysis the twin protections against branch economy status are a host government with a clearcut policy in respect of foreign investment, and a reasonable prospect of a prosperous and stable future in the market.

PREEMPTIVE BUYING OVER OF A RIVAL COMPANY

An issue related to that of the branch factory is one touched upon earlier, namely the possibility of a locally owned enterprise being bought over, not so much as a means of entering the local market, but in order to close down a rival company. The issue is rarely as clearcut as this: there are probably few, if any, provable instances of a foreign firm buying over to close down. On the other hand, if a newly acquired company is going to be incorporated into an international enterprise, it may find its markets and product policies violently changed – with the implicit assumption on the part of the buyer that a relative failure in their newly acquired company may not be an unqualified loss if the effect is to kill off a rival firm while securing its markets.

In theory, of course, guarantees can be sought: these will be discussed in terms of codes of conduct in the following chapter. At the risk of anticipating what will be said there, it has to be recognized that agreements about continued production under the new ownership can never be watertight. While, therefore, a government may welcome foreign direct investment if this means building new productive capacity, it ought to consider carefully whether a proposed takeover of an existing local company is likely to be a preemptive buying out of a potential rival, with the purpose of decreasing output and competition.

THE TECHNOLOGY GAP

The early part of the chapter made the point that one type of industry which was most likely to attract international investment was that with a heavy and growing expenditure on research and development. This is hardly surprising: a company which has to commit considerable amounts of its turnover to research and development has every incentive to market, even to produce, on as wide a scale as possible and is therefore likely to 'go international' at an early stage. From the viewpoint of the potential host government there is a real dilemma. To admit a foreign enterprise is to ensure that some sort of industry is created which might have been too costly on a purely national basis: on the other hand, the presence of the foreigner, particularly if he/she is allowed to buy over existing local companies, may inhibit locally financed and directed research and development. It is, for example, difficult to imagine any country which permitted the establishment of IBM or another advanced electronics firm ever being able to develop an independent national company competing on equal terms over the product range of the American multinational: and in Britain the only substantial mainframe computer company, ICL, in time succumbed as an independent company. In this sense, the more readily available are the results of research and development carried out elsewhere the less easy will it be for local enterprises to 'grow their own'. A technological gap which appeared to be being closed by the introduction of modern technology may be narrowed rather than closed; and the narrowed gap may become stabilized.

Technological dependence may be created and sustained in three ways:

(a) Research and development will not be a planned activity of the subsidiary. Where facilities had existed in a local form which has been taken over by the foreign enterprise these may be closed down. Such research and development as is permitted will tend to be jobbing contracts, with nothing of a very fundamental nature. At the same time, in the case of American takeovers, many of the brightest talents in any local research and development terms will be tempted to the lusher pastures of the USA.

(b) As a result, the subsidiary is perceived merely as a production plant manufacturing components to job specifications and designs supplied from headquarters.

(c) Even more perniciously, there may be the tendency already remarked on to use obsolescent equipment reconditioned after having been phased out at home. The rate of change of equipment, i.e. the rate of investment and technological development in the subsidiary, is then determined not so much by conditions in that particular market as by the rate of replacement in the more advanced home factories.

Thus, though the host country enjoys a reasonably high standard of technology, there is no obvious incentive for the supplier of technology to close the gap by installing the latest machines and processes simultaneously throughout the worldwide operation when obsolescent technology can still be made to work more profitably for the enterprise. This particular problem of a technological age gap being perpetuated is most likely in industries already having to operate on such a large scale in order to sustain research and development costs that there is room for only one such company per host country.

Another factor in the admittedly complex and unquantifiable situation is the nature of any new foreign investment, which, it has been argued, is as likely to come from Japan as traditional sources. Thus far the Japanese have been reluctant to undertake research and development work outside their own frontiers, but it is likely that even on cost grounds alone, some at least of this work will be 'farmed out' to research centres elsewhere in the developed world.

THE FOREIGN EXCHANGE DRAIN

The converse of the initial capital investment followed by export earnings is the possibility of a foreign exchange drain through payments of profits and royalties. From the host government's viewpoint there is little practical distinction between the two, as repatriation is freely permitted in both bases.

8 Alternative Policies

INTRODUCTION

This section has started with the avowed proposition that foreign direct investment is neither inherently good or bad: that on balance, for most host governments with an administrative machine sufficiently sophisticated to keep an eye on the situation, foreign enterprises are bringing more advantages than disadvantages; and that it might be possible to derive even more benefits if governments considered dispassionately what they wanted from foreign investment rather than merely reacting to situations as they develop.

Three points have to be made at this stage in the argument. First, no one can demonstrate objectively where the balance of advantage lies, just as no one can demonstrate the inherent economic superiority of a free enterprise system vs the corporate state (or *vice versa*) in terms of economic efficiency. One's attitude tends to be influenced by opinions on human behaviour and motives, i.e. by the political premises from which one starts. Arguably it could be said that a relative freedom from state plans to limit foreign investment and the simultaneous economic prosperity that West Germany has enjoyed demostrates the advantages of a liberal attitude to foreign investment. But equally, the sustained Japanese drive to limit foreign ownership of productive facilities while freely admitting foreign technology proves the opposite case may be at least as valid. The foreign enterprise is but one element in a vast cultural complex.

An important point was alluded to earlier about the relationship between ownership and control of foreign subsidiaries. There is little doubt about the scope of, for example, the British bureaucratic machine and its potential, if not always its performance, in regulating the conduct of private enterprise. In less developed countries where the administrative machine is more primitive any attempt to control enterprises may have to involve ownership. Nationalization of foreign enterprises at one extreme, or legislation to increase local equity participation (as is increasingly the practice in countries like Nigeria or India) are in this sense more than political gestures of disapproval of foreign influence. They may be necessary to ensure that national policy, whether wise or foolish, can be implemented, because it is not merely enough to decree a policy to assume it is thereby enforced. The United Kingdom, for example, has at times suffered from overgovern-

249

ment and too much law making, but the point still remains that if a
government wishes to impose controls on the activities of foreign
enterprises it can do so reasonably effectively, without the political
crisis which is likely to follow the forced nationalization or expropriation of foreign assets which is so often the scenario of the Third World
country in political crisis. Forced nationalization to achieve a political
end is not necessary in a developed country: in the final part of the
chapter it will be argued that it is almost certainly counterproductive –
even more counterproductive than the results which have followed
from hastily imposed price controls of the kind already discussed.
Provided it is prepared to consider the issues dispassionately and with
adequate time to consider all the implications of legislation, any host
government with a technologically sophisticated economy can mould
the policy of foreign enterprises without the nationalization which
tends to be necessary in the Third World. With these qualifications
noted, it is now useful to consider the options open to the government
policy maker.

A 'DO NOTHING' POLICY

One course of action is simply to carry on as before. There is an
obvious case for such a government policy. There are, however, at
least two counter-arguments against such a policy: the first of these is
the 'peaking' of the foreign investment boom by the 1970s and the
possibility of disinvestment from the traditional sources; and the
second is the changed nature and probable source of any future
investment.

(a) Economic forecasting is a remarkably hazardous occupation but
    there is evidence that the boom period for overseas investment in
    Western countries is over. All the major US corporations which
    are likely to do so have established themselves. The need in the
    future so far as the traditional investors are concerned may be to
    limit disinvestment in the more desirable industries as much as to
    encourage fresh investment.
(b) The second factor depends on the validity of the theory already
    advanced that the only new source of investment in most parts of
    the world which might remotely rival the Americans in the past, is
    Japan. It is, of course, perfectly possible that Japanese enterprises
    will never invest in any very significant quantities outside

South-East Asia, but there are grounds for supposing that Japanese multinationals in the 1990s will be a good deal commoner than today and that the United Kingdom may be a base for such investment. Additionally, if marginally, the newly industrializing countries of the Pacific Rim, which have replicated many of the Japanese successes, may be compelled in turn to increase their direct investment in North America and western Europe. The Korean Hyundai's decision to build a car plant in Canada may well be a harbinger of what is to come.

The legal basis for the requirements now being imposed by the British government (and Britain is one of the areas being considered by the Japanese for increased investment), and discussed in the next section, is as vague as the legal basis of the much tougher conditions about licensing or joint venture imposed by the Japanese government. In the context of Japanese enterprises, however, it seems to work.

LICENSING, ASSEMBLY, JOINT VENTURES

The points made in the following section are based largely on the Japanese experience, which has proved to be a haunting mirror image of another offshore island which pursued a radically different course from the United Kingdom. The Japanese successes were no doubt helped by the alien nature of the culture, in Western terms. In spite of the long post-war American occupation they succeeded in resisting any significant change to the cultural patterns which had determined the pre-war pattern of Japanese industry. In these days they had a reputation – substantially justified – of imitating Western designs. In the post-war years they pushed forward from slavish imitations to the wholesale importation of Western, mainly American, technology. It comes, perhaps, as a shock to realize how relatively little innovation there has been in the Japanese system. But they have shown a superb gift of taking the best of Western concepts, amending and improving on them. Again, one might perceive the mirror image of Britain which has produced a remarkable flow of original concept and pioneering work, which has then been exploited by others.

It would be interesting to speculate what might have been the prospects for the British economy if in the immediate post-war years governments had followed the Japanese policy of insisting on foreign patents and technology being exploited as far as possible through licensing arrangements rather than through direct investment; whether Britain would have experienced anything like Japanese growth; or whether the absence of some vital factors in the British culture would have frustrated British successes as much as has happened under an 'open door' investment policy. The present pressure within UNCTAD for freer access to patents and technology use, i.e. intellectual property rights, by the Third World and discussed in an earlier chapter shows that the Japanese as much as the British approach is seen to have possible advantages; though whether the average Third World country has the ability to repeat the Japanese success is open to doubt. The very scale of Japanese success in exporting, as has been seen, poses considerable difficulties for them throughout western Europe. These in turn may encourage them to seek at least a half-way house as an alternative to continued exporting, e.g. assembly and partial local manufacture, particularly if such a policy affords greater ease of access to the European Common Market. The tendency to assembly or manufacture overseas is now well established as a response to political pressures in their markets or overfull employment at home. In the latter context the Japanese do not permit immigration on the 'guestworker' scale of Europe in the late 1960s: rather, they will farm out work, initially in South-East Asia but as far afield as Latin America or Portugal.

There is, on the face of it, no reason why a readiness to export employment should lead to anything like joint ventures. Nevertheless, some Japanese industrialists may be rather more susceptible to pressure to enter a joint venture than, say, the Americans or the Germans. The tough domestic policy of excluding foreign investment wherever possible in favour of licensing or at most joint venture makes them psychologically more receptive to the idea that investment in another relatively developed country will be permitted only under very specific conditions. Such investment as is now being permitted in Britain appears to lay down a minimum value added on the price of imported components and a requirement to export at least half of all production. Although, as has been noted, there can be no legal basis for such a requirement. Clearly, however, relatively large investment such as the Nissan car plant in the north of England, is subject to pressure from the British government to ensure more use of British component manufacturers, rather than the traditional Japanese suppliers, or even European suppliers, against whom it would be impossible, legally, to discriminate.

Future limitations might well be made to apply to joint ventures or licensing of other processes to British firms as a condition for being allowed to manufacture within the United Kingdom as experience is amassed. The other type of investment in which it might still be possible to secure joint venture arrangements is in one of the few bright spots in the British economic situation, i.e. the technology related to offshore oil exploration (industry of the fourth group categorized in Chapter 7). The implications of this have already been discussed: there is at least a possibility of the granting of equipment – a factor which could increase the attractiveness of a joint venture approach.

RELATING BENEFITS TO SPECIFIC PERFORMANCE

An earlier section discussed the advantages which could be expected from the establishment of a foreign subsidiary, in terms of jobs, knowledge transfer and foreign exchange implications. Although as yet no attempt has been made to resolve any conflict between the objectives or at least to list them in order of priority, it is useful to explore the implications of this categorization by considering how government policy decisions could be used to further these aims. Again taking them in the order already established, we have:

a. Job creation as a policy aim

The major problem faced by a host government in the issue of job creation arises from the confusion of aims and methods which have been allowed to grow up over regional policy. The general problem has already been stated, but the confusion can be said to exist at two levels. Governments are never quite sure how to deal with regional aid, neglect the situation until a specific political crisis arises when a major foreign company is about to pull out, and then tend to extend operations hurriedly with lavish financing during the period of the crisis. Experience suggests that even when such expenditure induces the company to remain, the respite is temporary.

b. The generation and transfer of knowledge reconsidered

To encourage knowledge transfer by government fiscal policy is rather like placing an order for the creation of great art or literature. There are in fact two problems: can any government action facilitate this transfer and, if it can, how is it to be measured?

First, however, to define the type of knowledge being discussed: what is required is to ensure that research and development in an appropriate technology will be carried out in the host country, and not merely imported; and second, that the results of research and development carried out here or elsewhere are made available immediately in the host country instead of at the time which appears most expedient to the foreign enterprise, i.e. when production machinery will have to be scrapped in any event. The other types of knowledge transfer, i.e. marketing and cultural attitudes discussed earlier, are rather unquantifiable and presumably not susceptible to fiscal action by the host government.

If it is in practice difficult to define or quantify the knowledge which is to be generated locally or transferred, it can be at least averred that there is a rough correspondence between new knowledge on the one hand and research costs and capital investment on the other. By treating such expenditure sympathetically for taxation purposes and allowances, government is doing as much as it can directly to encourage technology. It follows therefore that if the job creation aspect suggests a regional policy based on investment grants and regional employment premiums, then knowledge generation and transfer implies investment allowances and accelerated tax depreciation.

It is not possible to make an objective judgement: all that can be said is that if a government sorts out its own political priorities in regional aids and does not then yield to short term expediences in a crisis, it has gone far to making a decision about its treatment of foreign enterprises. There is however not such a conflict between jobs and capital development in the context of international enterprises as in the context of regional policy in general. One can seek job creation industry and at the same time attempt to persuade the foreign enterprise to carry out research and development here.

So far it has been assumed that any encouragement to foreign enterprises is carried out in the context of regional policy by a host government, i.e. that finance is made available only for certain regions and that additionally the benefits are not merely available to foreign enterprises. This is probably realistic enough except for the awkward fact that not all foreign enterprises operate only in these areas. It is however worth considering whether the distribution of technologically advanced industries is such that a high correlation exists between innovative potential and regional location. For this purpose it is helpful again to make use of the fourfold categorization: namely,

industries with high technological innovation; those with 'slowing
down' technology but massive capital investment; those where
innovation has an element of fashion or marketing considerations;
and finally those where technology is less highly advanced, than
unfamiliar, in the host market. The two most relevant here are
recognizably the first and fourth of the categories, i.e. those with a
contribution to make to technology in the host government by
generation or transfer are possibly better established in the declining
regions where government help is freely available, while the second
and third categories may be found more in the more prosperous areas
where traditional skilled labour and mass markets are readily
available.

What does emerge from this is that regional policy is only an
imperfect method of achieving the results sought; but it is doubtful
whether any other method would achieve more. Given, therefore,
that any government may have its own ideas on priorities – and it is a
point of this chapter that a government should have its own priorities
clear – then either the investment grant/regional employment
premium system or investment allowance/tax depreciation method
could be employed. It is not beyond the wit of an administrative
machine in a host country with a developed economy to administer a
policy where both patterns could be applied so that each enterprise
could be treated in the most appropriate manner, depending on the
type of industry and how far it was deemed possible for it to generate
or transfer technology: even perhaps to allow the foreign subsidiary
to opt for that system which seemed in its best interest, with the
government then using the responses as a measure of how far it was
achieving the right mixture of more jobs and new technology.

c. Encouraging improved export performance

The problem of encouraging more exporting by the subsidiaries of
foreign owned enterprises is a complex one. There are legal pitfalls in
terms of international treaty obligations, as well as the technical
problem of measuring efficiency.

It has to be said from the outset that the export record of these
subsidiaries is good. In the first instance, as has been suggested, their
very international nature is an indication of their management's
awareness of the importance of foreign markets. But the great
stumbling block is the one already alluded to, namely that if exports
are going to another unit of the same enterprise in another country

they may not be valued 'at arm's length' if it is not expedient for taxation or currency transfer reasons.

This is a situation where mythology may be as important as reality: i.e. the suspicion that foreign enterprises are able to manipulate costs and prices can be enough to poison relations between government and subsidiary. The 1970s furore which followed the report on price charges for drugs sold in the United Kingdom by the Swiss Hoffman-La Roche illustrated the same problem, albeit in terms of excessive profits rather than overt transfer prices. The problem was that official sources in the United Kingdom simply did not have the information available to check on pricing policy – and not unnaturally drew the worst conclusion. Governments have power to disregard recorded prices and access profits at arm's length – in the case of the British government, at least since 1951, with powers substantially strengthened by the subsequent Finance Acts. A group of specialist staff now appear to have been set up by the Inland Revenue department largely, it is to be suspected, because British enterprises operating abroad were being rigorously scrutinized, particularly by the American tax authorities.

On the assumption that host governments' tax authorities have considerable discretion in their dealings with foreign owned subsidiaries, what scope is there for government action to improve export performance or at the very least cut imports? The major precedents are in the actions followed by some of the less developed countries; the major limitations, the problem of treaty obligations.

The standard import controls used elsewhere turn on relating tariff concessions to export performance. There may be provision for a local content value added, with the prospect that tariffs or various subventions will vary according to how quickly exports are reduced and local content substituted. It is on this basis, for example, that countries like Spain have been able to build up car manufacturing capacity, attracting foreign multinationals by a system of incentives and payments.

It can be argued that such policies flout both the spirit and the letter of the treaty obligations of GATT and the European Community where the host government is a member. Certainly this route is not likely to remain open to Spain in the light of its access to the European Community. In fact, many of the rules of these bodies are already observed more in the breach than in the observance. Presumably every motor vehicle which is exported from a loss making company in receipt of government aid is tainted. The problem was graphically illustrated in the late 1980s by the efforts of the British government to dispose of the Rover Car Company, then effectively state owned, to a private company in circumstances which effectively involved a substantial subsidy to the proposed purchaser. In the face of EC opposition the British government had to modify the terms, but the final deal was a compromise rather than a victory for the policy of no subvention.

The methods adopted by Spain in the 1970s and, arguably, Britain in the late 1980s are scarcely any more objectionable than those adopted by other countries to preserve and increase their industrial base – in the process weakening that of someone else – or arguably than those of a price code which inhibits prices and profits on domestic sales while giving *carte blanche* on export practices. The more overt export incentives are well enough known. VAT itself permits repayment of taxation on value added in the processes of manufacture: in some instances, national governments will effectively free exports entirely from taxation.

Finally, of course, if adverse balance of trade figures persuade a weak government to give way to the trade union demands on import controls and limiting the repatriation of profits by foreign subsidiaries, the export performance itself can be used as a measure of how generous on profit repatriation to be. This is a method commonly used in Third World countries. Profit repatriation is permitted only at a fraction of the export earnings of the subsidiaries. What is being described here, however, is a type of siege economy inappropriate for a Western developed economy.

LOCAL EXECUTIVE RECRUITMENT

It is received wisdom in most multinational enterprises that as far as possible locally born executives should be used in the subsidiaries, for reasons which have been discussed in an earlier chapter. Such a policy not only makes the foreign enterprise more acceptable in the host country, but insofar as these enterprises tend to originate in developed countries and set up subsidiaries in less developed, it is probably much cheaper to use a local national.

The actual number of these executives, particularly compared with the total of personnel employed in the subsidiaries, may be tiny, but they are almost invariably key posts. To wrench a political slogan out of its context 'One is enough', provided that one is the chief executive. Indeed it may be better in maintaining headquarters control that there should be only one key man who can be briefed on policy under conditions of tight security on a visit to the parent company. The major problem therefore is that in a conflict of interests between the foreign enterprise and the host government there is no doubt where the loyalties of the key executives lie. In other parts of the world where local managers hold the key posts and so have to implement decisions, the foreign enterprise may be restrained to some extent by an awareness that if a quarrel between the enterprise and the host government was ever pushed to the point of a showdown, local executives would in the last analysis accept directives from their own government and operate the subsidiary on the lines laid down by the government.

In most parts of the world pressure to appoint local managers is, if anything, increasing. The Japanese, comparative newcomers to the international scene, appear, as so often happens, to have been more resistant to change, operating on the principle that any post filled by a non-Japanese is lost permanently. In time they too will have to conform to local practice: at the moment, however, it can be said that the American policy in the United Kingdom, insofar as there is an overall pattern, bears a remarkably close similarity to that of the Japanese in the Third World: and the Japanese practice elsewhere may give a hint of their future policy towards British subsidiaries.

Should a host government like Britain be more nationalistic in its approach, particularly to the Americans and in time to the Japanese companies, on the subject of key posts? There is at least a *prima facie* case for requiring more often that key posts be reserved for local nationals and that as far as possible it should be practicable to run the subsidiary without foreign executives in a crisis situation.

LOCAL EQUITY HOLDING

The idea of encouraging local participation in foreign subsidiary ownership, discussed in an earlier chapter under the catch-all title of 'indigenization', is a politically attractive one. Like most attractive ideas in the field of international business, it has its complications. Before considering these in detail it is, however, worth reiterating the point made earlier that a share in ownership of local subsidiaries is politically attractive but strictly unnecessary in terms of control. It is possible to divorce ownership of assets from control in a modern industrial society if the government is sufficiently resolute and clear in its own mind about what it wants from the foreign enterprise.

Local equity holding requires that a foreign owned subsidiary is converted into a joint stock company under host country company law, with a proportion of the equity, presumably a controlling share, kept by the original parent company and the remainder of the shares being bought and sold in the open market like any wholly domestic company. In theory, of course, it would be possible to contemplate the parent company receiving the agreement of its original shareholders to the issue of more shares in the original company which would then be sold only in the host country. The practical complications which would arise from the existence of share certificates which were in effect claims on a foreign company subject to exchange control regulations would, however, as has been noted in an earlier chapter, be too great for the idea to be acceptable to most governments.

From the enterprise viewpoint, equity shares which are sold locally pose problems also. Initially, of course, selling such shares is an obvious way of raising local finance: the major problem is the restraint on the enterprise's freedom of action because the enterprise would find some options closed. As was noted in an earlier chapter on ownership strategies an export market could not be arbitrarily re-allocated between one subsidiary and another without one set of local shareholders feeling that however much such a decision was in the interests of the shareholders of the parent company, it was not in theirs. Equally, any of the pricing or taxation options which might move currency or profits out of particular states would be, by definition, inimical to local shareholders in the region.

Possibly the only situation where the issue of such local equity posed no great policy problems for the enterprise would be in those industries where production was largely limited to the domestic market.

CODES OF CONDUCT FOR FOREIGN OWNED SUBSIDIARIES

In a situation where foreign owned subsidiaries are at least in part out of the day to day control of host governments, it is not surprising that attempts are made to lay down objective rules of conduct in the form of a code of good behaviour. Such codes now exist at at least three levels: their effectiveness in two of these levels is rather open to doubt.

The three levels are:

(a) specific agreements relating to a particular company;

(b) national codes of conduct;
(c) international, at UN or similar level.

Specific agreements arise most commonly when a local company is being bought over by a foreign enterprise with the host government laying down conditions under which it will permit the foreign takeover. Generally the agreement, however dressed up, is that production facilities and employment in the United Kingdom will be maintained despite the change to foreign ownership. However reassuring such agreements may appear to be at the time, they are in practice worth very little, being cosmetic rather than effective.

In the first instance the agreements cannot and do not specify in exact quantitative terms what are the new owners' obligations. No company is in practice likely to give or honour an open ended commitment to carry on its payroll indefinitely X thousand employees regardless of wage costs or market demand; neither is it in any position to guarantee a certain level of manufacturing output of a product whose design must constantly be updated either in terms of units produced or value of production. It would in theory be possible to specify an output in terms of raw materials or of an undifferential homogeneous product; however, this is not the type of product to be found in the British situation. Finally, the distinction between manufacturing and assembly is one of degree rather than of kind. In this sense almost any type of industrial activity could be regarded as a continuation of manufacturing facilities. The British car industry provides illuminating evidence of the problems. Between the 1950s and the 1970s, a small British car company, Rootes, became partially then wholly American owned, and then French owned. Each dramatic move provoked a crisis. British government intervention, a patched up agreement, more often than not involving taxpayers' money being given to the foreign company to produce a transient solution which could be justified as saving jobs. But at the end of the day the rump of the company became an assembly plant for Peugeot, not all that different in technological status from the Iranian plants which assembled components from the British plant to produce the ostensibly Iranian car, the Peycan. In the same way, if less noisily, the Vauxhall company became largely an assembly operation for vehicle components produced outside the United Kingdom.

A specific agreement, then, is paradoxically often neither definable nor enforceable. It is not definable in the sense that a commitment of absolute rigid adherence to a *status quo* in terms of production and employment for an indefinite period into the future is simply impracticable. It is unenforceable in the sense that even if a government decides that the spirit if not the letter of the agreement has been broken, there is nothing effective it can do. There are no benchmarks by which it can measure month by month or year by year into the indefinite future whether the agreement is being honoured. It cannot demand compensation for failure to meet specific perform-ance if there is no performance specified. It can scarcely even nationalize in any effective manner if the foreign ownership have decided to pull out in any event and have effectively switched the foreign markets to other sources. At best a company agreement is a 'gentleman's agreement', at worst a political gesture virtually empty of content.

There is one type of specific agreement already alluded to which is more likely to have some meaning: significantly enough, however, it is not publicized as is the first type, although its legal basis remains as dubious. This is the type of agreement currently being made with incoming Japanese companies, trading off permission to invest and investment grants, etc. against guarantees of specific export perform-ance. Most governments do not appear to be overanxious to detail the conditions or the sanctions, which presumably include cutting off government aid or banning the import components. The lack of publicity also arises from a desire not to have too close an examination of such deals in terms of, for example, EC commit-ments. In spite of the decent obscurity in which such deals are buried, it may be significant that the deals which are best publicized are largely meaningless, and those which are not publicized appear to be effective.

National codes are a comparatively recent development whose effectiveness and relevance to local conditions cannot easily be judged. Previously, national responses to foreign investment had tended either to be violent, i.e. nationalization or expropriation during revolutionary conditions, or obscure rather than detailed, i.e. administrative pressures or bans on foreign investment of the form most obviously practised by the French or Japanese governments.

In the last few years some attempts have been made to systematize principles of good conduct for foreign owned enterprises. The most relevant of these experiments are those which are tried in states whose legal systems derive substantially from the English patterns; and the most interesting of these was in the now repealed Canadian Foreign Investment Review Act of 1974.

The background of the legislation was the belief by the Canadian government that foreign control of their industry had reached the point where it affected the ability of the Canadians themselves to maintain effective control of their economic environment. Provision was therefore made for the creation of a Foreign Investment Review Agency which was given the task of supervising fresh foreign investment. It must be apprised of any takeover proposals whereby Canadian enterprises would pass under foreign control and any proposals by foreign enterprises already in Canada to establish themselves in new industry, particularly in areas unrelated to their existing business. In effect, then, the agency had the power to prevent foreign investment being extended in the Canadian situation. The legislation was further detailed in guidelines issued for the benefit of the prospective foreign investor – the guidelines levelled against foreign enterprises in any country.

The guidelines called for a high degree of autonomy for the Canadian subsidiary of any foreign enterprise, including autonomy in technological development, while at the same time requiring for the subsidiary ready access to technological developments taking place elsewhere in the foreign enterprise. Where raw materials were involved, they were to be processed as far as possible within Canada instead of being simply shipped out for processing elsewhere. Canadian sources of supply were to be encouraged. Foreign markets were to be kept open for the Canadian subsidiary, which would in effect have freedom to seek new markets without any restraints. There should be retention of sufficient of the profits generated by the Canadian operation to permit adequate financing of growth, openness of information on pricing policy (presumably to ensure the avoidance of transfer pricing to the detriment of foreign exchange holdings and tax payments), as well as the possibility of Canadian participation in the equity holdings of the enterprise. The management would be substantially Canadian with adequate prospects of career advancement and a willingness to operate the subsidiary in the overall interests of the Canadian economy and Canadian culture.

In total the guidelines were intended to ensure that, regardless of foreign ownership, control and the operation of any enterprise operating within Canada should follow Canadian national interests.

In the event, the legislative intentions foundered by the end of a decade, partly as a result of the world recession and the very real fear that the American companies against whom the legislation was directed, would pull out if the conditions proved too onerous; partly too as a result of the fall of the liberal government, which was the more nationalistic of the two major political parties. Since it is unlikely that the issue will remain dead and buried, it is still worth considering some of the lessons to be learned from what was largely abortive legislation. First, the fact that guidelines have to be issued over and above the original legislation demonstrates how difficult it is to devise a code of conduct which will be so precise as to leave no room for dispute. The guidelines outlined above would be regarded as unexceptionable by the most ardent nationalist as points of principle: a few moments' consideration of any of the points made in the guidelines demonstrates how difficult it could be to establish that they were being violated deliberately. The problem was a diluted version of that discussed earlier in terms of undertakings given by foreign enterprises in taking over British companies. The major advance in the Canadian approach was that an *ad hoc* Foreign Investment Review Agency maintained a closer overview of the activities of foreign enterprises than is at present possible in the British context where, as has been suggested, there is no body with overall responsibility for dealing with foreign enterprises.

The second criticism normally levelled against the Canadian federal legislation was that is was both too severe and could militate against provincial or local interests. There is not the same division of power in, for example, non-federal Britain but there still exists room for conflict between, say, the central government and a development agency or regional authority.

The final point is that in many respects Canada might seem a relatively more attractive investment area to the foreigner, especially the American. The issue of foreign control in Canada was and remains acute; and the fact it is so acute is a demonstration of Canada's attractions as an area for foreign investment.

There are few other appropriate examples of national legislation so advanced as the Canadian which might have lessons. The US Foreign Investment Study Act of 1974 gave powers to the Secretaries of the Treasury and of Commerce to obtain information on foreign direct investment in the United States. The Department of Commerce was also authorized to establish an Office of Foreign Direct Investment, but its power would be small. There already exists under the Act a Cabinet Committee on Foreign Direct Investment.

Because of the very scale of US direct foreign investment elsewhere, it would be difficult for the US agency to pursue so overtly inquisitory a line as is likely to be followed by the Canadians. Certainly the scale of foreign direct investment, though considerable in absolute terms, is relatively small in the global context of US industrial and commercial power. The initiative leading to the Act appeared to derive more from fears of congress members who saw industries in their own states or constituencies passing into foreign control than a general concern on the part of the federal government. The Act had only an information gathering function. No doubt in time, if the situation warranted it, further legislation could be used to protect strategic industries from foreign takeovers or to nudge foreign companies with advanced technology with an application in the USA, to look to licensing or joint ventures as an alternative to complete ownership. Potentially the Act, by limiting competition, might on occasion run counter to anti-trust instinct in US government circles. If such a situation arose it is likely that anti-trust policies would prevail. And not least important in the situation is the relative strength of individual states, who, if they see advantages in more foreign investment as a means of creating employment, would in all probability attempt to oppose an application of federal powers on foreign direct investment.

International agreements: finally in this catalogue of codes of conduct there are those emanating from international organizations, mainly the UN and its satellite organizations, but also from OECD. The degree of hostility to the multinational company varies according to the source, with the so called 'non-aligned' Third World group as the most hostile, and OECD representing the industrialized countries as the least hostile, to international investment.

Two characteristics stand out about all these codes. They are written on the assumption that investment is taking place in Third World countries whose administrative machinery implicitly is not sophisticated enough to deal with aspects of multinational operations, and where bribery may well be something of the norm. They tend frequently to assume the foreign investor is the exploiter without taking account of the possibility that if some of the practices of the international enterprises in these regions are rather dubious, that fact is as much a comment on the morality of local officials as on the enterprise. Second, there is an element of window dressing in declarations of principles which are both voluntary and unenforceable. The only real remedy for bribery is an honest host government and civil service; the only remedy for most of the faults, real or alleged, of transfer pricing, tax evasion, etc. is a local civil service which is sophisticated and competent enough to be able to keep an eye on the activities of multinationals operating within the national territory.

ARBITRATION ON OWNERSHIP OR COMMERCIAL DISPUTES

In the last analysis, an international enterprise may find itself involved in a dispute in a foreign country, possibly with a customer, i.e. a commercial dispute, or more profoundly with the government, i.e. a political dispute: the latter arising either from a decision to nationalize or in some other way penalize the enterprise, or in a situation where the enterprise's offence is its particular nationality in a dispute between governments. In the first situation, a commercial dispute, there may be difficulties in obtaining legal remedy through foreign courts, in the latter case, there is probably no legal process in the commercial code of the country whereby justice can be obtained.

The major convention on the recognition and enforcement of arbitration was signed in 1958, and the effect of a country adhering to the convention is undoubtedly to facilitate the arbitration agreement. In this situation, however, it is very convenient, possibly for both sides, certainly for the injured party, to have some form of pre-agreed arbitration. There are a number of such arrangements, of which the most important is the UN backed International Centre for the Settlement of Investment Disputes, relating, as its title suggests to the problems and relationship of host government and international enterprise. The centre was set up under the aegis of the World Bank in the 1960s and can arbitrate on agreements which were in force before its creation, by mutual agreement of both parties, or its use in case of dispute can now be specified in new investment decisions. Rather more than half the countries of the world now recognize the validity of its activities by recognition of the convention by which it was set up, with Latin America being the major exception. Unfortunately, it is precisely in countries which do not recognize the convention, or revolutionary governments which may repudiate the agreements of their predecessors, where disputes are most likely to arise.

For more general, as opposed to straight, investment disputes there are two fairly recent sets of arbitration rules, one formulated by the UN Commission for International Trade Law (UNCITRAL) and a very similar one specifically applying to Latin America, drawn up in

1978 by the Inter-American Commercial Arbitration Commission (IACAC). Nevertheless, the willingness of individual nations to adhere to arbitration procedures varies enormously. What is involved in many instances is that national courts are being asked to accept without question an arbitration decision which may have been made elsewhere, according to a different code of laws: national sovereignty, and above all national pride and suspicion, are potent forces against arbitration.

NATIONAL CONTROL ACROSS FRONTIERS

One aspect of attempts at national control which is particularly controversial, and likely to become more so, is the situation where national legislation or supervisory bodies administering legislation attempt to impose a nation's mandate into another nation's territory, by attempting to control an enterprise's activities outside its own frontiers. There are varying degrees of sensitivity about these activities. In practice, a national government may in effect tell one of its own nationally incorporated enterprises what that enterprise may or may not do abroad even where its writ does not run. The enterprise, unless it faces contradictory instructions from a host government, or where it reckons it can keep the parent government in ignorance of what it is doing abroad, will find it expedient to obey specific instructions. If the host government objects to this indirect application of national sovereignty by another state, it can issue its own directives, in the knowledge that it can effectively be obeyed.

What is likely to prove more objectionable is when a government attempts to issue directives applying to what a foreign company may do outside the national territory, even indeed in the home territory of the company, i.e. an American law or agency might attempt to impose control on a British company's operatives in Britain, on the grounds that at some point American interests were involved. This so-called effects doctrine was originally intended to apply to legal actions involving other US states, but has increasingly been applied to foreign states. The American example is pertinent, because it has tended to be American legislation which gives offence elsewhere. The justification may be a trade embargo, or in more recent years an aspect of anti-trust legislation, but the effect is almost inevitably to cause a diplomatic storm between the USA and the nation within whose territories American jurisdiction is being asserted by the US investigative or regulatory agencies. The Australian, British and Canadian governments are only three of some 20 governments which have felt it necessary to protect their own companies by forbidding them to co-operate, if necessary by passing their own legislations against American jurisdictional encroachment.

In recent years the major impact of such legislation has related to the sale of products incorporating sensitive US developed technology, e.g. computer or data processing developments. A British company, for example, including US components or designs might find itself obliged to agree not to sell such equipment to customers in the Soviet bloc. A breach of this undertaking would result in an embargo of further sales of the components to the company.

It is difficult to believe that there is much future in this type of national control on international enterprises. Virtually every government except the US shows discretion in avoiding legislation to be enforced within another country's jurisdiction and it is highly unlikely, given the changing balance of power between the USA on the one hand and Europe and Japan on the other, that the latter nations will accede to US attempts to extend its national jurisdiction in this way.

The EC dimension

In time it is probable that the European Community will produce a coherent policy in respect of direct foreign investment, probably through developments in competition policy and a rationalization of its somewhat incoherent regional policies.

Two of the directives issued by the European Commission, and discussed earlier in a different context, have potentially long term effects on the role and room for manuoeuvre of the multinational corporations operating within the Community whether foreign or European Community in origin. One of these is the Fifth Directive which relates to Codetermination or Worker Participation in Management and has already been discussed in passing. At present, following its rejection by the European Parliament this directive is virtually in suspense, but probably not dead.

The other is the Seventh Directive, which requires standardization of the presentation of consolidated accounts by enterprises operating in different countries in the EC. At present, accounting practices and standards vary widely throughout the Community and it is difficult for individual governments or the European Commission to detect different financial practices being operated by the enterprise in different countries. This directive, if it becomes law, would enable discrepancies or differences to be detected.

At the moment, however, the Community still ranks as a comparatively minor factor in the development of codes of conduct. In summary, it appears that as yet there is little help in formulating policy to be obtained from existing agreements or codes of conduct at the national or international level. Only the Canadian government appears to have considered the issue in detail, even if, at the moment, its policy is muted.

THE IRRELEVANCE OF NATIONALIZATION

A previous section considered the possibility of nationalization as a method of resolving a dispute between host government and foreign subsidiary. In the last analysis of course nationalization or expropriation is always the prerogative of the host government. In the prevailing balance of power in the world, any act of nationalization against any foreign compnay is likely to enjoy a wide measure of support throughout the UN and its agencies. This section, however, is concerned to show that nationalization is very much a last resort, and even less relevant to the problems of foreign enterprises than of domestic companies.

The situation of the foreign owned company is significantly different from those of domestic companies in two respects: the shareholders have rather more prospect of being able to protect their interests, being non-resident; and, as important, if the key personnel of the enterprise also are non-resident and transient, they do not have any interest in acquiescing in a situation which is going to leave the shareholders who pay their salaries dissatisfied. They have often an incentive to resist nationalization or if it does come, to ensure that the price paid protects shareholders' interests.

A major element in the political equation of nationalization is where foreign international enterprises operating subsidiaries in its host country depend very largely on markets outside. The distribution chains of these enterprises handle not merely the local product range but other branch factories as well and possibly even products from the much larger home based plants. The consequence is that in the event of a dispute it is open to the headquarters company to prevent overseas sales by two methods. First, where the distribution network is particularly important, e.g. if there is a need for servicing via a distribution or sales company in the foreign market, it may be possible to inhibit sales taking place through the existing distribution channels, in the event of nationalization on unsatisfactory terms. The second method is a form of legal pressure, where the headquarters company publicizes its intention of taking legal action to secure payment for any products sold overseas by a nationalized former subsidiary, which involves patents, trade marks, etc. Rather similar action has been taken in the past by oil companies, e.g. BP threatened to sue purchasers of oil from their nationalized oil fields in Iran in 1952, and the US Occidental Oil Corporation used the same tactics in disputes with the Libyan government in 1976. It is in practice generally unnecessary to proceed to legal action. In most instances buyers, faced with the prospect of being sued if they purchase the disputed product, simply buy elsewhere and sales are choked off.

In the last analysis, neither of the methods described in the above paragraph is foolproof. Probably neither BP nor Occidental ever succeeded entirely in inhibiting sales, as refined oil is not very easy to trace to its source. But in the case of most foreign subsidiaries in the United Kingdom, the products concerned are manufactured, branded, perhaps trademarked – in a word, identifiable.

The only situation where power outside the United Kingdom is more evenly balanced between the British government and the foreign company is in the type of manufacturing process where supplies from a British subsidiary are necessary to keep another company going elsewhere, i.e. in the situation of car components from the United Kingdom being necessary for assembly plants elsewhere. As it happens, however, as a routine measure such international enterprises often duplicate sources in different national areas, so that difficulties or bottlenecks rather than an absolute standstill would be caused if one national subsidiary was pulled out of the system.

In one sense the political difficulties of nationalization without consent in the British situation are an extreme example of the point made earlier that international enterprises are not brought readily under day to day national control by governments, particularly of the host government, where the products are such as are normally produced by British based companies. The very advantage the subsidiaries pose in terms of a respectable export performance is the very thing which makes them relatively safe from unsought nationalization. British Leyland, while it remained substantially a British company, could be taken over and the interests of domestic shareholders virtually ignored. GM (Vauxhall) and Ford are a more difficult proposition, and are likely to remain so even if a left wing government is returned and nationalization becomes once again the panacea of Britain's economic problems.

The most significant aspect of this situation is that, while the foreign owned international company is most able effectively to resist nationalization if it chooses, it can use its freedom of manoeuvre to coerce governments into policies which suit it, using in the process the very trade union pressures which create the original situation. The Chrysler crisis of 1975 in the United Kingdom was a classic study of the dilemma thus posed. Chrysler was ready to pull out of the United Kingdom, being prepared even to give the government a financial sweetener in the process: they were apparently prepared to accept nationalization, even to the extent of offering a quittance payment to the British government – provided, by implication, they were left in undisputed control of the lucrative overseas markets. Chrysler dealers abroad would in this situation almost certainly opt for retention of an international enterprise's products rather than state produced ageing models from Britain. The trade unions of course favoured nationalization as a virtual guarantee of job protection regardless of the practical problems of breaking even financially. The British government, in spite of its zeal for nationalization in principle, frantically wanted to avoid it in this instance, presumably because it could foresee an open ended commitment, in competition with yet another open ended commitment with British Leyland, and an opinion from the Central Policy Review Board, the 'Think Tank', that there was excess capacity in car production. The patched up solution was quite remarkable even as an example of short term expediency from a British government. Chrysler were actually given freer access to the British market by converting much of the production facilities to assembly work on a French model: the only major export market apparently guaranteed for Chrysler (UK), and sustained by the British taxpayer rather than the Chrysler shareholders, was Iran, where the British subsidiary has a market in assisting the Iranians to build up their own home industry. That particular market will not only dry up in time but the Iranians will no doubt attempt to compete elsewhere. About the only cheerful aspect of the solution from the point of view of the British taxpayer was that nationalization had been avoided and so the hair-raising losses of British Leyland were not yet to be compounded. Nevertheless, the British taxpayer lost out; the US shareholders, however, had every reason to congratulate themselves on being extricated from a situation where, had they been unfortunate enough to be British, they would have received short shrift.

The situation was repeated again in 1978 when Chrysler in effect pulled out of Europe, selling off their remaining assets to Peugeot. The vague guarantees given to the British government and trade unionists proved to be no obstacle to a precipitate withdrawal, and the new French owners did not even trouble to make the same meaningless noises of goodwill and co-operation. In effect they set their own terms and the British government tacitly acquiesced in a development on which they had not even been counselled, with the choice of building up any part of the former Chrysler empire in Britain, France and Spain, or simply dismantling and cannibalizing the constituent parts in the Peugeot system.

A wave of successful nationalization throughout Latin America and the Middle East in the early 1970s, coupled with the overt approval of nationalization expressed by many international conferences dominated by the so-called non-aligned countries, has made nationalization, superficially at least, an easy answer to many of the problems caused by foreign enterprises. The political and economic difficulties, however, are immense.

CONCLUSIONS

It is now possible to draw up what might be termed an interim report on the role of foreign owned international enterprises. The evidence suggests that their presence has been much more to the advantage than the disadvantage of many host governments and that these net benefits may be expected to continue. On the other hand it is difficult to avoid the conclusion that some countries like Britain could have done much better if anyone had foreseen the level of investment which was to build up in post-war years and had thought ahead on the long term implications. Finally, in practical political terms it is probably too late to achieve dramatic results by a change in policy, except in the longer term.

The reasons for this somewhat bleak conclusion are twofold. First, the vast amount of probable investment has already been made and it is very improbable that future investment will be on anything like the same scale. Although this means that there is a large amount of fixed investment which the enterprises are in no position to liquidate in the short run, if new policies were imposed, their ability to resist substantial changes against their interests is now significant. They are far more able to resist hostile policies by government than are purely domestic companies. In the longer run, moreover, they can still liquidate without too much loss: i.e. they can simply cease to renew investment and by the use of transfer pricing, tax strategies, etc. extricate assets over time – taking with them the lucrative overseas markets which are at present allocated to the four subsidiaries.

Second, this decade is now one of retreat by the multinationals or, more strictly, the American multinational – not necessarily a retreat because of recession but from a growing sense among multinationals that they are no longer so eagerly welcomed, that they are convenient stock villains in the international scene. This is in United Kingdom terms, at least, a gross caricature, but it is important to reflect on how much fashion played a role in the whole post-war foreign investment wave. A generation ago it was fashionable for companies, especially US corporations, to go international: now it has become fashionable for them to stay at home and seek alternative methods of increasing profits to replace direct foreign investment. For a host government therefore to be particularly hostile to international enterprises while there is an attractive alternative strategy for the latter to invest at home is to invite their withdrawal. Only where there are, for example, raw materials to be exploited will they remain: and these are hardly the type of enterprise on which inward investment into Britain traditionally depends.

The emphasis so far has been on political expediency in short term crises and there has been in fact a manifest confusion of aims: it is fairly obvious that the three desirable objectives, namely job creation, knowledge creation and transfer and foreign exchange capability are not *per se* compatible. Arguably at least the first two conflict, in that labour intensive industry is not likely to encourage technology innovation or *vice versa*. The problem has arisen because in many potential host countries no government department has overall responsibility or perceives foreign investment as a single issue: and most significantly no department appears until recent years to have considered export potential in any systematic way, let alone contemplated shaping incentives accordingly.

It is hardly surprising, therefore, that in a situation where governme: t departments do not know what they want and do not apparently agree policies with other government departments, they do not succeed in matching the skills of the negotiators for the enterprise.

The situation does appear to be changing, but typically perhaps, without any publicity, in countries like Britain. There now appears to be the inter-departmental committee on Japanese investment, discussed earlier. Such a committee might have played a very significant role in shaping the all-important American investment 25 years earlier. And even today the committee, if it exists, is almost certainly an intermittent affair. If there is room for an Office of Fair Trading, there is at least as much room for an Office of Foreign Investment. Such an office, whose principles might derive from those of the former Canadian Foreign Investment Review Agency or the Technology and Investment Boards which act as a filter in the Third World, particularly Latin America, could have a twofold purpose. It could decide, in consultation with the present government departments which have a stake in the issue, what types of industry were to be encouraged and under what conditions. Second, it could decide, on the basis both of government attitudes towards particular nations and the conditions under which domestic and direct foreign investment were treated within their own frontiers, the conditions in which foreign companies would be permitted. This would in practice mean that nations which imposed restrictions on UK direct investment would, if necessary, be similarly treated, at least as a bargaining counter. Finally, it would ensure that foreign investment would not be of such a nature that it would be banned in the home territory for pollution or safety reasons.

The major merit of such an institution would, however, lie in its existence rather than its specific policies, for it would effectively be an institution whose very existence would provide an ongoing review of foreign investment, where none exists at present, and which would compel governments to reflect seriously on the issue of foreign investment; and above all perhaps would avoid the 'quick fix' fudge which so often passes for policy, when a crisis unexpectedly blows up.

The problem has deeper roots than the absence of institutional arrangements. This absence reflects the marked reluctance of successive host governments to think through what it is that they want from multinationals. Until they do so, it is not surprising that the multinationals tend to get the conditions they themselves want.

For anyone who accepts the concept of a social market it is difficult to postulate any other principle than export earning capabilities. Job creation itself may be humanitarian, but considering the inbuilt inertia to change and vigorous defence of the *status quo* as a policy, it is merely pandering to the very instincts which have done so much to hold the

United Kingdom back. Technology and general knowledge transfer by itself, without a clearly defined objective, is almost as dangerous. The fantastic expenditure on prestige technology has cost countries like the United Kingdom or France dear – witness Concorde, a form of technological machismo which is likely to be matched or surpassed by a new generation of wild excess of government policy. Hundreds of millions of pounds – all taxpayers' money are likely to be spent on the so-called infrastructure, on the destruction of the environment in order to encourage so-called high technology foreign investment which by its very dynamism is likely to be outdated almost as soon as complete – and which creates only a handful of jobs. If in present conditions a foreign company or consortium announces a new project in a host country with an expenditure of millions of dollars, perhaps tens or a hundred, it is a safe bet that the backers are not going to pay most of the bill – the local taxpayer is.

The point about export earnings is that it poses in a clear form the question which faces so much of Western industry. If a project cannot compete in a world market it has no future, whether it be locally or foreign owned; and the appropriate employment level and technology derives from that. In the long run it is only in the world marketplace, rather than a protected and cossetted home market that the efficiency and relevance of an industry can be judged.

Further Reading

Abegglen, J. C., *Strategy of Japanese Business* (Ballinger, Mass., 1984).
Brooke, M. Z. and H. L. Remmers, *The Strategy of the Multinational Enterprise*, 2nd edn (Pitman, London, 1978).
Brooke, M. Z. and M. Van Beusekom, *International Corporate Planning* (Pitman, London, 1979).
Buckley, P. J. and M. Casson, *The Future of the Multinational Enterprise* (Macmillan, London, 1976).
Casson, M., *Alternatives to the International Enterprise* (Macmillan, London, 1979).
Eiteman, D. K. and A. I. Stonehill, *Multinational Business Finance* 4th edn (Addison Wesley, 1986).
Farmer, R. N. and B. M. Richman, *Comparative Management and Economic Progress* (Cedarwood, Bloomington, 1970).
Fayerweather, J., *Multinational Business Strategy and Administration* (Ballinger, Mass., 1982).
Fayerweather, J. (ed.), *Host National Attitudes towards Multinational Companies* (Praeger, London, 1982).
Franko, L., *The Threat of Japanese Multinationals* (J. Wiley/IRM, New York, 1983).
Gladwin, T. N. and I. Walters, *Multinationals under Fire* (J. Wiley, New York, 1980).
Harbison, F. and C. A. Myers, *Manpower and Education* (McGraw Hill, New York, 1965).
Hawryshlyn, B., *Road Maps to the Future* (Pergamon, London, 1980).
Kapoor, A., *Planning for International Business Negotiations* (Ballinger, Mass., 1975).
Kapoor, A. and J. Fayerweather, *Strategy and Negotiations for the International Corporation* (Ballinger, Mass., 1978).
Kinsey, J., *Marketing for Developing Countries* (Macmillan, London, 1988).
Livingstone, J. M., *The International Enterprise* (ABP Ltd, London, 1974).
Ohmae, K., *Triad Power* (Collier Macmillan, London, 1984).
Paynter, A. T., *Multinational Enterprise and Government Intervention* (Croom Helm, London, 1985).
Perlmutter, H., 'The Tortuous Evolution of the Multinational Corporation', *Columbia Journal of World Business*, January 1969.
Robinson, R. D., *International Business* (McGraw Hill, New York, 1985).
Stopford, J. M. and L. T. Wells, *Managing the Multinational Enterprise*.
Terpstra, V., *The Cultural Environment of International Business*, 2nd edn (S.W. Publishing Co., Cinn, 1985).
Tsurumi, Y., *Multinational Management* (Ballinger, Mass., 1984).

Index